D0148214

THE GREEN CITY

NICHOLAS LOW is Associate Professor of Environmental Planning at the University of Melbourne.

BRENDAN GLEESON is Professor of Urban Policy and Management at Griffith University, Brisbane.

RAY GREEN is a landscape architect, environmental planner and Head of Landscape Architecture at the University of Melbourne.

DARKO RADOVIĆ heads the Masters of Urban Design Program at the University of Melbourne.

To the memory of John Iremonger,
publisher, who inspired this book.

THE GREEN CITY

Sustainable homes, sustainable suburbs

Nicholas Low,
Brendan Gleeson,
Ray Green and
Darko Radović

UNSW PRESS

Routledge
Taylor & Francis Group

A UNSW PRESS BOOK

Every effort has been made to ensure that the advice and information in this book is true and
accurate at the time of going to press. However, neither the publisher nor the authors can accept
any legal responsibility or liability for any errors or omissions that may be made. In the case of
drug administration, any medical procedure or the use of technical equipment mentioned within
this book, you are strongly advised to consult the manufacturer's guidelines.

Simultaneously published in

Australia and New Zealand by
University of New South Wales Press Ltd
University of New South Wales
Sydney NSW 2052
AUSTRALIA
www.unswpress.com.au

National Library of Australia
Cataloguing-in-Publication entry:

Low, Nicholas, 1941– .
The green city: sustainable homes,
sustainable suburbs.
Includes index.
ISBN 0 86840 693 7.
1. City planning – Australia. 2. Sustainable
development – Australia. 3. Housing –
environmental aspects – Australia. I.
Gleeson, Brendan, 1964–. II. Title.
307.12160994

Page design Lamond Art & Design
Cover design Di Quick
*Cover image Classified Quickbird satellite image
showing vegetation cover and growth vigour in an
urban area.* Created from a satellite image
provided by DigitalGlobe, Victoria.
© CSIRO 2004
Printer Kyodo, Singapore

The rest of the world by
Routledge
2 Park Square, Milton Park, Abingdon Oxfordshire,
OX14 4RN

Taylor & Francis Inc
270 Madison Avenue, New York, NY 10016

Routledge is an imprint of the Taylor & Francis Group

British Library
Cataloguing in Publication Data
A catalogue record for this book is available from
the British Library

Library of Congress
Cataloging-in-Publication Data

The green city : sustainable homes, sustainable
suburbs / Nicholas Low ..
[et al.].-- 1st ed.
p. cm.

Includes bibliographical references and index.
ISBN 0-415-37231-3 (pb : alk. paper)
1. Urban ecology. 2. Sustainable development.
3. Urban policy. I. Low, Nicholas.
HT241.G74 2005
307.76--dc22

2004029443

CONTENTS

AUTHORS

NICHOLAS LOW

Nicholas Low is Associate Professor of Environmental Planning in the Faculty of Architecture, Building and Planning at the University of Melbourne, Australia. He is the author or editor of eight books. His book (with Brendan Gleeson) *Justice, Society and Nature* (Routledge, London, 1998), won the Harold and Margaret Sprout Prize of the International Studies Association in 1998 for the best book published on ecological politics. Nick is a Fellow of the Planning Institute of Australia, a member of the editorial team of the international journal *Urban Policy and Research*, and on the editorial board of three other international journals of planning and environment. Nick is working with Brendan Gleeson (below), Carey Curtis (Curtin University, WA) and Emma Rush (University of Melbourne) on transport institutions and policy in Sydney, Melbourne and Perth.

Email: npl@unimelb.edu.au

BRENDAN GLEESON

Brendan Gleeson is Professor of Urban Policy and Management at Griffith University in Brisbane, Australia. Before joining Griffith in March 2003, he was deputy director of the Urban Frontiers Program at the University of Western Sydney. His research interests include urban planning and governance, urban social policy, disability studies, and environmental theory and policy. He has also co-edited three books with Nicholas Low on aspects of urban and environmental policy. Brendan's urban social policy interests were reflected in his 1999 book, *Geographies of Disability* (Routledge, London). In 2001, his book (with Nicholas Low) *Australian Urban Planning: New Challenges, New Agendas* (Allen & Unwin, Sydney) received the Royal Australian Planning Institute's National Award for Planning Scholarship. His latest book (co-edited with Nicholas Low), *Making Urban Transport Sustainable*, was published by Macmillan in March 2003. Brendan is currently a member of the Planning and Land Council of the Australian Capital Territory.

Email: brendan.gleeson@griffith.edu.au

RAY GREEN

Dr Ray Green is a landscape architect and environmental planner, and head of the Landscape Architecture Program in the Faculty of Architecture, Building and Planning at the University of Melbourne, Australia. Ray's research interests focus on understanding relationships between community environmental perceptions and issues of environmental sustainability, and in developing methods for facilitating community participation in environmental planning and design. He publishes his research findings in a range of planning, landscape architecture and environmental psychology journals. One of his primary concerns is using his research findings to inform design actions so that they will be sensitive to local ecological and cultural conditions. In addition to his academic background, Ray has had extensive professional practice experience in the United States, Mexico, Australia and several Southeast Asian countries, where he is credited with a range of implemented projects focusing on tourism, housing and open space developments.

Email: rjgreen@unimelb.edu.au

DARKO RADOVIĆ

Dr Darko Radovic´ heads the Master of Urban Design Program and teaches in architecture at the University of Melbourne. He received his doctorate in Architecture and Urbanism from the University of Belgrade, Yugoslavia. Darko has taught, researched and practised architecture and urban design in Europe, Australia and Asia. He is interested in situations where architecture and urban design overlap, and argues that neither the path of ecological sustainability nor that of cultural sustainability can be undertaken separately – environmental responsibility means cultural sensitivity and cultural sustainability must include ecological awareness – and that there is no viable future without their harmonious synthesis.

Email: d.radovic@unimelb.edu.au

ACKNOWLEDGMENTS

Today in Australia there are many magnificent efforts being made to implement sustainable urban development in housing, open space, workplaces – many more than we can do justice to, or even mention, in this short book. We salute you and acknowledge your inspiring work. We hope that you will not judge us too harshly for the omissions in this book, which are inevitably multiple.

This book is truly a collaborative research effort among four professions: urban planning, geography, landscape architecture/planning and architecture. It also represents collaboration amongst these disciplines within the Faculty of Architecture, Building and Planning of the University of Melbourne. The book, based on our research, grew out of a conversation with John Iremonger in 2001. He articulated the need for such a book and suggested what eventually became the subtitle. Since then the authors have drawn on many immensely helpful sources of advice. Nick Low spent a period of study leave in 2003 working on the book at the Oxford Centre for Sustainable Urban Development (Oxford Brookes University in the UK). Professor Mike Jenks, Dr Katie Williams and Professor Susan Roaf gave essential advice. Liz Low, you were always present to provide critical support and the photograph of Ginkaku-ji. Vinca Low provided the photograph of Mount Cook that is in the background of the carbon cycle diagram in chapter 1 (Figures 1.1 and 1.2). Nick was also able to visit BedZed and talk to its visionary architect, Bill Dunster, tour the ING Bank Headquarters, and join a group of English planners visiting the Västra Hamnen development in Malmö, Sweden. Nick learned a lot about housing from Professor Terry Burke and Dr David Hayward at Swinburne University of Technology in Melbourne. They provided unpublished course notes that proved invaluable in understanding the Australian housing system – but we take responsibility for our interpretation of these notes. Michael Mobbs was kind enough to provide photos of his pioneering Chippendale house. Val Plumwood's work continues to challenge and inspire us.

In 2003 Ray Green spent a period of time at the University of Michigan's School of Natural Resources, where he worked on his contributions to the book. Professor Joan Nassauer, a leading advocate of the need to link the study of environmental perception with the design of ecologically sustainable open spaces, is gratefully acknowledged.

Likewise, Professor Rachel Kaplan, also at the University of Michigan, supplied Ray with helpful suggestions in terms of the psychological benefits that having contact with nature can provide for urban dwellers. Professor Terry Daniel at the University of Arizona, a pioneer in the field of environmental psychology, and Associate Professor Mark McDonnell, Director of the Australian Research Centre for Urban Ecology, are also acknowledged for providing useful advice. Finally, Ray is immensely grateful to the late Professor Paul Shepard for his inspiration and prophetic vision about the place of humans within the natural world.

The City of Melbourne and Mick Pearce provided valuable assistance in understanding the new Melbourne Council building (CH2). Alistair Mailer helped us with the Green Building at 60 Leicester Street, Carlton. Vuk Radovic and Michael Roper made the clear and easily read drawings that we use to illustrate these and other buildings, as well as the diagram of the Montpellier city centre plan. We thank architect Rajko Petrovic for his photograph of the Cultural Centre in Noumea. We would also like to thank Elahna Green, who provided us with informative and artistic photographs of the River Torrens Greenway, Royal Park and Merri Creek, and helped with the design of the cover.

Brendan Gleeson is grateful for the support and encouragement given to him by Griffith University's Vice-Chancellor, Glyn Davis, since his relocation to that institution in 2003. He is immensely happy in the warm company of the Faculty of Environmental Sciences and pays particular tribute to Dr Neil Sipe and Professor Lex Brown for their friendship and collegiality. Other colleagues from whom he continues to learn much include Patrick Troy, Bill Randolph, Ruth Fincher and, of course, his old chum Nick Low. And above all he treasures the love and encouragement of his wife, Ulrike, and son, Julian. He was immensely gladdened by the arrival of his beautiful daughter Alison during the writing of *The Green City*.

The University of Melbourne has been very supportive of the project. It generously provided a publication grant to assist with inclusion of the colour plates. The Faculty of Architecture, Building and Planning provided funds for the drawings and index. Nick also thanks the School of Environmental Planning and its Urban Policy Program at Griffith University, the Head of School, Dr Neil Sipe, and Professor Brendan Gleeson – friend and co-worker from way back – for supporting a visit to the School in February 2004. Dr Sipe gave helpful advice on transport and Dr Kristen Lyons advised us on matters concerning food distribution and production. Carey Curtis of Curtin University helped our understanding of transport planning in Perth. For his advice on the relationship between climate change and water supply we thank Professor John Langford, Director of the Melbourne Water Research Centre and Chair of the Board of the Cooperative Research Centre for Catchment Hydrology.

Finally, all of us want to acknowledge the fine work of UNSW Press and its publishing manager, John Elliot; managing editor, Heather Cam; and our copy editor, Sarah Shrubb, whose critical eye and detailed engagement with our project have made this a much more reader-friendly and intelligible text. Finally, our thanks go to Di Quick, who designed the cover, engaged with us on ideas for it and came up with just the right inspiration.

THOUGHTS IN A GARDEN

How vainly men themselves amaze
To win the palm, the oak, or bays,
And their uncessant labours see
Crown'd from some single herb or tree,
Whose short and narrow-verged shade
Does prudently their toils upbraid;
While all the flowers and trees do close
To weave the garlands of repose!

Fair Quiet, have I found thee here,
And Innocence thy sister dear?
Mistaken long, I sought you then
In busy companies of men:
Your sacred plants, if here below,
Only among the plants will grow:
Society is all but rude
To this delicious solitude.

No white nor red was ever seen
So amorous as this lovely green.
Fond lovers, cruel as their flame,
Cut in these trees their mistress' name:
Little, alas! they know or heed
How far these beauties hers exceed!
Fair trees! wheres'e'er your barks I wound,
No name shall but your own be found.

When we have run our passion's heat,
Love hither makes his best retreat:
The gods, that mortal beauty chase,
Still in a tree did end their race;
Apollo hunted Daphne so
Only that she might laurel grow;
And Pan did after Syrinx speed
Not as a nymph, but for a reed.

What wondrous life in this I lead!
Ripe apples drop about my head;
The luscious clusters of the vine
Upon my mouth do crush their wine;
The nectarine and curious peach

Into my hands themselves do reach;
Stumbling on melons, as I pass,
Ensnared with flow'rs, I fall on grass.

Mean while the mind from pleasure less
Withdraws into its happiness;
The mind, that ocean where each kind
Does straight its own resemblance find;
Yet it creates, transcending these,
Far other worlds, and other seas;
Annihilating all that's made
To a green thought in a green shade.

Here at the fountain's sliding foot,
Or at some fruit-tree's mossy root,
Casting the bodies vest aside,
My soul into the boughs does glide;
There, like a bird, it sits and sings,
Then whets and combs its silver wings,
And, till prepared for longer flight,
Waves in its plumes the various light.

Such was that happy Garden-state
While man there walk'd without a mate:
After a place so pure and sweet,
What other help could yet be meet!
But 'twas beyond a mortal's share
To wander solitary there:
Two paradises 'twere in one,
To live in Paradise alone.

How well the skilful gard'ner drew
Of flowers and herbs this dial new!
Where, from above, the milder sun
Does through a fragrant zodiac run:
And, as it works, th' industrious bee
Computes its time as well as we.
How could such sweet and wholesome hours
Be reckon'd, but with herbs and flowers!

– ANDREW MARVELL (1621-78)

CHAPTER 1

WHAT DOES 'SUSTAINABILITY' MEAN FOR CITIES?

'Sustainability' is the word of the moment. It's everywhere – in the press, in government reports, on business websites, all over the internet. Adjectives proliferate: ecological, environmental, economic, social, cultural, political, architectural, urban, rural – whatever next? With all the variety of meanings splashing around, does sustainability mean much at all? Is it just another fashion of the intelligentsia, or merely a useful cover story for business as usual?

Sustainability does mean something both important and new.[1] It speaks of the greatest change in human thought and behaviour for 3000 years. It is fundamentally about the global environment. It is also about cities. A simple metaphor may be useful. Think of having a good soak in the bath. Before getting out and grabbing a towel, lie there a moment longer and pull out the plug. The water level immediately begins to drop. A colder perimeter creeps round your body. A little whirlpool or vortex forms above the plug hole. Now think of the bathwater as the environment. The city is the vortex created by swallowing up the environment – it is the energy, the water and the materials consumed by city dwellers. There are two ways of keeping water in the bath. Put the plug back in, or run the taps at the same rate as the water going down the waste pipe – or do some combination of the two: stem the flow, run the water. Maintaining the water level and keeping the water at a comfortable temperature is what 'sustainability' means in the world of this little metaphor.

What people have begun to appreciate over the last 20 or 30 years is that the environment is, like a bathtub, of limited capacity. When humans were launched into space in the late 1960s, they – and then we – were for the first time able to view the planet Earth as a blue globe, utterly bounded in extent, moving in the infinite and hostile darkness of space. The limits of the environment became immediately clear. Since then the image of Earth from space has become trivialised through overuse, but what that image told us is continuing to have a profound effect on human knowledge about the relationship between the human species and the planet.

For 3000 years, human knowledge in Europe was shaped by the project of understanding the natural world in order to consume it more efficiently. In the last 100 years that project spread worldwide. The staggering success of the growth project is reflected in the exponential expansion of the world's human population. The population is growing because more people are surviving, and for longer. Experts hope that improved survival chances will bring about a levelling of population growth in the poorer countries as it has in the rich ones; but even so the world's population is expected to reach 10 billion within 50 years. The same 'science' that made growth possible is also telling us that consumption is already crashing up against environmental limits. Under present circumstances, the prosperity of the rich cannot be spread to the whole world's population. It has been calculated, for example, that if all countries consumed as much energy per person as Britain does, the world would need seven extra planets.[2] Since Australians consume more than twice as much as the British, the corresponding figure for this country is 14 extra planets. The world has the span of just a single lifetime, 70 or 80 years, to turn human behaviour around from *growth* to *sustainability* before the planet's population spirals back towards decline, ill health and shortened lives.

This change would not be a return to a simpler world, which some romantics might welcome, but rather a cataclysmic scenario marked by a sudden reversal in human health and massive disruptions to settled populations, cities and societies. The spectre of 'environmental refugees' – people forced to flee ecologically ravaged areas – has already been foreshadowed in Africa, where large numbers have been unsettled by local wars, desertification and the destruction of food-producing habitats. Translate these 'regional' disruptions to a global scale and we have an appalling outlook. This may not be a 'doomsday' prophecy – people are remarkably adaptive in the face of even the worst forms of change – but it signals a future which sees humanity, or major parts of it, forced back to raw survival and the constant threat of suffering. Is this where our economic progress is taking us? Or should we use the intellectual capacities and technologies that we have developed as a species over the past three millennia to secure a sustainable future? There is time, but not much.

We are today living through a crisis of knowledge: much of what we thought before about how to get along in our human societies, especially what we learned through the study of politics and economics, and even what we knew about how to do science itself, is now obsolete. One of the finest of Australian philosophers, Val Plumwood, calls this the 'ecological crisis of reason'.[3] For thousands of years the principal purpose of science was the mastery of nature. Now we find we are not masters but partners with nature – and junior partners at that – in a project of mutual survival.

CITIES CONSUME THE ENVIRONMENT

Enough has been spoken and written about the environmental crisis. This book rejects the politics of doom – the 'do nothing because nothing helps' outlook – and charts the way to a brighter, sustainable future for our cities. Nevertheless, in this opening chapter we must speak about the environmental crisis in terms of the two most serious threats that confront the world today: the threat to the atmosphere, and the threat to the biosphere. We will then move on quickly to the core of our argument, which is about what we who live in cities can do about these threats. Frightening though these threats are, there is no cause for despair, because the solutions are known and clearly understood. They are also fundamentally urban. They start from where we Australians mostly live: in cities and suburbs.

One feature of urban society is the extreme separation of everyday life from the natural world on which human life depends. Most people know what chicken fillets look and taste like. Also, hens clucking and pecking about the farmyard are engaging creatures familiar to us from children's stories or even first-hand experience. What people know almost nothing about, and probably resist thinking about, is how vast numbers of hens become chicken fillets. Even less is known about the effects on the natural world of that process of mass production. The same applies to almost all food. Today consumers are being asked to take on trust genetically modified food whose long-term impact is completely unknown.[4]

What applies to food applies to just about every item we use in our everyday life. The word processor I am using to write this chapter is the end result of a long chain of production. Every part of the computer originates in nature and will eventually return as waste. But of the effects of this chain of production and waste on the natural world I have little knowledge. As we approach the limits of what the Earth's environment can provide, we must allow technology to move forward only with great caution.[5]

The symptoms of environmental damage appear far and wide – in the paddocks and fields, the mountains and deserts, the oceans and forests, and the plains, rivers, lakes and glaciers of this extensive planet. So it is easy to assume that the environmental problem is 'out there'. Environmental problems are rarely experienced – or at least not fully – by the people who cause them, as economist Michael Jacobs points out.[6] This remoteness is emphasised by the frontline troops of the city-based green movements who take their protest to the endangered forests and the high seas, bringing with them the attention of the world's media. But the production processes that cause the damage in remote places would not exist without cities in which to consume the end products. Urban industries draw in environmental 'raw' materials and spew out waste.[7] Japanese whale meat ends up on city tables. Rainforest timber adorns city boardrooms and urban boardwalks. Consumption is certainly only part of the problem – production is the other part – but consumption is crucial. It's also easier to tackle the environmental problem at the urban consumption end.[8]

The globalisation of production now puts even greater distance between the people who consume and the land and sea that ultimately produce. In Australia, the vegetables on supermarket shelves may come from Brazil, the canned tuna from Thailand, the timber from Malaysia, and most manufactured goods from China. The most voracious consumers on the planet live in cities and work in office jobs processing clean information. Unlike the situation in the early industrial cities, the factories (and associated pollution) may be thousands of miles away from the consumers of their products. We may live in the virtual 'information society' but we can't eat information. Everything the virtual society depends on for survival comes from and returns to the real environment.

Most people on the planet now live in cities remote from agriculture and the extractive industries that feed the factories that, in turn, feed the homes and offices. Many more will do so in future. Cities are the way that human societies have found convenient to create the division of labour necessary to produce goods and services for human consumption. City dwellers do a multitude of different jobs, and in cities all these different jobs are co-ordinated to make up a vast collective effort – it's rather like a human anthill. Cities themselves are beginning to connect to other cities across the globe in networked systems, creating an urban universe that seems totally separated from nature, or at least oblivious to its dependence on nature. Modern cities are wonderfully efficient machines for consuming nature, and many people owe their lives to this consumption machine. The problem today, though, is that *efficient* consumption of nature is no longer what is most needed; *sustainable* consumption is what is needed. Unless cities themselves become focused on and designed for sustainable consumption, environmental damage will multiply. The cities will be the last to know, and by that time it will be too late.

What does it mean to 'consume' the environment? Obviously the global environment is much more complex than water in a bathtub. But there are significant parallels. There is a 'tap' for stored sources of energy. The sun provides a constant energy flow to the Earth and that energy is stored in solid forms of carbon through plant growth. Fossil fuels are huge stores of organic material deposited in the rocks at times of extreme global warming. The last two epochs of algal deposition that eventually turned into oil occurred about 90 and 145 million years ago.[9] Fossil fuels are easily converted to heat (as in the hot water tank for the bath), but using up fossil fuels is like drawing hot water for the bath without reheating the water in the tank.

More importantly, the environment provides services. The service the bathwater provides is keeping us warm and comfortable while we wash our bodies, or just relax. One of the services the environment provides is a stable climate in which to live and work. When the bathwater is dirty it is discharged into a waste pipe, and where it goes after that most people don't think about. But there is no convenient waste pipe to outer space for polluted air – it just stays in the atmosphere until it is broken down (over millennia) by natural processes. The atmosphere therefore provides the service of a waste dump, or 'sink', for pollution.

What is the relationship between the environment, society and the economy?[10] A student in Nick Low's 2003 graduate class at the University of Melbourne, David Mitchell, pointed out that the 'economy' is the term that describes the dominant way in which society, any society, interacts with the natural environment. In our obsession with 'the market', which describes human-to-human interactions, we have forgotten that the most fundamental fact of all real economic systems is human exploitation of the environment. Mitchell was absolutely right.

The implications of this insight are as obvious as they are momentous. First, if human behaviour is despoiling the environment, it is the economy that has to change, because the economy is the sum total of all interactions with the environment. Of course people interact with the environment in ways other than economic, just as they interact with each other in ways other than economic. But material support for human life comes from the environment. And this life support is provided collectively by the set of real relationships called 'the economy'.[11] Unfortunately, our material relationships with the environment have now developed into a threat – both to the environment and to all those who depend upon it. The threat takes two main forms.

THE THREAT TO THE ATMOSPHERE

The political world has, since the 1980s, been worrying about the impact on the Earth's climate of 'greenhouse gases' released into the atmosphere through human activity. With the support of many national governments, the United Nations (UN) has put an enormous scientific effort into understanding this impact. The UN Intergovernmental Panel on Climate Change (IPCC) was set up in 1988 to bring together the world's leading specialist climatologists to investigate and report authoritatively on what was happening. The IPCC's first report, in 1990, suggested (cautiously) that a generalised global warming, though with highly variable local impacts, was probably occurring. Every IPCC report since, using new and better data, has confirmed those findings.

The evidence for climate change has thus become steadily firmer. Its impact already seems manifest in Australia, where citizens witness and experience with mounting concern the increased frequency of drought and extreme heat. The cities cannot escape this judgment of nature, and most of our capitals now seem to be moving to permanent water restrictions and a generally heightened 'water insecurity'. For instance, water expert Professor John Langford says that 'Perth in Western Australia, located on the margins between a large dry region and the wetter southwest corner of the state, is particularly sensitive to climate change. Perth has experienced a decline in average rainfall of 15 per cent over the past 35 years compared to the previous 70 years, resulting in a 50 per cent reduction in average stream flow into Perth's water storages' (John Langford, personal communication).

Many urban Australians may already believe that 'the weather is changing'; scientists, in contrast, are cautious people and not inclined to follow or reflect conventional wisdom. They deal in observed phenomena and the theories, built into mathematical models of processes, that tell us why the phenomena are happening. The core of the IPCC work

is directed towards finding out whether or not the records of temperature observations confirm that global warming is occurring, and
whether or not observations of the Earth's atmosphere correspond with
what the models predict.

Now any scientific endeavour is attended by uncertainty. It is well
known that the Earth has warmed and cooled naturally at intervals over
its lifespan of billions of years. What is new and dangerous about the
current phenomenon is the extraordinary speed with which the new
warming seems to be happening. Over a million years, or even perhaps
10 000 years, the Earth's inhabitants – plants and animals (including
humans) – stand a chance of adapting to the changing climatic conditions. Though we humans are very adaptable creatures and can live in
very hot or very cold climates, we are still dependent for food on the
adaptability of the plants and animals in the ecosystems that support
human life. There is little chance of adaptation if the change takes place
over a few hundred years or less.[12] The Earth's biosphere will itself
adapt, by simply shrugging off the cause of global warming: humans.
For us global warming means much more than a change in the weather.
Failure to adapt our economy to reduce global warming will bring death
and misery on a scale never seen before in human history. The scale of
death will enormously exceed the plagues of the Middle Ages and the
persecutions and wars of the 20th century. Every single one of us on this
planet should be frightened by this prospect.

Reliable surface temperature records have only been kept since about
1860; satellite observations of the upper atmosphere for little more than
a decade. The warming signal from the atmosphere has only become
noticeable in the last century, with an upturn from about 1915 to 1940
and another larger upturn from 1970 to the present. This is a very short
time span over which to assess what is normally a very slow-moving
event. Not surprisingly, a few scientists dispute the findings. One of these
is Professor Richard Lindzen, a meteorologist from Massachusetts
Institute of Technology, who has challenged the interpretation of the
data. These challenges, including the arguments of Lindzen, have in fact
been very carefully and cautiously assessed by the IPCC and – unfortunately – refuted. While many people, some of them scientists, dispute
global warming, there is near consensus among those scientists who
specialise in the study of climate that global warming *is* being observed,
even over the short time so far available for observation.[13]

Nevertheless, there is still uncertainty and debate, just as there was
over the ozone hole forming over the Antarctic (see Box 1.1). At the

time of the ozone debates a new principle was applied: the 'precautionary principle'. This principle states simply that if a predicted event has serious enough consequences, lack of scientific certainty does not justify lack of action. The depletion of the ozone layer, which protects the Earth's upper latitudes from harmful ultraviolet radiation, was considered to have such consequences. As a result, even before the processes of ozone destruction were fully understood, the world took action to ban the production and use of the family of chemicals believed to be causing the problem, chlorofluorocarbons, through the Montreal Protocol (and subsequent amendments). The consequences of rapid global warming are likely to be more terrible than the loss of the ozone layer. The precautionary principle must be applied again.

Box 1.1 CLIMATE CONTROVERSY

Debate and controversy are how science typically proceeds. The world is largely unaware of the debates that rage within most scientific fields. But because climate change affects us all, the media seize upon any climate controversy as extremely newsworthy. A challenge to the mainstream consensus on global warming caused by human intervention is rapidly reported, and the reports can then be adopted by vested interests as a reason for political inaction. For example, on 17 January 2004 *The Age* headlined an Insight piece by Stephen Cauchi: 'A load of hot air?', and continued, 'Despite freak weather and looming extinctions, scientists are divided by a new row over whether global warming matters – a row the world's politicians have been quick to exploit as the Kyoto treaty approaches deadline' (Insight, p. 1).

Needless to say, the career of a scientist whose work proved conclusively either that global warming was not occurring or that the result was benign would receive an immense boost – ultimately, a Nobel prize. So there is very good reason for scientists to challenge the consensus. These challenges show that science is in a healthy condition! But those of us who care about the future should *not* take them as a reason for inaction.

Cauchi reports that geologists have tried to show that fluctuations in climate are a natural phenomenon. A recent challenge (2003) comes from two Canadians, statistician Stephen McIntyre and economist Ross McKitrick, who have been reinterpreting existing data and seeking to show that the period of warming that happened about 1000 years ago was actually warmer than the present. Since this period was before industrial development started adding carbonic gases to the atmosphere, their conclusion is that the Earth's climate shifts naturally, and therefore the current observations of warming may not be caused by human intervention at all. Bob Carter, Professor of Geology at James Cook University, wrote in the *Australian Financial Review* (November 2003) that, 'The 20th century temperature rise is seen in proper perspective to lie well within the bounds of historic temperature change.' Sceptical environmentalist Bjørn Lomborg disagrees: he believes climate change is real.

These controversies are quite peripheral to the main discovery and its consequences: namely that the Earth's climate is unstable, that humans are adding massively to a key element, atmospheric CO_2, and that a rapid climatic shift would almost certainly impose a colossal burden of adaptation and mass death within species, including our own.

The most important discovery about the Earth's climate in the last 50 years is actually not the warming trend but the fact that the climate is highly unstable and subject to patterns of change that resist straightforward prediction. The debates in the 1950s that led to the discovery of global warming were mostly about the cause of the ice ages, periods of extreme cold when ice sheets spread from the poles into what are now temperate latitudes. Very small changes in the balance of the many elements that affect the climate can tip the climate rapidly into a new phase. Whether in the longer run the phase will be much warmer or much colder cannot be predicted with certainty.

For instance, one possible result of global warming could be the melting of the polar ice. A deep and very slow ocean circulation called the 'thermohaline conveyor' brings warmer water near the equator gradually to the polar latitudes. The conveyor is thought to be driven by cold polar water sinking to the ocean floor, moving slowly along the depths. Warmer water correspondingly flows along the upper ocean layers from equatorial to polar latitudes, warming the polar climate. If this happened, the water's saltiness at the poles would be diluted by melting ice sheets. This, plus the fact that water that is less salty is also lighter, could counteract the tendency of colder water to sink, capping the thermohaline and switching it off. This in turn could lead to a sudden cooling at the poles, which may trigger a new ice age even while temperatures at the equator become hotter.

Another alarming possibility is a massive and sudden warming caused by the release of vast bubbles of methane from the ocean floor. Methane is a greenhouse gas that can trap about 20 times more heat than carbon dioxide. Enormous quantities of the gas exist in solid form as methane hydrates, or 'clathrates'. These are 'ice-like substances found in the muck of seabeds around the world'.[14] They are kept solid by both immense pressure and the cold of the ocean depths. The heat from a warming atmosphere, however, will gradually be transferred down through the ocean layers in ways we do not yet perfectly understand. If the water in the bottom layers warms enough to melt the clathrates, methane will be freed and bubble to the surface, causing a rapid spike in global warming.

The gradual build-up of carbon dioxide in the atmosphere – which we know for certain is occurring – could become the trigger for a sudden and profound climatic change over a time span as short as 10 years. The evidence from ice cores drilled kilometres down into the Antarctic show in fact that volatility is not abnormal. The Harvard physicist and science historian Spencer Weart thus arrives at a startling conclusion: 'The entire rise of human civilization since the end of the Younger Dryas [a prolonged cold period lasting about 1200 years, beginning about 9600 BCE] had taken place during a warm period that was far more stable than any other period in the last 400,000 years. The climate known to history is a lucky anomaly.'[15] So all human civilisation may have been made possible by an unusual climate system that humans are now in the process of destroying. We can now expect climate change to be not a gentle and gradual warming, but instead periods of slower change leading to massive, rapid and highly unpredictable shocks.

While much of the debate over global warming has been about observations, a different way of looking at the matter, which is perhaps not so well known, brings the problem into sharper focus. The Earth sustains what is called the 'carbon cycle', in which carbon in the form of gas is transferred between places where carbon is stored.[16] Such places are the atmosphere (which contains carbon dioxide gas), the land biosphere (the Earth's cover of vegetation on land, which contains solid carbon in plant and animal matter), and the oceans (which contain both plant and animal matter and dissolved carbon dioxide). These are the main storages of carbon: 'carbon pools' or 'carbon sinks'. An exchange of carbon is continually occurring among these carbon sinks.

Over the billions of years of the Earth's existence a rather fine balance has developed, so that the flow of carbon into the atmosphere has been approximately equalled by its reabsorption by the other carbon sinks – the ocean and land biosphere. In fact the balance is tilted slightly in favour of the absorption of gas from the atmosphere by the other pools. Thus in a study of the period 1980–89, the surface layer of the ocean each year absorbed about 92 gigatonnes (billion tonnes) of carbon and gave up about 90 gigatonnes into the atmosphere. The land biosphere absorbed about 61.4 gigatonnes from the atmosphere and gave up about 60 gigatonnes into the atmosphere. There was also an exchange of carbon between the deep ocean and the surface layer: the surface ocean absorbed 100 gigatonnes from the deep and sent back 91.6 gigatonnes (Figure 1.1).[17]

Into this system comes human activity. According to the International Energy Agency, emissions of carbon dioxide from the burning of fossil fuels sent 6.14 gigatonnes of carbon dioxide into the atmosphere in 1999 (with zero being returned to the source, as power stations do not absorb any greenhouse gas!). Changing land use, including land clearing, sent another 1.1 gigatonnes net into the atmosphere. It is very clear that the major factor upsetting the existing balance is the emission of carbon dioxide and other greenhouse gases, and most of it comes from cities.

It is not just people that produce greenhouse gas through domestic activities such as heating and cooling their homes. It is also the production of commodities and services, including travel: fossil-fuelled economic growth. But of course economic growth can occur with different amounts of greenhouse gas emissions. We need to know how much greenhouse gas is emitted per dollar of growth, and how that is changing over time. Is the world now emitting less greenhouse gas in the drive for growth, or more? Is the rate of economic growth itself overwhelming any improvements in greenhouse emissions per dollar?

With the support of its General Assembly, the UN has created a Framework Convention on Climate Change to co-ordinate the actions

Figure 1.1 The carbon cycle 1989: natural exchanges and human impacts.

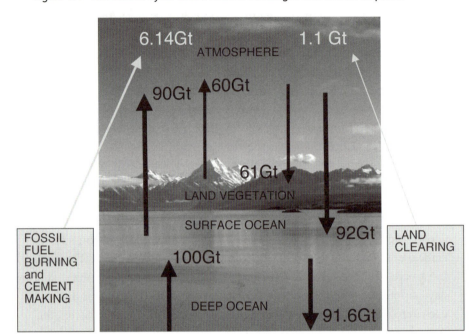

Source of the numbers: J.T. Houghton, L.G.M. Filho, B.A. Callander, N. Harris, A. Kettenberg & K. Maskell (eds), *Climate Change, 1995: The Science of Climate Change*, Cambridge University Press, Cambridge, 1996 (Figure 2.1, p. 77). Note that the components of the carbon cycle are simplified and subject to considerable uncertainty. The figures represent average values and may vary from year to year *(photograph of Mount Cook, New Zealand, by Vinca Low).*

nations are taking to reduce greenhouse emissions. The aim is to reduce them – over the next 100 years – to a level that will avert catastrophic global warming. A 'protocol' was drawn up at the conference of the parties to the Climate Convention held in Kyoto, Japan in December 1997 (see Box 1.2). This protocol defines mandatory targets for each nation to reduce greenhouse emissions to, using 1990 as the base year. Australia was granted an exception from this regime, and was in fact allowed an 8 per cent increase till the end of 2012. The Kyoto Protocol comes into force (that is, becomes international law) when the developed countries ratifying the protocol together account for at least 55 per cent of all developed country emissions.

Adherence to the Protocol will not save the world from global warming, but it will be a small first step on a path that will see nations strengthening their actions over the next 50 years to reduce greenhouse emissions to the necessary low level by the end of the 21st century.

One hundred and eighty-eight nations (plus the European Union) have signed the Framework Climate Convention, including Australia and the United States.[18] As of 20 October 2004, 125 nations, which together account for 44.2 per cent of global carbon emissions, have signed, the Kyoto Protocol. But Australia, in lockstep with the United States, has refused to sign the Protocol and thus refused to 'take the lead in combating climate change and the adverse effects thereof', as the Climate Convention requires its signatories to do. Australia has abandoned its global responsibility, cocking a snook at the world and the future. These two spoiler nations refuse to take even the first step in global co-operation: both seem to value smokestacks over sustainability.

The intransigence of spoiler nations will not, however, stop the Kyoto process. As we write, 85 nations have signed. The US still refuses to sign, thus preventing Russia and the US from trading carbon credits. Under the protocol Russia could trade its reduced level of carbon emissions since 1990 (when the Soviet system collapsed) with the US, which

Figure 1.2 The carbon cycle 2059: natural exchanges and human impacts in a 'business as usual' scenario, 2059.

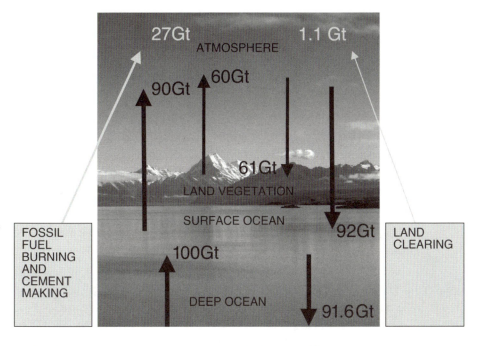

Based on scenarios used in J.T. Houghton, L.G.M. Filho, B.A. Callander, N. Harris, A. Kettenberg & K. Maskell (eds), *Climate Change, 1995: The Science of Climate Change*, Cambridge University Press, Cambridge, 1996 *(photograph of Mount Cook by Vinca Low)*.

Box 1.2 THE UN FRAMEWORK CONVENTION ON CLIMATE CHANGE
AND THE KYOTO PROTOCOL

FRAMEWORK CONVENTION

Article 2:

'The ultimate objective of this convention and any related legal instruments that the conference of the parties may adopt is to achieve, in accordance with the relevant provisions of the convention, stabilization of greenhouse gas concentrations in the atmosphere at a level that would prevent dangerous anthropogenic interference with the climate system. Such a level should be achieved within a time-frame sufficient to allow ecosystems to adapt naturally to climate change, to ensure that food production is not threatened and to enable economic development to proceed in a sustainable manner.'

Extract from 'Principles':

1 The Parties should protect the climate system for the benefit of present and future generations of humankind, on the basis of equity and in accordance with their common but differentiated responsibilities and respective capabilities. Accordingly, the developed country Parties should take the lead in combating climate change and the adverse effects thereof.

2 The specific needs and special circumstances of developing country Parties, especially those that are particularly vulnerable to the adverse effects of climate change, and of those Parties, especially developing country Parties, that would have to bear a disproportionate or abnormal burden under the Convention, should be given full consideration.

3 The parties should take precautionary measures to anticipate, prevent or minimize the causes of climate change and mitigate its adverse effects. Where there are threats of serious or irreversible damage, lack of full scientific certainty should not be used as a reason for postponing such measures, taking into account that policies and measures to deal with climate change should be cost-effective so as to ensure global benefits at the lowest possible cost. To achieve this, such policies and

measures should take into account different socio-economic contexts, be comprehensive, cover all relevant sources, sinks and reservoirs of greenhouse gases and adaptation, and comprise all economic sectors. Efforts to address climate change may be carried out cooperatively by interested parties.

THE KYOTO PROTOCOL

Extract from Article 3:

1 The Parties included in Annex I [the developed countries] shall, individually or jointly, ensure that their aggregate anthropogenic carbon dioxide equivalent emissions of the greenhouse gases listed in Annex A do not exceed their assigned amounts, calculated pursuant to their quantified emission limitation and reduction commitments inscribed in Annex B and in accordance with the provisions of this Article, with a view to reducing their overall emissions of such gases by at least 5 per cent below 1990 levels in the commitment period 2008 to 2012.

Source: http://unfccc.int/resource/conv/conv.html.

has increased its emission level. But despite this, President Putin has now (12 November 2004) confirmed Russia's ratification of the Kyoto Protocol bringing it into effect. Trading of 'carbon credits' can begin – but not with the world's biggest polluter, the US. Unfortunately, Russia is also threatening to turn 843 million hectares of natural woodland over to 'private enterprise' (mostly run by the former numenklatura of the Communist Party) for logging.[19] Twenty-two per cent of the world's forests are in Russia.

The IPCC has developed 40 scenarios, based on a variety of assumptions about world economic growth. The scenarios are wildly diverging, but all of them indicate that unless the world takes immediate action, emissions are going to grow to dangerous levels in the next 50 years. Depending on the scenario, the level of global greenhouse emissions by 2059 is predicted to be between 9 gigatonnes per year and 27 gigatonnes per year (Figure 1.2). The first amount, from the most optimistic scenario, is dependent on full adoption of the Kyoto Protocol and continuous progress under the Framework Climate Convention to reduce greenhouse emissions. However, all these scenarios are just informed guesses, really, and all could turn out to be overoptimistic.

China and India are two vast nations, and growth in both of them over the past 10 years has been spectacular. Suppose that the economies of China and India continue to grow for the next 50 years at the same average rate as they have in the last 10 years. For the sake of world prosperity, as well as their own, we must hope that this happens. These nations have also been reducing the amount of greenhouse gas emitted per dollar of growth, but they are still a long way behind the US. The US is by far the world's largest greenhouse emitter, but even its vast economy emits much less greenhouse gas per dollar than China's. Let us further suppose that these two rapidly developing nations reduce their greenhouse performance (emissions per dollar) to the US level during the next 50 years. The result would be that China and India alone, just two nations (albeit with 30 per cent of the world's people), would be emitting about 23 gigatonnes of greenhouse gas per year.

Turn back now to the carbon cycle. To stabilise the balance in the global climate system, the atmosphere must retain the capacity each year to absorb some of the carbon already deposited there by industrial growth over the last 100 years. Fortunately, in this respect we have nature on our side. Climatologists of the IPCC tell us that the world has to get its greenhouse emissions down to about 2 gigatonnes per year within 50 years. This figure is now accepted by the Royal Commission on Environmental Pollution in the UK and by Dr Graeme Pearman, the chief atmospheric scientist of the CSIRO.[20] In contrast, all credible scenarios (notably, those generated by the IPCC) suggest that in 50 years' time the world will be emitting between 9 and 27 gigatonnes – and maybe much more. Even the lower, optimistic figure, when compared with the total global exchange between the atmosphere and the surface of the planet (about 150 gigatonnes), represents an enormous disturbance of the carbon cycle. Worse still, that disturbance may cause positive feedback effects that turbocharge global warming: an increase in water vapour, itself a potent greenhouse agent, for example. Therefore, given what we know today about the greenhouse effect and the climate system, it is highly improbable that a disturbance of such a scale would *not* cause a global climate catastrophe. If such a catastrophe is to be averted, action to meet the real target – a 60 to 70 per cent reduction in emissions (from the 1990 figure) over 50 years – must begin immediately.

There is total agreement among climate scientists on the effect that carbon dioxide and other greenhouse gases have on the atmosphere. There is total agreement that the amount of these gases accumulating in the atmosphere is steadily and regularly increasing every year. Under these circumstances, the dispute over whether or not global warming has yet been observed is a little like a dispute over the functioning of the speedometer among the occupants of a car speeding towards a brick wall. The arguments about the timing and nature of 'collateral' damage obscure the sure consequence of inaction. The journey may not harm us but the sudden stop at the end most definitely will.

THE THREAT TO THE BIOSPHERE

Cities contain what urban ecologists call 'remnant' vegetation. These remnants are scraps and pockets; all that remain of plants, animals and ecosystems that occupied the land before the city developed on it. How far are we from a state on Earth in which remnants are all that remain anywhere of the natural ecological heritage of 4 billion years of evolution?

The environment contains a great variety of plant and animal species whose potential environmental services to humanity are unknown and largely unexploited. Humans have been content to domesticate a very few species and cultivate them as monocultures, to the exclusion of most others – which become designated 'weeds' or 'pests' if they interfere with human activity. The term 'biodiversity' refers to the range of different species, from slime moulds to pandas, bacteria to gorillas, and the ecological systems of relationships that have evolved among these creatures.

Cities are both directly and indirectly responsible for the destruction of biodiversity: directly in that urban development replaces the habitat of non-human species with habitat for humans, and indirectly and far more seriously through the city's agricultural 'footprint' on the land. This footprint overwhelmingly consists of monocultures, and means that natural ecological habitats are forced to the margins and small remnant pockets.

Predicting climate change is an exact science compared with investigating the extinction of species. There have been mass extinctions before on the planet. Since the Cambrian period in the Earth's evolution (500 million years ago) there have been five major extinction events when between 30 and 50 per cent of all species were wiped out over a relatively short period – from a few hundred to a few thousand years.[21] The last event, about 65 million years ago, destroyed the ruling order of dinosaurs. Humans are today the ruling order, and of course there are significant differences between these two ruling orders. First, whereas the dinosaurs numbered thousands of species of enormous variety, humans number just one. Second, and this is also both quite unlike the dinosaurs and quite unprecedented in the Earth's 4 billion year history, the ruling species is becoming the probable cause of extinction of many of the rest of the Earth's species.

There have been some extravagant claims made about species extinction caused by human destruction of forest habitat. In 1979, Oxford University ecologist Norman Myers claimed, in his book *The Sinking Ark*, that with the rate of loss of forest habitat continuing at 2 per cent per year, one-quarter of all species would be lost by the year 2000, an extinction rate of 40,000 species per year. 'Sceptical environmentalist' Bjørn Lomborg argues that Myers' estimate is just a guess about the consequences of deforestation, based on no hard evidence. Species are very gradually evolving and becoming extinct all the time, so the rate of extinction is important. Lomborg admits that contiguous large areas of forest habitat are disappearing rapidly, but claims that this does not necessarily lead to species extinction – well, not yet. Even so, he endorses a more recent study that suggests that the current extinction rate of all species worldwide is about 0.7 per cent every 50 years, which is something like 1500 times the 'background' rate of extinction (what would happen without human or extra-terrestrial impact).[22]

Unfortunately, it is not easy to discover the truth with any precision, for all sorts of reasons. What counts as a species? How many species are there? We can only make the roughest of estimates, because the largest categories are the orders that biologists rarely want to examine, such as fungi and insects. Do the tiny moulds and bugs count as much as the larger animals and the bigger and more beautiful plants? A certain sense of fairness suggests that perhaps they should, but should all species be necessarily regarded as equal? Is it reasonable to regard the mosquito as the equal of the tiger?

The evolution and extinction of species moves extremely slowly, and human population in today's numbers has never occurred before, so it is quite possible that the greatest extinction is yet to come. All we have to go on are a limited number of case studies, which scientists call 'anecdotal evidence'. This evidence comes from a series of locally specific scientific studies (it is not just people telling stories!). If the scientifically reliable studies in particular places around the world are representative of the loss of species worldwide, species extinction is running at a rate of between 1000 and 10,000 times the background rate. Even if we assume that the studies are not representative of species extinction worldwide, it can still be argued that the rate is still 200–1000 times higher than the background rate. This qualifies as a mass extinction – 'the sixth great extinction, the one generated by humankind'.[23] Interestingly, Lomborg and those who believe mass extinction is on the way, such as Richard Leakey, do not disagree substantially on the rate of extinction.

Will species extinction continue for many hundreds of years to come? Lomborg thinks that as humanity gets richer, it will have more spare cash to care for other species. Unfortunately, humanity has been getting richer for 100 years and still does not know how to share out the wealth fairly within its own species. The enrichment of humanity has so far also come at the expense of the environment, which is why we now face a species extinction crisis. And we have hardly seen the effects of global warming yet. A new scientific study, 'the largest collaboration of scientists yet to have investigated the impact of climate change on biodiversity', published in 2004 in the world's most prestigious scientific journal, Nature, reports that the effect of global warming, based on IPCC data, will be the extinction of a million species by 2050.[24]

Klaus Toepfer, the Executive Director of the UN Environment Program (UNEP), commenting on the report, said:

> If 1 million species become extinct as a result of global warming, it is not just the plant and animal kingdoms and the beauty of the planet that will suffer. Billions of people, especially in the developing world, will suffer too as they rely on nature for such essential goods and services as food, shelter and medicines.[25]

If these predictions are to be believed, species extinction will occur much faster than even Leakey believes. So the future extinction rate may well approach Myers' 'unlikely' estimate. At the UN Rio Earth Summit in 1992 a global agreement was drawn up to conserve biodiversity (the Convention on Biological Diversity). The Convention has been signed by 188 nations to date, including Australia. Although it does not specify urban biodiversity, it covers both urban and non-urban areas (see Box 1.3). It is not just a matter of conserving biodiversity within urban areas, though this is critically important (see chapter 3); it is also about the impact of urban systems on ecologies far from cities – the diverting of water from non-urban areas to urban areas, for instance (Box 1.4).

Box 1.3 THE UN CONVENTION ON BIOLOGICAL DIVERSITY

The UN Convention on Biological Diversity is a global development convention agreed to at the Rio Earth Summit (UN Conference on Environment and Development) in 1992. It has been signed (to date) by 188 nations, including Australia. Although the convention does not specify urban biodiversity, its scope is inclusive of both urban and non-urban areas.

Article 1 of the convention (Objectives) states:

> The objectives of this Convention, to be pursued in accordance with its relevant provisions, are the conservation of biological diversity, the sustainable use of its components and the fair and equitable sharing of the benefits arising out of the utilization of genetic resources, including by appropriate access to genetic resources and by appropriate transfer of relevant technologies, taking into account all rights over those resources and to technologies, and by appropriate funding.

In **Article 2** the meaning of the term 'biological diversity' is explained:

> 'Biological diversity' means the variability among living organisms from all sources including, inter alia, terrestrial, marine and other aquatic ecosystems and the ecological complexes of which they are part; this includes diversity within species, between species and of ecosystems.

This convention is designed to foster international cooperation, so **Article 5** states that 'each Contracting Party shall, as far as possible and as appropriate, cooperate with other Contracting Parties, directly or, where appropriate, through competent international organizations, in respect of areas beyond national jurisdiction and on other matters of mutual interest, for the conservation and sustainable use of biological diversity'.

Article 6 speaks of the general measures to be taken. These include national strategies for conservation and sustainable use of biological diversity. Importantly for *urban* biodiversity, each nation shall also: 'integrate, as far as possible and as appropriate, the conservation and sustainable use of biological diversity into relevant sectoral or cross-sectoral plans, programmes and policies'.

Article 7 requires nations to engage in 'identification and monitoring' of biological diversity:

- Identify components of biological diversity important for its conservation and sustainable use.
- Monitor ... the components of biological diversity identified, ... paying particular attention to those requiring urgent conservation measures and those which offer the greatest potential for sustainable use.
- Identify processes and categories of activities which have or are likely to have significant adverse impacts on the conservation and sustainable use of biological diversity.

Source: *United Nations Convention on Biological Diversity,*
http://www.biodiv.org/doc/publications/guide.asp.

Box 1.4 MELBOURNE'S WATER AND THE THOMSON RIVER

Metropolitan Melbourne depends for the largest part of its water supply on the Thomson Reservoir, which has a capacity of 1068 gigalitres (about 59 per cent of the city's total water storage capacity). The reservoir has been artificially created by the Thomson Dam, which retains the waters of the Thomson River. The Thomson is one of several rivers that flow into the Gippsland Lakes, and before the dam was built the Thomson flushed water through the lakes system. The lakes are regularly subject to blooms of toxic blue–green algae; these are not flushed out when flows are very restricted. The ecological health of both the river and the lakes depends on these flows at times of peak rainfall. A scientific assessment of the river system has recommended that in order to restore the system to health, an additional 40 gigalitres per year be released from the reservoir into the river. It is now understood that such 'environmental flows' have to be maintained.

The drought reduced Melbourne's water storages to 49 per cent full in January 2003. They increased to 54 per cent full by

Box 1.4 continues over page

the following year (January 2004). Metropolitan Melbourne used 483 gigalitres of water in 2002–03, and mild water restrictions were brought in in 2002, with a target of saving 13 gigalitres per year. As a result of the restrictions, Melburnians saved a total of 46 gigalitres in the 14 months between November 2002 and January 2004. Even though December 2003 was the hottest December for 130 years, Melburnians still managed to save 20 per cent more than the target.

It is clear that there is great scope for metropolitan water saving and that consumers respond very well to calls to save water. People understand that water is not in endless supply and that there is a need to share water with the more than human environment.

The Australian Bureau of Statistics estimates that around Australia's regions of major urban growth (Sydney, Melbourne, Brisbane and the Queensland growth areas, Perth and Adelaide) there are 1625 species of plants, 12 species of mammals, 110 species of birds, 107 species of reptile and 29 species of fish at risk. Insects and fungi, as usual, don't rate a mention![26]

The greatest threat to species comes from the conversion of land from wilderness to cultivation: agriculture and forestry. Biologists Leakey and Lewin point out that a single species (humans) uses 40 per cent of all the energy available to sustain all life (all species) on Earth. If we are to reduce species extinction, we must stop converting land to cultivation. But at the same time, there is pressure to increase the food supply for humans. Life in cities, as presently constructed, cannot continue without food from elsewhere on the planet, and water from regions surrounding the cities. Both food and water supply are themselves now global problems.

Australian cities are fortunate in being well supplied with food. Most of what is consumed could be produced locally – but much of it isn't. But population growth in developing countries is placing pressure on food supplies worldwide, and Australia is a key player in the world trade in food. Feeding a future 9 or 10 billion people is a global problem which no country can escape. Put crudely, if people are starving, they will move to where they can eat. Australia itself attracted people who were doing just that; they displaced the indigenous culture and people, taking what was known as the 'geographical cure' to economic ills – men, sometimes whole families, 'going on the wallaby' in search of food and security. Many of us are their descendants. The constant drift to our cities from rural areas, especially in times of agricultural downturn, is a less dramatic example of this. But mass movement driven by the need for food and 'environmental security' in today's populous world would cause enormous ecological and – more worryingly – geopolitical disruptions. If the scale of movement is big enough, only enormous expenditure on border protection, and even perhaps mass killing, will prevent people's entry. War becomes a distinct and evil possibility.

Heavy cropland losses are expected during the next 50 years in developing countries with big populations and food needs – India and China, for example. India has already tripled its wheat yield and doubled its rice yield. It will find it difficult to sustain an increase in land productivity that will offset the shrinkage of the area devoted to grain growing, though. China is in a slightly better position. Its population is not growing as fast as India's, but even its land area devoted to grain production is expected to shrink to 0.06 hectares (a plot just 25 metres square) per person. China's area of productive land may be able to support its population at current standards, but it won't support it if, with growing affluence, there is a tendency to eat more meat products.[27]

The most serious problem comes for nations in the second tier of size: Pakistan, Nigeria and Indonesia, which are all projected to pass the 300 million mark by 2050, and Ethiopia, which will cross the 200 million mark. Pakistan is expected to grow in population to 357 million by 2050; this is more than today's population of the US and Canada together. Pakistan's crop area is expected to shrink to 0.3 hectares per person. So far, increased productivity of land for food has been possible, largely because of the so-called Green Revolution: new, more productive crops have been developed. But the new crops have a huge appetite for nutrients and water, and both are directly and indirectly supplied by petroleum – a fuel that will be priced out of reach within 50 years.[28]

So during the next 50 years or so Australia faces a choice: either the country welcomes in peace a very large influx of migrants (millions) who will settle here and work the land, or it must cultivate enough food to feed the urban populations of countries that cannot grow enough locally. No more land capable of producing food must be lost, especially good-quality agricultural land around cities. This is a strong argument for stopping metropolitan growth extending further and further into the rural hinterland. Our rural cities must be revived as part of a new settlement strategy that aims to secure a more sustainable use of our productive land.

Sustainability is not just a banner flying over environmentalism. It marks a larger agenda of improvement and hope for humankind that must be realised at a variety of geographic scales, including – but not limited to – the city. It involves much more than simply improving the local environment. Though the two may overlap, sustainability is not the same as local liveability. Sustainability is about the protection of the global commons: the atmosphere, the natural ecologies of land and water, the evolved species – the elements of nature in the midst of which all people belong. The move from growth to sustainability is one that every society in the world has to make. But it will not come easily. It requires a gradual but radical change, not so much in our lifestyles, because there will remain a great deal of choice about how we live, in what degree of material comfort and with what degree of mobility, but, as this book hopes to show, in the means of achieving those lifestyles. One aspect of the change will be the recovery of an attitude to the relationship between humans and nature that has been submerged by today's economic culture: that is, the environment not only provides services for us humans; it has its own value independent of human use.

PEOPLE ARE NOT MAN-MADE

People are not man-made; we are an integral part of a natural world of great complexity and (still) considerable mystery. What we know about this world through science is dwarfed by what is yet to be known. We take spectacular risks when we assume that we know all the consequences of new technologies or social practices that change our relationships with nature. Caution is not a brake on change but a sensible insurance against our seemingly inbuilt tendency to overreach ourselves and thus compromise healthy natural relationships. As the celebrated German sociologist, Ulrich Beck, warns us, we need to remind ourselves continually of the value of self-awareness – of 'reflexivity' – and of the consequences of our actions, especially radical shifts or innovations that have profound impacts on the natural world. We must constantly practise the habit of reflexivity – we too often abandon self-awareness in the euphoria that arises during the emergence of new technologies and their social supports. Sometimes these have terrible consequences. So many new industries and technologies which were assumed to liberate us from our human and natural limitations, for example, ended up chaining us to terribly despoiled ecological conditions. The city can be deployed for good or for bad, but it can never be used to 'free' us from nature. A reflexive city contains a citizenry that is always aware of its direct and indirect relationships with nature.

Human systems of production, consumption, government and culture are subject to the ecological resources of the planet, a closed system containing wealth accumulated over 4 billion years, but with just one energy input – from the sun – and no outlet for waste. Given that awareness, what do we humans owe nature?

This question of justice – what is due to whom, what is deserved, and what are rights – has been posed in different ways in different cultures for millennia. Some ancient cultures have treated the natural world with respect and compassion, including humans and nature within the same moral sphere. The Chinese Daoist and Japanese Buddhist philosophies, for example, show reverence for the natural world, as is evident from their gardens and paintings. Australian indigenous culture links the human person and community to the land ('country') and its non-human inhabitants in quite specific ways. But these cultures have been inundated by the tide of modern Euro-American culture, which is focused exclusively on the growth of the human species. This culture contains the depleted and dangerous central idea that we live only to work, breed and die efficiently. Only islands of the old cultures remain in an ocean of commercial economy, and these remnants have for the most part been turned into pleasing aesthetic objects to be visited, collected and traded.

The economic culture rules nature out of the moral question by casting human beings as fundamentally different from the rest of the natural world. Only humans are believed to have value. The economic culture goes further, making the welfare of the 'individual' person the only matter of moral concern. And, in a yet more extreme version of this philosophy (in Australia called 'economic rationalism'), the key social relationships of production, consumption and government are expected to be conducted under a single set of moral rules, the market, in which individuals pursue their own 'self-interest', the self being a homunculus shrunk to the simple register of pleasure and pain. It is a morally warped view of our position in the world.

But despite the glorification of the pursuit of self-interest, the economy could not function without a corresponding social solidarity – people helping each other and working together for reasons that have little to do with the homunculus featured in economic philosophy. It is now becoming clear that such solidarity is also felt beyond the human species, and even though our ties with the 'more than human' world may be weak, they are nevertheless essential to the survival of our species.[29]

Many people intuitively understand that human self-interest can extend to include the more than human world. People care for animals and other elements of nature and feel that they deserve moral consideration. It is absurd to reduce the value of conserving the orang-utan or blue whale to its potential future utility for humans. So the question of what, in justice, is owed to nature is a real and pertinent one. Answering it is a much more difficult matter, one likely to occupy philosophers increasingly as the natural world comes to be viewed as a partner rather than a slave. However, it is perhaps the first step that is the most important one: treating the whole of nature, and any part of it, as valuable in its own right.[30]

In modern times there are two features of human society that enable the illusion of detachment to be maintained. One is the application of science to the production of a vast array of goods that enable us to live without direct contact with nature. The other is the placing of geographical distance between production and consumption. The first can be called 'substitutability', the second 'remoteness'.

In cities and towns, human societies surround themselves with the products of human ingenuity: buildings, roads, cars, pipes and wires, machines of every conceivable kind, electronic gadgets, communication devices (mobile and fixed), recreation devices, money, information, weapons, food. All of this can be called 'capital': the sum total of human products. It amounts to an impressive pile of stuff; it is so impressive, in fact, that it can appear to be a substitute for the natural world. Under this delusion, all our needs are met by the things humans produce. What further need do we have of natural objects?

Nature, it is even argued, is just a human idea. It is nature that is illusory. So dominant has the pile of capital become in our minds that some environmental economists, concerned to bring nature to the attention of their more conventional colleagues, use the term 'natural capital' to describe nature itself. But consider this: most of the capital that is around today, and the technological knowledge that made it possible, has been produced within the last 100 years. Let's suppose that the evolution of life on the planet has been going on for 1 billion years. The supporters of substitutability (which is basically the idea that everything can be solved by humans making more technology) argue that what humans have created is somehow equivalent to, and may now replace, what has evolved naturally over a period of time ten million times as long as the time in which humans have been busy building things. But substitutability, as a solution to the problem of how humans in ever-increasing numbers can survive on this planet, must be viewed rather in the way that we now look on the belief, held not so long ago, that a flat Earth is the centre of a universe of revolving musical spheres. It is a 'solution' that will surely fail us.

The best way of keeping distasteful events out of mind is to keep them out of sight. Australia, sometimes thought to be a civilised and compassionate country, has managed to introduce a form of concentration camp for refugees by placing it out in the desert. When members of the public and media arrived to have a look, an exclusion cordon had to be thrown around it to keep it from view. Despite that, the media have done a remarkably good job of revealing the frightening reality. Modern developed cities live under the illusion that they are 'post-industrial' and have now entered the Information Age, when in fact all that has happened is that the industrial filth and pollution of production has been moved to developing countries such as China and India.

The long-term remedy for these delusions is to bring people back into contact with nature, both aesthetically pleasing nature and productive nature, and to make transparent all the processes by which the natural world is turned into things for our use – so that it becomes possible for people to understand how hens become chicken fillets. This is not going to be a matter of moving people out to farmland or bringing the farm and other industries to town (though some of both may help). It will certainly involve communication – press, radio, film, TV and the internet. Cities will continue to be the main habitat of human life, and the world is going to see them continue to grow and proliferate. The task at hand is making contact with nature in the city a thoroughly pleasurable and self-expanding experience.

THE GREEN CITY

Cities as mass societies can function in glorious ignorance of their demands upon nature. But cities are also the loci of much of our most insightful critiques of consumerism and its harmful ecological (and social) consequences. The challenge is to connect these critical insights to people's everyday experience. This book makes a modest contribution to that task.

In the chapters that follow we do not look at the city from the perspective of the orthodox planner – the plan and the aerial perspective. Our view is, as far as possible, from ground level – we use the perspective of the citizen. Of course cities in reality contain an enormous multiplicity of elements, but we have pared them down to just four: houses, open spaces, workplaces and transport. Homes – or 'dwellings', to be accurate – are people's castles. They are the truly private domain of the person living alone or with others, and potentially of the primary social group, the family. A great area of the city is made up of 'housing' of one sort or another. All the rest is the public domain of the citizen. To maintain our suburban lifestyles we need only one-tenth of the environment that we now use. We explore just how this can be achieved in the next chapter.

It is sometimes easy to forget that there is usually more open space than enclosed, walled and roofed space in the city. This open space is of course permeable to nature – sometimes intentionally (as in parks and gardens), sometimes not. It is easy to forget that though private gardens may keep out people, the more than human city dwellers neither know nor respect the rules of property. As far as the natural world is concerned, the city is just a part of their territory. In what has been written so far there is a strong concern for the impact of cities and humans on nature. But what of the reverse: the impact of nature on humans? Insofar as we humans have evolved from nature and are still part of this wider whole, the more than human world still has an impact on our needs. These impacts are discussed in chapter 3.

There is no real privacy in workplaces. Work is generally public. Workplaces, as a category, cover just about all the other kinds of buildings (apart from homes) found in cities: offices, factories, shops and supermarkets, schools and universities, libraries and cinemas, casinos and churches. In this book we will not be so much concerned with work itself. Work, or what is usually termed 'industry', makes enormous demands on the environment, but that is the subject of other books. In this book we devote chapter 4 to what contains 'industry', the architecture of the built environment. Like homes, workplaces can be designed to reduce the drain on the environment and at the same time inform their users (workers, customers, clients) of their impact on and relationship with the environment.

All the preceding elements are tied together by lines of transport. Cities occur because large numbers of people interact, visit, journey, seek, find, and get together in myriad combinations. Likewise, goods are constantly on the move around cities, stocking shops and supermarkets, victualling offices and factories. These flows of people and goods represent the fastest-growing threat to the environment in terms of greenhouse gas emissions. In chapter 5 we discuss how urban transport systems can become more sustainable.

In chapter 6 we start to think about how the green city can be made to happen. Too often responsibility is laid at the feet of individuals to 'change their behaviour'. This is utterly wrong. Individualising responsibility is a scurrilous attempt by the immensely powerful collective institutions of our society to shed their own responsibility for the dangerous and unsustainable path they are treading. We are collectively responsible, and it is through the collective institutions of states and corporations that we can most effectively act to effect a change of path. Finally, chapter 7 offers some reflections on the 'green-shaded' city, acknowledging that there will be many different cultural ways of making the city sustainable.

SO NOW, BACK TO WHERE YOU LIVE – THE HOME AND THE SUBURB.

FURTHER READING

A good background to the global environmental situation in its various dimensions is provided by the books produced annually by the Worldwatch Institute, edited by Lester Brown & Christopher Flavin: *State of the World* (Earthscan, London) and *Vital Signs* (Earthscan, London). An overview of the environmental crisis from an Australian perspective is by Graeme Aplin and seven other authors: *Global Environmental Crises, An Australian Perspective* (Oxford University Press, Melbourne, 1999). Bjørn Lomborg's *The Skeptical Environmentalist* (Cambridge University Press, Cambridge, 2001) brings together in a thoughtful way the best of the arguments opposing the environmental enthusiasts. It is not unbiased in its interpretations, but it is a critique that must be taken seriously. One of the most readable books on global warming is *The Discovery of Global Warming* by Spencer Weart, Director of the Center for the History of Physics of the American Institute of Physics (Harvard University Press, Cambridge MA, 2003). A more technical text, representing the IPCC consensus, is Sir John Houghton's *Global Warming: The Complete Briefing* (Cambridge University Press, Cambridge, 2nd edition, 1997).

Those who want to know why faith in economics is misplaced, and are prepared to persevere, should read Steve Keen's *Debunking*

Economics: The Naked Emperor of the Social Sciences (Pluto Press, Sydney, 2001). This book has an unfortunate subtitle, because it is in fact a very substantial economics text in its own right. But it does make clear that economics is a philosophy fraught with internal inconsistency and uncertainties. Clive Hamilton's *Growth Fetish* (Allen & Unwin, Sydney, 2003) demonstrates how possessions are so often substituted for what is truly valuable. For a look at economics through the eyes of environmentalists, see Michael Jacobs, *The Green Economy* (Pluto Press, London, 1991), and Herman Daly, *Beyond Growth* (Beacon Press, Boston, 1996). Val Plumwood provides a masterful analysis of environmental philosophy in *Environmental Culture: The Ecological Crisis of Reason* (Routledge, London, 2002).

CHAPTER 2

SUSTAINABLE HOMES AND SUBURBS

What you mostly see when you fly down in a jet over a city are houses and suburbs. Looking down out of the window as the crew prepares for landing, there appear to be endless hectares of housing reaching out to a distant periphery where houses become fewer, merging with more and more paddocks, forests, meadows and gaps of nondescript open land which seem to be merely waiting to be filled up with urban development.

In some cities the housing is densely packed blocks of flats; in others, like those of Australia, single houses in gardens dominate. Every one of those houses is a little whirlpool of environmental consumption. Together they create a giant vortex, swallowing materials and energy and spewing out waste – and, in the process, providing citizens with a decent quality of life. Can we maintain our much-vaunted quality of life with much less environmental consumption and waste?

In the 20th century, town planners had visions of whole cities. Their visions were of ideal spatial and social patterns. These ideas stemmed from observed geographical patterns of settlement, hierarchies of villages, towns and cities in which town and countryside lived in harmony. Planners with an engineering background thought about patterns of infrastructure – great reservoirs supplying reticulations of channels and pipes for water supply, and of drainage and sewerage conveying soiled water to remote treatment plants, or sometimes just discharging into the ocean. Gas and electrical power were thought of in a similar way, with distant gas holders and power stations supplying energy for heating and lighting. Above all, perhaps, transport systems with vast networks of railways and roads were planned. Sometimes the patterns embraced by architect planners seem to have been chosen for their aesthetic quality, as abstract designs. Always the viewpoint was from high above the real city. A 'city plan' is in fact an abstraction of a city, viewed from 10,000 metres above that city (see Figure 2.1).

Figure 2.1 An orthodox planner's view of the city

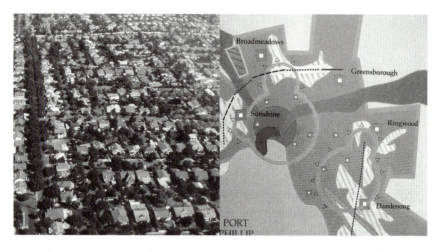

Source: Ministry for Planning and Environment (MPE), *Shaping Melbourne's Future*, MPE, Melbourne, 1987.

These visions of heroic social and physical engineering have had a powerful effect on the structure of cities worldwide, with mixed results. They have brought into being new towns and green belts, but they have also encouraged forms of urban growth that are oblivious to their effects on the environment. When you can simply 'plug' a new suburb into a set of large and abstract resource grids, there is little incentive to consider the overall impact of such a decision on the natural resource base. Incremental urban expansion made possible by giant utility networks can never adequately sense or take responsibility for the real costs of growth. This is another example of the city that lacks self-awareness, which we drew attention to in chapter 1. The reflexive city, in contrast, would localise the impacts of growth by insisting that as many resources as possible (water, energy and food, for example) are sourced, processed and disposed of locally. This localised, 'self-aware' system of resource use and waste disposal would instil in urban communities a real sense of the ecological demands they generate through everyday activities. If the consequences of resource use are immediately manifest and always known to us, we are much less likely to waste our natural capital.

Of the energy used to light one incandescent light globe, 97 per cent is wasted; 70 per cent is used up before it reaches the light globe, as heat generated by the power station and in heating the cables and transformers through which the electricity passes. Once the 30 per cent of the energy that becomes electricity reaches the light globe, only 10 per cent is converted into light. Similar wasteful use of energy and materials can be found in most other chains of supply of products and services that end up in the house. The localisation of supply and disposal will do much to reduce the waste that seems inevitable in big utility systems.

The point is to reduce waste, not wellbeing. The services that people want from housing can still be supplied – and in fact improved – while we cut down what is taken from the environment by a factor of at least four and quite feasibly ten. A tenfold reduction in damaging greenhouse emissions, for example, can be achieved without reduction in quality of life; on the contrary, it can be done while making an improvement in quality of life. But achieving such a result means adopting a different perspective and making changes – not so much to the citizens' lifestyles, but to production systems.

The vision for the green city has to be shaped in a different way; it needs to come not from the air, but from ground level, in the street, from the front door. The aerial perspective biases planning in favour of the whole system, to the neglect of the small parts, the microtexture of city life. Building the green city does not mean that the system-wide perspective should be abandoned, but that the order of consideration should be reversed. Instead of starting with the whole pattern and working down to the units of which it is composed, it is best to start with the units and work up to the systems into which they are organised. Doing things this way introduces an entirely new way of thinking about the urban system, a way of thinking that is not primarily geographical patterning. It also encourages planners to think first of the city in terms of the way people experience it every day, in the street on foot, in the house, car and train, on the ground. Thinking of the city in this way, as a system of places and local environments, might just make for a better result. By refocusing our attention on the scale of the everyday – the ordinary environment of our senses – we would begin to sensitise the city generally to the real nature of its resource use and environmental impact.

Let's start with the green house, and then move up in scale to green suburbs. This way it is easier to judge whether the lifestyle changes the green city entails are acceptable, and whether life in the green city will be better or worse than it is in the city of the present.

THE GREEN HOUSE

Michael Mobbs is one of a growing number of people around the world who have built 'green' houses. He has written up his experiences in a book which also works as a useful manual: *Sustainable House*.[1] Mobbs is a Sydney lawyer specialising in environmental law. He has also been a policy consultant to the government of New South Wales, and a Sydney City councillor. In the late 1980s serious episodes of water pollution occurred because of sewage discharged into Sydney Harbour and the ocean. These pollution events started Mobbs thinking about the water problem. Although the Water Board had taken steps to reduce pollution, the basic technology remained unchanged – sewage was collected from houses and piped to treatment plants, and thence into the ocean. As more houses were connected to the sewers, the problem became worse. Mobbs started redefining the problem from the ground up, thinking about the origins of sewage: the house. As he researched the possibility of attacking the problem at source, he also started thinking about the other systems to which the house is connected: the water and energy supply networks.

At the same time the Mobbs family was considering renovating their house in the inner-Sydney suburb of Chippendale. The family decided to make this house as independent as possible of the city's supply and disposal systems. Mobbs and his family took three years to research the technology necessary to make the house self-sustaining and ecologically undamaging (Plate 1). The renovations entailed rebuilding and refitting two rooms and installing a new roof over part of the building as well as installing waste treatment, water collection and energy-generating equipment. The construction itself was quick. Building work began in early September 1996 and the house was occupied by the end of November the same year.

The aim was to achieve four things: no rainwater to leave the property, no sewage to leave the property, water needs to be met from water falling on the roof, and all electricity and heating needs to be met from solar panels (solar hot water and an array of photovoltaic cells). In addition, plantation and regrowth timber only would be used in construction (no rainforest timber); only building materials produced by pollution-free manufacturing processes would be used; no materials that discharge toxic chemicals (for example formaldehyde) would be used in the construction; and PVC plastics would not be used.

The three main systems contributing to sustainability are the waste treatment and drinking water systems and the solar energy system. To work well for the household, all these systems had to require little maintenance, be capable of running themselves without attention by technical specialists, have reasonable installation costs, low operating costs and be constructed with widely available technologies.

Water is collected from the roof, so the roofing material needs to be suitable. A metal, ceramic tile or slate surface works well. Some houses have difficulty with leaves and sticks falling on to the roof from surrounding trees. In the inner city, though, toxic dust was the main problem. Even though leaf litter wasn't a serious problem for the Mobbs house, guttering was fitted that allowed for material falling onto the roof to be blown off the gutters instead of clogging the water flow into the downpipe. From the gutters, rainwater is directed through three filters before it reaches the storage tank. The first, at the head of the downpipe, is a sloping metal grid that sieves out crude litter. At the downpipe base, a length of pipe drains off the first 10 litres of water whenever it rains, removing the 'first flush' of rainwater. This pipe contains a lightweight ball that floats to the top of the diverter pipe when it is full and blocks entry to that pipe. The diverter pipe drains slowly into the garden. A further small settling sump with a mesh grille provides a last chance for any remaining sediment to drop out before the water enters the 10,000 litre storage tank. From the tank – designed to hold as much water as the household requires – clean water is pumped into the house. The electric pump is inexpensive and silent.

It is worth noting that the rainwater collected is not regarded as 'grey water', as it would be in Europe, but as drinking water. Not only did the roof water supply system have to meet the stringent requirements of the Water Board, but the Mobbs family was naturally concerned to monitor the water quality to make sure that it did not threaten the family's health. It was assessed according to the standards set by the National Health & Medical Research Council of Australia for heavy metals and other toxic pollutants. While other heavy metal content was well below safety limits, tests showed that the tap water contained more dissolved lead than the current recommended minimum of 0.01 milligrams per litre (mpl), varying from an undetectable level to 0.03 mpl. Such a level is in fact not uncommon in ordinary tap water, but the Mobbs family fitted a further filter for the taps most often used to drink from.

If the drinking water supply system seems remarkable, the sewage treatment plant is even more so. All waste water is processed through a 'wet compost system' developed in Australia by Dean Cameron and based on his design for a composting toilet. The system was approved by the NSW Department of Health for experimental use on the Mobbs site only. The system, which Cameron calls a 'biolytic filter', was manufactured in Australia by Dowmus Inc.[2] The Dowmus system consists of a concrete tank – in this instance rectangular, to fit the site – containing three layers of filter beds, each about 7 metres long. Each bed is composed of a sandy peat-like mixture containing micro and macro-organisms and worms that sift, sort, digest and treat the putrescible material and waste water. The flush toilet, shower, bath, dishwasher, washing machine, sinks and tubs drain into a single sewer pipe. This pipe then empties into the top filter bed of the tank. Everything is broken down by the living creatures that not only digest the sewage but also keep the filter beds porous by tunnelling through them. The remaining water trickles down into the sloping floor of the tank, where it is pumped up past an ultraviolet lamp to kill any remaining bacteria.

Not only sewage goes into the biolytic filter; any food waste and organic material that one might normally put in the compost bin goes in there as well. Even cold ashes, condoms, facial tissues, house dust, cardboard, paper, steel staples, steel wool and tampons can be thrown into the Dowmus tank. The system does not break down plastics or disposable nappies, but neither does it require a grease trap, unless large amounts of oil or fat are regularly poured down the sink. The system is aerobic, which means it is not smelly, and the effluent water is reasonably clean and can be recycled. Monitoring of the effluent for bacteria (faecal coliforms) showed that when the filters were working properly, the level was zero. The bacteria level, however, did occasionally rise. Monitoring was carried out fortnightly by Dr Huu Hao Ngo, of the School of Civil Engineering at the University of Technology, Sydney. Failure occurred when the vegetable and other organic matter was not spread evenly along the narrow top filtration bed. The system does not yet function reliably enough to produce water of drinking quality, but Mobbs says the recycled water is certainly good enough for flushing toilets, clothes washing and watering the garden.[3] Mobbs writes:

> To us the Biolytic Filter is something of a miracle. The key players in this system are creepy crawlies and minute living animals: it is they that process all the rubbish and sewage and turn it into a renewable resource: water. There is no odour. There is no maintenance except for what we expect will be the occasional replacement of one or two parts in the pumps (once every three to five years we anticipate). We live in cities where agencies spend billions of dollars a year trying to eradicate creepy crawlies because they interfere with our activities but here is a case where they are benefiting us … and it's free.[4]

Remarkably, the whole water treatment plant fits into a tiny backyard no bigger than the ground floor area of the house itself, and still leaves space for a small garden and wetland nursery for frogs.

The house had been fitted with a rooftop solar hot water heater sometime after 1979. This two-panel, 300-litre water heater with an electric booster (to top up the heat at times of peak demand and at night) provided hot water for the whole household. Each year this heater harvests 3123 kilowatts of energy direct from the sun, saving about 4 tonnes of greenhouse gas. During the renovation, the electric booster was replaced by a gas booster which contributes less greenhouse gas than electricity. Mobbs also installed 18 solar panels of photovoltaic cells that produce electricity from sunlight. The capacity of the rooftop electricity power station is only limited by the roof space available – which in a terrace house is small – and the efficiency of the photovoltaic technology. Even so it is enough to provide about 70 per cent of the electricity used in running the house, saving about 3 tonnes of carbon dioxide emitted by a coal-fired power station.

Mobbs has monitored the performance of the Chippendale house. Each year the house saves 102,000 litres of water that would otherwise be taken from the Shoalhaven River and Warragamba reservoir. The sewage treatment system keeps 100,000 litres of sewage from flowing into the Pacific Ocean, and the same amount of stormwater from draining into Sydney Harbour. It cuts the waste that would otherwise be taken to landfill by the local authority by several tonnes. It reduces carbon dioxide emissions from electricity generated at coal-fired power stations by 8.3 tonnes – about 7 tonnes from solar hot water and electricity and the rest from energy-saving appliances – and saves the household more than $1000 in energy costs each year. Mobbs writes: 'Since we did the renovation in 1996, we have not changed our lifestyle from the one we enjoyed previously.'[5]

Mobbs has now taken his ideas a step further. He has joined up with Brisbane property developers Scott and Mark Elsom to sell designs for affordable kit homes (priced from $60,000) that have high quality environmental performance, based on the principles of Mobbs's experiment in Chippendale. These houses will typically use thick straw bale insulation for protection of west-facing walls, carefully designed natural ventilation to cool the roof space with air from below the floor, solar panels for hot water and electricity, rainwater tanks and onsite sewage treatment plants (http://www.salahomes.com.au/). SALA expects eventually to be able to build a three-bedroom sustainable house for a little over

$100,000 – some $30,000 less than an equivalent conventional house anywhere in Australia – and such a house would save hugely on energy and water bills.[6]

At the opposite end of the world, a house designed for her own use by Susan Roaf, a Professor of Architecture at Oxford Brookes University, also generates electricity from a rooftop array of photovoltaic cells; so much electricity, in fact, that the excess power is enough to fuel an electric car (Plate 2). But the water system is not as elaborate as the one in the Mobbs house. Sue Roaf and her team have written a manual for the sustainable house: *Ecohouse 2*.[7] More than the Mobbs house, Roaf's 'ecohouse' is designed to maintain an even temperature inside even on the coldest and hottest days. England's maximum temperatures in winter regularly go down to 4°C – and, judging from the heatwave of 2003, it seems the nation must now expect top temperatures at times nearly comparable with the hottest reached in our own major cities (over 40°C).

A comfortable internal temperature is maintained by a combination of orientation to the sun, trapping the sun, insulation, ventilation and clever use of 'thermal mass'. Thermal mass is the 'heat bank' principle: heavy materials warm up and cool down slowly. So if heavy materials – bricks, concrete floors, concrete block walls, stone, even water – are located inside the house, the construction acts like a heat bank, heating up slowly during the day and releasing the warmth at night. The ecohouse has concrete floors and high-density concrete block internal walls.

The main windows of Roaf's ecohouse face south, to catch the sun. The advantage of a north–south orientation is that the low-level winter sun can shine right into the house, heating the heavy internal construction materials, while the summer sun, higher in the sky, does not penetrate and can easily be kept out by overhanging eaves or pergolas. The idea of a glass sunspace or conservatory is now very popular in the colder latitudes and could be attractive in winter even in warmer climates. The two-storey ecohouse has a sunspace that rises from floor to roof level on the south side, trapping the warmth of the sun like a greenhouse. But of course good ventilation of the sunspace is essential. Sometimes it is necessary to lose heat quickly. Twenty per cent of the glazing of the sunspace can be opened, and hot air can be quickly drained out of the top.

The Oxford ecohouse is designed with good cross-ventilation but little infiltration. Infiltration is uncontrolled movement of air through a building. Up to half the heat loss from buildings can come from infil-tration: air leaking in or out where it is not intended or wanted. Air movement is always important to clear stagnant air, but it needs to be controlled. Ventilation need not be through openable windows. Opening windows in winter can let in air that is too cold, and on very hot days in summer the windows are also best kept closed. An experi-mental 'Passivhaus' in Darmstadt, Germany, takes air in through plastic pipes buried 3–4 metres underground. The thermal mass of the earth warms the air to at least 8°C before it enters the house. A heat exchanger then warms the fresh air to 70 per cent of the temperature of the stale air leaving the house. Even though the Passivhaus is sealed off from direct contact with the outside air, there is a constant flow of fresh, warm air through the house. In effect this is a passive method of air-conditioning. Not surprisingly, use of the house design to save energy is called 'passive solar design'.

High 'R value' insulation is always a key ingredient of the sustain-able house. Insulation is needed to stop the cold or hot air outside adversely affecting the temperature inside a house. Insulation does not store heat; it prevents heat passing through it. The R value given to insulating material is a number which represents the material's resis-tance to heat transfer. The higher the R value, the greater the insulat-ing effect. The aim should be to wrap the entire house in a blanket of insulation so that as little active heating or cooling as possible is needed to maintain a comfortable inside temperature. This means not only that insulation of sufficient R value is placed in the walls, roof and floors, but also that no gaps are left where heat can leak through. These gaps are known as 'cold bridges', and they can occur at windows, window frames, corners, and through metal ties linking inside and outside walls.

Insulation comes in two forms: bulk and reflective insulation. Air itself is the best insulator. Bulk insulation stops the conduction of heat by means of lightweight fibres or particles that trap pockets of air – typi-cally batts and blankets made of rockwool, fibreglass, acrylic fibre, wool or even eel grass. Reflective insulation reflects radiant heat on the warm side. Radiant heat travels through air but not solid material (which absorbs it), so reflective insulation must have an air space adjacent to it. Reflective insulation is usually aluminium foil with a stiff backing (such as reinforced building paper [heavy paper used in walls or roofs for damp-proofing]) or a reflective coating on the underside of corrugated metal or on the back of plasterboard.

It should be noted that solid, heavy material is not a good heat insulator unless it is thick and transfers heat slowly. Lightweight materials, on the other hand, are good at stopping heat transfer, but do not stop noise. Noise insulation requires density and mass. Windows must also be insulated. This is usually done by interposing layers of air or other gas between panes of glass: double or triple glazing. This also cuts down on noise because of the density of the glass. The ecohouse is equipped with triple-glazed windows.

Roaf carefully monitors the daily temperature of the rooms in the ecohouse, and the readings for the internal rooms show that an extraordinarily steady, comfortable temperature of 20–21°C is maintained at all times of the year. Standards for sustainable housing are best measured in terms of the energy required to maintain a comfortable internal temperature. These standards vary hugely from country to country. In Germany, for example, the 1990s building standards permitted the heat loss from an average dwelling to be 200 kilowatt hours per square metre. In Sweden at the same period the permitted heat loss was about one-quarter of that (50–60 kilowatt hours per square metre).[8]

In Australia there are no transparent quantitative standards of this kind at all. It is time we all demanded higher standards from our regulators and builders. Many will trumpet noisily the alleged high costs of tougher energy standards, but do they consider the cost to households of running poorly designed and constructed dwellings – the needlessly high electricity bills, the expensive home heaters and coolers, the fevered nights and the achingly cold days, year after year? Is this really 'affordable housing'?

Different ecohouses emphasise different qualities. The Chapmans' house in Footscray in Melbourne is equipped with a solar hot water system, photovoltaic panels, a water collection and recycling system and has been built to an energy-efficient design. But the existence of the Rolls Royce of all sewage treatment plants at Werribee, in Melbourne's west, means that sewage composting with the Dowmus system, as in the Mobbs's Sydney house, is unnecessary.

Design for the local climate is also critically important. In tropical conditions of more or less constant high temperature and high humidity, internal thermal mass will not be used; making the most of cooling breezes will be more important. In Australia it is not just heating and cooling that consume energy. In fact the Australian Greenhouse Office has estimated that 53 per cent of greenhouse emissions from the domestic (home) sector come from the use of electric appliances and equipment.[9] That is because most electricity in Australia is generated by coal-burning power stations, which emit prodigious amounts of greenhouse gas. It is particularly important, then, that Australian housing be equipped with alternative renewable sources of electricity: the obvious candidate for the job is photovoltaic panels.

Houses designed on passive solar principles can now be found in all regions of Australia. Owners of over 100 homes around Australia open their doors to visitors on one day of the year. Examples can be found on the solar house day website (http://www.solarhouseday.com/): the Parker house in East Perth, Kawanda Muna in South Australia, the Lever house in New South Wales, the Gillam house in Victoria, the Sunbird house in Cairns, Eagle Eye in Darwin.

Traditionally, Australian homes have been based on designs imported from the US. Most of these designs have paid considerable attention to style – some would say with dubious success – but scant attention to comfort. The notion that one design fits all has to be abandoned, but there are some general design principles for the 'green house'; these can be summarised as follows:

- Design for the local climate.
- Orientate the house so that main windows face north (south in the northern hemisphere).
- Make good use of thermal mass.
- Provide high R value insulation.
- Design for good ventilation but minimise leakage of air or heat.
- Manage water wisely.
- Use localised energy systems with the national or local grid as backup.
- Aim at zero greenhouse gas emission from daily life in the house ('operational energy').

With 'green suburbs' we can add some further principles, without losing sight of those above. Green suburbs are a step up in scale and therefore involve such matters as social interaction, community and transport.

GREEN SUBURBS

Green suburbs have already been built in some European cities, and experiments are under way worldwide. These new suburban housing developments combine all the elements of green housing described above. They also contain a mixture of activities: affordable housing, workplaces, shops, cafés, sports facilities, child-care centres and schools. They leapfrog over the minimal conditions for greenhouse gas reduction laid down by the Kyoto Protocol. They even go beyond the 60 per cent reduction in greenhouse emissions recommended by the scientists of the United Nations' (UN's) Intergovernmental Panel on Climate Change (IPCC). These new city extensions aim, in fact, for zero net greenhouse emissions. Three examples are: the Beddington Zero (Fossil Fuel) Energy Development (BedZed) in the London Borough of Sutton; the new suburb of Kronsberg in the city of Hannover, Germany; and the waterside development of Västra Hamnen (Western Harbour), in the city of Malmö, Sweden.

BedZed was jointly designed by environmental consultant company Bioregional and the architect Bill Dunster for The Peabody Trust, one of the largest and oldest organisations in Britain providing affordable housing.[10] BedZed is a medium-density development consisting of 82 flats and houses and 1600 square metres of workspace (Plate 3). It was built on a former sewage works and so saves undeveloped land at the urban fringe (greenfield land). Renewable building materials were chosen from sources, wherever possible, not more than 35 miles (56 kilometres) from the site, thus reducing the energy consumed in long freight journeys.

The housing is designed to conserve energy and provide a comfortable interior climate. The buildings face south, with south-facing glass conservatories (sunspaces) to trap the sun. Thick internal walls prevent overheating in summer and store warmth in winter. An 'overcoat' of insulation in roofs, walls and floors retains heat from sunshine, lights, appliances, hot water, and everyday activities such as cooking (Plate 4). Windows are triple-glazed, and the frames are designed to prevent cold bridges through which warmth could leak out. Britain has cold winters and quite short summers, so for much of the year heat loss is the issue. In some Australian climates where there are hot days and cooler nights (Melbourne, Adelaide or Perth, and to some extent Sydney and Brisbane, for example), the same principles apply in reverse. What works to keep warmth in also works to keep out excessive afternoon heat.

Heat exchangers in the wind-driven domestic ventilation system recover 60–70 per cent of the heat in outgoing stale air. Kitchens are fitted with energy-saving appliances and low-energy lighting. It is estimated that residents can expect to reduce their need for energy by up to

60 per cent and for heat by up to 90 per cent. All BedZed's needs for additional heat and electricity are met by a single central combined heat and power unit (CHP, or co-generation unit). Trees in people's gardens and local parks around Sutton produce a great deal of excess growth. This would normally be lopped and dumped in the Council's landfill tip. BedZed's CHP unit, however, uses the material as fuel. The CHP unit has been designed to generate as much electricity as will be used at BedZed. It will generate electricity and distribute hot water via insulated pipes to domestic hot water tanks positioned centrally in every home and office, so that they can double as heaters during cold weather. The CHP is linked to the national electricity grid, so that at peak times, electricity from the grid supplements that generated by the CHP unit. At other times, excess electricity is exported from the CHP unit to the national grid.

BedZed's water conservation aims are quite modest: a reduction of water consumption by one-third is hoped for. This will be achieved partly by water-efficient washing machines, smaller baths and water-saving taps. A clearly visible water meter is installed in the kitchens so that it is easy to check how much water is being used. Dual-flush toilets – an Australian innovation – are used throughout. Nearly one-fifth of water use on the site is met by rainwater and recycled (grey) water stored in large tanks built into the foundations of the buildings. Waste water is treated onsite by a small-scale sewage treatment plant known as the 'Living Machine'. This is a biologically based system which extracts the nutrients in the water and treats the water to a standard that allows it to be recycled back to the underground water tanks to supplement rainwater for flushing the toilet. Extracted nutrients are recycled for plant food. The Living Machine is kept in an upper-floor greenhouse that is filled with plants. The car parking spaces on the site are laid with porous block paving over gravel, to minimise surface run-off. Run-off from roof gardens, roads and pavements is drained to the front of the development, where a formerly dry ditch has been made into a water feature to attract wildlife.

A perhaps more controversial and innovative aspect of BedZed's plan is to cut fossil fuel consumption from car use by 50 per cent (in comparison with a conventional development) over 10 years. Providing workplaces on the site means that there is an opportunity for some residents to work locally. If all new developments in the region followed suit, many long commuting journeys might be saved, though there is no guarantee that the residents of a particular development would work at that place. Onsite facilities such as child care and shopping cut out other unnecessarily long journeys. The developers are negotiating with a local supermarket to provide regular deliveries of bulk goods ordered over the internet. BedZed is located within easy reach of public transport, including two railway stations, two bus routes and a tram link to adjoining suburbs. To encourage alternatives to car use, BedZed provides generous space for bike storage, and bikeways linked to the local bike path network. The development is designed on the principle of 'walkers first', with generous, well-lit footpaths, drop kerbs for prams and wheelchairs and a road layout that limits vehicles to walking pace.

With the aid of a grant from the European Union's Thermie project, all homes are equipped with photovoltaic solar panels. The electricity produced is used to charge the batteries of electric vehicles for local trips, and onsite charging points are provided for electric cars. The target is to produce enough solar electricity to power forty electric vehicles – some private, some in pooled use. People do not need to give up their car. The aim is simply to provide enough convenient alternatives so that people will choose to use it less.

One option that BedZed hopes to develop is car pooling. Car pooling is a growing trend in European cities. An Edinburgh car pooling club estimates that one pool car can displace about five privately owned vehicles. The great incentive here is cost saving. A motorist travelling between 17,000 and 20,000 kilometres per year can, it is estimated, save up to $3600 (£1500) in motoring costs per year by car pooling.

Let's move now to a much larger scale. In the late 1990s the city of Hannover in Germany decided to create a new city district on a greenfield site long designated for the city's expansion and close to the Hannover World Expo 2000 site.[11] The Kronsberg development is part of the city's contribution to the Expo and a contribution to its obligations under the UN's 'Agenda 21' and the Aalborg Charter (Box 2.1). The whole development is co-ordinated by the Kronsberg Environmental Liaison Agency (KUKA). The development will eventually provide some 6000 homes and accommodate about 15,000 people. Three children's day care centres, a primary school, a district arts and community centre, a health centre and a shopping centre are already operating. This city extension is laid out on a grid pattern that uses avenues, parks, urban squares and planted courtyards to frame the buildings. In keeping with the scale of the development, and to ensure a diversity of approach, many different architects, developers and building contractors have been involved in different projects on the site. Each

Box 2.1 THE AALBORG CHARTER OF EUROPEAN CITIES AND TOWNS TOWARDS SUSTAINABILITY, Part 1

1.1 The Role of European Cities and Towns

We, European cities & towns, signatories of this Charter, state that in the course of history, our towns have existed within and outlasted empires, nation states and regimes, and have survived as centres of social life, carriers of our economies, and guardians of culture, heritage and tradition. Along with families and neighbourhoods, towns have been the basic elements of our societies and states. Towns have been the centres of industry, craft, trade, education and government.

We understand that our present urban lifestyle, in particular our patterns of division of labour and functions, land use, transport, industrial production, agriculture, consumption, and leisure activities, and hence our standard of living, make us essentially responsible for many environmental problems humankind is facing. This is particularly relevant as 80 per cent of Europe's population live in urban areas.

We have learnt that present levels of resource consumption in the industrialised countries cannot be achieved by all people currently living, much less by future generations, without destroying the natural capital.

We are convinced that sustainable human life on this globe cannot be achieved without sustainable local communities. Local government is close to where environmental problems are perceived and closest to the citizens, and shares responsibility with governments at all levels for the wellbeing of humankind and nature. Therefore, cities and towns are key players in the process of changing lifestyles, production, consumption and spatial patterns.

1.2 The Notion and Principles of Sustainability

We, cities & towns, understand that the idea of sustainable development helps us to base our standard of living on the carrying capacity of nature. We seek to achieve social justice, sustainable economies, and environmental sustainability. Social

Box 2.1 continues over page

justice will necessarily have to be based on economic sustainability and equity, which require environmental sustainability. Environmental sustainability means maintaining the natural capital. It demands from us that the rate at which we consume renewable material, water and energy resources does not exceed the rate at which the natural systems can replenish them, and that the rate at which we consume non-renewable resources does not exceed the rate at which sustainable renewable resources are replaced. Environmental sustainability also means that the rate of emitted pollutants does not exceed the capacity of the air, water, and soil to absorb and process them.

Furthermore, environmental sustainability entails the maintenance of biodiversity; human health; as well as air, water, and soil qualities at standards sufficient to sustain human life and wellbeing, as well as animal and plant life, for all time.

1.3 Local Strategies Towards Sustainability

We are convinced that the city or town is both the largest unit capable of initially addressing the many urban architectural, social, economic, political, natural resource and environmental imbalances damaging our modern world and the smallest scale at which problems can be meaningfully resolved in an integrated, holistic and sustainable fashion. As each city is different, we have to find our individual ways towards sustainability. We shall integrate the principles of sustainability in all our policies and make the respective strengths of our cities and towns the basis of locally appropriate strategies.

Source: http://www.iclei.org/Europe/ECHA RTER.HTM.

section of the district contains about 1000 dwellings grouped around a neighbourhood park.

The energy target set was at least a 60 per cent reduction in greenhouse gas emissions compared with current standards for conventional housing. Like BedZed, Kronsberg combines low-energy housing, on principles of good passive solar design, with district heating and the use of renewable energy. The City Council of Hannover maintains a high standard of low-energy design – called the Kronsberg Standard – by frequent site inspections backed up by a training program for all contractors working on the site. KUKA offers certificated 'fast response' courses to upgrade the builders' skills. Thus in addition to building a green suburb, a newly skilled building profession is also being created. Some ninety of the dwellings will be built as 'passive houses', like the Darmstadt experimental Passivhaus, requiring extremely little energy to keep the temperature inside the house at a constant comfortable level.

The scale of the development is much bigger than BedZed, and the city sector draws power from many different sources. In the southern part of Kronsberg a 1 megawatt gas-fired power station supplies heat and power to 2700 dwellings. In the northern sector another station powered by fuel cells is situated in the basement of a building occupied by housing, offices and shops. This power generator, which is virtually silent in operation, provides heat and power for 600 dwellings and a primary school. In another section, about 100 dwellings draw half their heating requirement from solar energy and the other half from the district heating network. Three large state-of-the-art wind turbines feed energy into the local grid, providing enough energy for up to 3000 dwellings and reducing greenhouse emissions in that area by a further 20 per cent (that is, 80 per cent in total for that area). The district arts and community centre and the primary schools also draw electricity from rooftop photovoltaic arrays.

Rainwater management has had a large influence on the design of the Kronsberg district. A conventional development would seek to discharge rainwater from the site as quickly as possible. Instead, in Kronsberg, rainwater is viewed as an environmental resource and retained. The aim is to disrupt the water ecology of the surrounding area as little as possible, and in particular not to change the water table in the nearby Mastbrucher woodlands. A stream running through the district has been 'renaturalised' to make it flow more slowly through the site. The balance of the natural water regime has been largely maintained using a new method of rainwater management called the Mulden-Rigolen system. Rainwater is collected from public areas and fed into soakaway trenches. Rainwater is also collected from roofs and private paved areas and gradually released into ponds and wetlands, or recycled to flush toilets. Water-saving measures are implemented to substantially reduce water consumption in dwellings and offices: the target is 100,000 cubic metres of water to be saved within the development per year. The water ecology is incorporated into the urban landscape. In an echo of the 'garden city' vision of Ebenezer Howard, the father of modern town planning, the City of Hannover has adopted the theme of 'City as Garden' to govern its future urban design.

A key aspect of the scheme is the intermeshing of social and communication programs with design and construction. The designers of the development hope that the arts and community centre will be used for meetings and social events. Old people's housing is dispersed around the neighbourhoods, and accommodation is provided for kindergartens and after-school child care, clubs and residents' associations. The Fokus housing project provides housing for the disabled, also dispersed throughout the development. This project is staffed by a network of specialist carers who can respond quickly to any calls for help. Housing is also provided for immigrants, who have in recent years become an important part of German culture. This development tries to meet the broad sustainability challenge by providing living environments that are ecologically sound and socially inclusive. Increasingly, international evidence shows us that possession of these two qualities is likely also to guarantee the security and stability needed for an urban community's economic wellbeing.

The landscape has an educational role as well as an environmental and an aesthetic role. It is hoped that residents, who see water around them and live with the landscape beauty it produces, will come to value water as something much more than a liquid that comes out of taps. The primary school, for example, retains all water falling on its grounds. The gently sloping roof of the school is grassed to slow down run-off. Children see the water cycle that they learn about at school in action around them. As with the construction program, KUKA runs training schemes for water engineers so that working at Kronsberg becomes a practical opportunity to learn about new techniques for safe water management.

Rather more than BedZed, Kronsberg is literally a green settlement, full of tenants' and allotment gardens, neighbourhood parks and sports-grounds. At the southeastern edge of the site a farm that runs on organic principles has been established (see chapter 4 for information on organic farming). The farm's produce will be processed in its own slaughter-house, brewery, dairy and bakery, and sold from farm shops direct to the consumers in Kronsberg and Hannover. The aim is to 'counteract the high degree of specialisation caused by agribusiness and the increasing remoteness of the agricultural base from regional economic cycles'.[12] The farm also has a strong educational focus, as it brings the population closer to where food is produced and to the processes of its production.

The City of Hannover has contracted with the developers of the

Kronsberg site to use only building materials that are environmentally friendly, do no damage to ecosystems elsewhere on the planet, and are healthy for the residents. Recycling and waste minimisation principles are applied at all levels of construction and use of the scheme. Building waste is sorted onsite and a recycling rate of about 80 per cent has been achieved. Household appliances are not thrown out when they break down; they are repaired. There is a network of repair, adaptation and alteration services for residents, creating a range of new jobs. Residents are encouraged to compost green food waste and sort and recycle plastics, bottles and solid household waste. Excavated soil for the new buildings (about 700,000 cubic metres) was reused on the site to create viewpoint hills and noise buffer embankments alongside a nearby motorway.

The new suburb is built around an environmentally responsible transport concept. A new tramline will connect Kronsberg and the Expo site to Hannover's city centre. This tramline is designed to generate development along the track, physically connecting the new settlement with the old. Eventually there will be strip shopping streets along tramlines (much as there are in Melbourne). No dwelling will be more than 600 metres from a tram stop. Residential density increases closer to the tram stops, and the streets are laid out so as to channel the heaviest traffic flow along service roads parallel to the tramline, to minimise disruption by vehicles. From the main service road, the district is covered by a network of minor streets. There will be no through traffic, and all vehicles will have to drive slowly (including 30 km/h zones). A specially constructed cycle path crosses the district from north to south. A finely branched network of footpaths is laid out through the quiet inner courtyards, offering safe play spaces for children.

Throughout the district there will be trees on both sides of the street and in front gardens. All house front doors face the street and most have generously proportioned entrance areas that make the addresses easy to find and impart a feeling of security among residents. Two avenues with open watercourses alongside them run downhill to the main road. To minimise car ownership, a car pool scheme is planned for Kronsberg, as an extension of the system already operating successfully in Hannover.

Our third example is the new suburb of Västra Hamnen in Malmö, Sweden. It was designed as a 'city of tomorrow' in conjunction with Bo 01, the city's international housing exhibition of 2001.[13] The new neighbourhood is built on an industrial site formerly used by a major shipyard (Kockums) and the vehicle manufacturer Saab. When these activities contracted, a polluted wasteland was left behind. The new city district built on this old industrial land fronts the sea on one side and the harbour on the other. The district will eventually combine housing for 10,000–20,000 people with commercial and social services. The section already built is a new neighbourhood on the most attractive seafront site. It is made up of about 559 dwellings: houses, terraces and blocks of flats up to six storeys (Plates 5 and 6). The six-storey flats are built along a seafront promenade and boardwalk that has a breathtaking view across the Öresund (The Sound) to Denmark and the bridge to Copenhagen. These flats make a felicitous and necessary barrier against the wind and weather, providing a less blustery interior of the neighbourhood, which contains smaller-scale houses and flats.

The sustainable alternative, says the literature, 'must prove itself to be at least as convenient, financially advantageous, comfortable, pleasant, exciting and beautiful as any conventional housing scheme'.[14] With waterfront housing being popular almost everywhere in the world today, and being within easy reach of the city, Västra Hamnen has something of a head start in terms of financial viability and excitement. The dwellings are expensive (between 1 and 4 million kronor – $250,000 to $1 million in Australian dollars) and are selling well. Some of them are in fact selling to commuters from Copenhagen, which is just across the water and now easily accessible by train. When the entire dockland district is developed it will include a large proportion of affordable housing provided by the public sector and by community (non-government) housing associations, but the strategy was to build the high-income housing first.[15] The seaward promenade and rocky beach have become a favourite resort for the people of Malmö. Many thousands of visitors stream through the area on hot days in summer – this might not be to the pleasure of the overlooking residents, but it does add to the social mix of the neighbourhood's users.

The new district is linked to the old town centre of Malmö by a large university campus (Malmö Högskolan), and the city is marketing the site as a location for new knowledge-based businesses. However, the docklands district is by no means empty: some 6000 people are already working in the area. There is a huge convention centre (Malmö Mässan) made from the old Saab factory, and a former shipyard is manufacturing massive steel poles for wind turbines. So housing is being developed jointly with workplaces, providing the opportunity for shorter journeys to work. Schools, child care facilities, shopping centres, parks and playgrounds are also included. Historic industrial buildings, such as the former foundry and nearby buildings next to the bridge, are being preserved and will be used for club, cultural and leisure activities.

Västra Hamnen is supplied entirely by renewable sources of energy, mostly generated onsite, and can therefore claim, like BedZed, to be a zero fossil fuel energy development. Warmth is extracted by heat pump from an underground aquifer and from the seawater, as well as being generated in large-scale solar collectors (1400 square metres). Electricity for the neighbourhood is generated by a single wind power station, the biblical-sounding 'Boel' in the North Harbour a kilometre away, and by a limited array of photovoltaic cells (120 square metres). Biogas (mostly methane) from the city's waste is used to heat homes and to power vehicles. In addition, the homes in the district are built according to passive solar design principles, so they have minimal energy demands for heating. All the power sources onsite are connected to the city's energy and the district's heating–cooling grid. The 100 per cent renewable energy equation is based on an annual cycle. At some periods the neighbourhood borrows from the city and at other times the reverse, but over a year it achieves a net zero fossil fuel balance.

Providing an integrated system of greenspace that encourages habitats for non-human species is part of the plan. A number of habitats are being created for different plant and animal species. Rabbits, a pest in Australia, are now at home in the neighbourhood's greenspace. A 'green points' list provides ideas about how construction companies and developers can help as many species as possible become established in the district. Each apartment may have a bird-box, frog havens are established so that frogs can survive the harsh local winters, and nesting boards for swallows have been set up on the sides of buildings. A large semi-mature tree has been planted in each courtyard. This supports the microclimate until other trees and shrubs have grown up and become well established. A so-called green area factor guarantees that all courtyards are planted up with plenty of vegetation – on walls and roofs and in courtyards. Rainwater and melted snow are collected in small pools and mini-channels. This is also a means of creating the special conditions for species of flora and fauna that depend on watery environments. There was a rich bird life here in the Bo 01 area before building began. A comparable biotope is now being created out in the harbour area of Malmö, and an ecologist is employed to oversee the development of the site's biodiversity.

Sweden has for some time aimed to become 'an ecocyclic society', a society in which nothing is wasted. This means that recycling of waste is at an advanced stage in Malmö. Plastics, glass and metal are sorted and deposited in containers onsite. Nutrients and heavy metals are extracted from sewage sludge and reused. Most of the organic waste produced in the area is transformed into energy by biogas digesters, and the gas is used for heating. Remaining organic material is burned to help provide district heating.

The neighbourhood gives priority to walkers and cyclists, and is designed to minimise intrusion by the private car. Only 0.7 car parking spaces per dwelling are provided – this has not proved a deterrent for purchasers. Foot and bike paths are designed to make walking and cycling attractive for short journeys and to connect to the old city. The public transport system connects seamlessly with Malmö's already efficient network, and the system has become the first choice for most residents' travel needs. Every flat is within 300 metres of a bus stop. Public transport and vehicles used for the area's maintenance run on environment-friendly natural gas and biogas (which minimises fossil fuel use). The district is developing a car pool for residents, which they can book from home through the local computer network. It will be a car or a minibus powered by both gas and electricity.

One of the authors (Nick Low) visited in 2003, and had a little criticism of three aspects of Västra Hamnen. The daytime public transport connection with the main city is good, with buses running at roughly 10 minute intervals during the day from 5 am until 9.45 pm Monday to Saturday, and every half hour on Sundays. The service stops too early to be much use for an evening out – surely Swedes don't go to bed that early? There is also a reasonable cycle path. However, the pedestrian connection with the city centre is a long, ugly tramp through an industrial wasteland. There is apparently a philosophy that unfinished development is somehow invisible. In surrounding areas, and in a few cases within the neighbourhood itself, sites waiting for development are left like … well, like building sites waiting for development, full of old tarmac, weeds, builders' junk, bits of concrete and parked cars.

A second issue is the use of rainforest timber in the main boardwalk, which is surprising. The timber comes from Cameroon, where, the developers were assured, the rainforest is 'managed sustainably'. We are sceptical on that count, since such a claim is frequently heard for the 'management' of old growth forest in Australia, where habitat value is in fact devastated by logging and woodchipping. The final criticism relates to the seafront. This is built up with huge granite rocks, some of which are polished, as a sculptural installation. This is a wonderful idea, but unfortunately for sustainability, the rocks were sent to China to be polished – with major expenditure of greenhouse gas in transit. It comes as something of a relief to find that the Swedes, who provide many of the best examples of green policy anywhere in the world, are not perfect.

These three developments do not just contain wish lists for environmental conservation. All of them have quantified targets and all are being carefully monitored to see that they achieve them. Importantly for Australians, these European examples show that we don't all have to live packed together into space-saving high-rises to live sustainably. Australians have long enjoyed living in lower-density suburbs. There is no reason why we can't build sustainable new suburbs that meet the needs of some households – especially families – for house and garden landscapes. Certainly, some of the ways we have created and lived in our older suburbs have been wasteful of land and resources and not sustainable, but the Europeans have shown us that it is possible to produce diverse, inclusive and ecologically efficient neighbourhoods without us all having to retreat into high-rise towers or dreary villa developments.

In recent years, the trend to higher-density living in Australian cities has often been marked by mistakes that contemporary Europeans would never make, such as replacing green space with buildings and producing 'car-dependent' medium and high-density residential landscapes. There is no necessary relationship between ecological sustainability and crowding people into smaller spaces. We need a range of types of dwellings and living environments for our increasingly diverse population. Neither high-rise nor low-rise is inherently 'good' or 'bad': it comes down to sensible layout, design and use.

GREEN SUBURBS IN AUSTRALIA

Australia has produced some of the world's leading eco-pioneers: philosophers, political scientists, activists, lawyers and designers. So it should not be surprising that there are also some excellent examples of 'green suburbs', or eco-housing, already built in Australia (See Box 2.2).

The Olympic Village at Newington in Sydney, developed and constructed by the Mirvac Lend Lease Village Consortium with the declared intention of encouraging environment-friendly technology, is one of the largest developments to adopt design principles based on 'ecologically sustainable development'. When fully completed in 2005, the suburb is expected to house around 5000 people and include a range of housing types: three and four-bedroom 'family houses', courtyard houses, 'townhouses' (usually terrace houses), and two and three-bedroom apartments. The housing is equipped with photovoltaic panels to generate rooftop electricity (connected to the main grid) and gas-boosted solar hot water systems. Passive solar design was adopted to save up to 50 per cent of the energy needed to heat and cool a conventional house. Ninety per cent of homes are oriented approximately north–south, to make the best use of the sun. High R value insulation is included and the houses all have good cross-ventilation. Deciduous tree planting is designed to let in the winter sun and provide shade in summer. The expected saving in greenhouse emissions is of the order of 7000 tonnes per year.

The village also supports a dual water supply system to all dwellings. Drinking water is supplied in one pipeline while another pipeline supplies fully treated recycled water for flushing toilets and for landscape and garden irrigation. The public space is planted predominantly with drought-resistant indigenous species. The development aims to reduce waste of materials both in the construction phase and in use. Waste separation bins are provided and the target is to recycle 90 per cent of hard waste (plastics and so forth) and 60 per cent of soft waste. Surrounding parklands covering 440 hectares include walking and cycle paths, mangrove forests and wetlands.

The development shows what an innovative commercial developer–builder willing to take a small risk can do. One shortcoming, which was perhaps out of the builder's hands, is the village's connection to the rest of Sydney, and especially to Homebush railway station. It is only a 10–15 minute walk to the station, but anyone who wants to get there on foot has to walk along roads designed exclusively for vehicles: there is no foot or cycle pathway, and the walker has to struggle across sweeping intersections, and risks turning an ankle in the gutters. In this sense, the village is not integrated with the rest of the urban fabric and its transport system.

Aldinga Ecovillage, set on 34 hectares on the coast of South Australia, 44 kilometres south of Adelaide, is designed to be something of an enclave of artists, and includes galleries, performance spaces, a sculpture court, an amphitheatre, studios and tuition rooms. These facilities will also be able to earn income from use by the wider community. The settlement plans to grow its own produce, using the 'permaculture' principles developed by Australian Bill Mollison in Tasmania. Permaculture is a now worldwide philosophy and practice of growing plants and animals for human use in a locally self-sustaining system in which all parts benefit one another in perpetuity.

Box 2.2 USEFUL WEBSITES ON SUSTAINABLE HOUSING IN AUSTRALIA

Solar houses:
http://www.solarhouseday.com

SALA Homes (Sustainable Affordable Living Australia):
http://www.salahomes.com.au

Permaculture:
http://www.permaculture.net

Aldinga Ecovillage can be found on the website of the Global
Ecovillage Network Oceania and Asia (GENOA) Inc.:
http://genoa.ecovillage.org

Christie Walk (Adelaide):
http://www.urbanecology.org.au/christiewalk/factsheet

Halifax Ecocity (Paul Downton):
http://www.urbanecology.org.au/halifax/evolution.html

Water Sensitive Urban Design:
http://wsud.melbournewater.com.au/content/case_studies
/matrix.htm

Inkerman Oasis:
http://www.loc-gov-focus.aus.net/2000/october/stkilda.htm

Landcom New South Wales:
http://www.landcom.nsw.gov.au

Permaculture projects are based on three principles. Every part of the system performs multiple functions: a tree, for example, might provide shade, food, a cash crop for exchange, mulch, and wood for kindling. Every function in the system is supported by other elements also providing similar functions: shade might be provided by a vine on a trellis, which also provides food, for example. Finally, plants and animals are selected precisely for their mutually supporting properties. In the Aldinga Ecovillage, which is one of a network of eco-villages around the world, there are areas for intensive organic horticulture and market gardening, nurseries for indigenous plants and community gardens, and an environmental education centre.

A word of warning, though: a critical eye is needed. The pressure on fragile coastal ecosystems is intense, and some so-called eco-villages just should not be where they are at all. Applying permaculture principles is not enough to justify a settlement's existence if the settlement is so placed as to damage the larger ecosystem. Moreover, the term 'eco-village' may be applied to just about any piece of speculative, second home, coastal development around Australia. Eco-villages can be the thin end of a very fat wedge. These settlements merely increase the pressure from human habitation, putting endangered species of birds, animals and plants at further risk (see comments on 'greenwash' in chapter 6).

Adelaide has an inner-urban green suburb called Christie Walk. This small development stemmed from Paul Downton's Halifax ecocity project in the 1980s. Christie Walk is a small mixed-density community housing project. It includes onsite sewage and grey water treatment which allows recycled water to be used for local subsurface irrigation. Stormwater is used to flush toilets. Both wind power and photovoltaic cells provide electricity, and solar collectors provide hot water. The well thought-out solar design, plus high R value insulation and ventilation, makes air-conditioning unnecessary even in Adelaide's hot summers. Like London's BedZed, Christie Walk has roof gardens, pedestrian spaces and is well linked to public transport. It is perhaps better integrated than BedZed into Adelaide's inner-urban fabric. The project consists of 14 dwellings – four linked three-storey townhouses with full solar orientation, a three-storey block of six apartments with east–west orientation, and four stand-alone cottages – and a 'community house'.

Particularly interesting is the social aspect of the housing. The project was designed for a development co-operative, Wirranendi Inc., itself created by a non-profit educational association, Urban Ecology Australia Inc. The co-operative structure enables people to build for themselves in urban environments where single house blocks are rarely available. The clients include 'first-time home buyers, investment purchasers, experienced home owners seeking the advantages of an urban lifestyle and older people wanting to retire in the context of an active, mixed community'.[16]

Melbourne's Inkerman estate, in the City of Port Phillip, is an example of a local council acting as instigator and director of the 'water sensitive' urban redevelopment of a site the council had previously wanted to dispose of. All domestic grey water (water from baths, handbasins and showers) is recycled to irrigate a small wetland planted with native species. Stormwater is also captured and used for subsurface irrigation. The project is one of the first in Australia to combine stormwater capture and domestic water recycling.[17]

The State Government urban land corporations have been active in leading sustainable urban development in Australia. The land corporations are the product of the Whitlam Government's effort in the 1970s to introduce public land banks or public development agencies to reduce land speculation and provide affordable housing. They fulfil a function similar to local government ownership of land for future development, and though they control much less land than the local governments of many European cities, they have been remarkably successful in setting standards and limiting speculation.

For example, Landcom, the NSW Government's land developer, has adopted 'triple bottom line' reporting, which means that along with profitability (in this case for the community) must go socially responsible policies and ecologically sustainable products (see chapter 6, Box 6.3). This sounds like the sort of managementspeak with which all government reports are overburdened. But digging beneath the rhetoric, we also find that Landcom has set its housing program praiseworthy quantitative targets. On water conservation the target is to reduce the use of drinking water by 40 per cent over the five years 2003–08. An estimated 22.3 per cent reduction was achieved in 2003, so the corporation is reasonably on track. Likewise, its greenhouse gas emission target is a reduction of 40 per cent over the five years, with an achievement by 2003 of a 10 per cent reduction – must do better. Landcom develops site-specific solutions to energy conservation and greenhouse mitigation. In a large-scale development at Edmondson Park, for example, the solution combined high R value insulation, solar water heating, ceiling fans in living areas and bedrooms, evaporative cooling in houses, cogeneration (the simultaneous production of heat – usually in the form of hot water and/or steam – and power, using one primary fuel) and an offsite wind generator (comparable with Boel, in Malmö). Landcom also takes care to preserve all indigenous cultural heritage, and to preserve native vegetation on the sites it develops, and consults indigenous communities to prepare plans to achieve this. It is committed to consultation with local people in preparing plans for site development.

GREEN HOUSING

The following principles can be distilled from these examples, and they apply to both the design of new neighbourhoods and the refurbishment and retrofitting of existing urban areas:

1   Minimise the use of resources: the atmosphere, water, land, and rare or toxic materials. All housing should seek to become self-sufficient in renewable energy, whether the 'self' is the house, the neighbourhood or the whole city district. The era of the national grid is passing.

2   Be responsive to the local environment, and integrate landscape into the plan for the neighbourhood; make open space useful and attractive, and acknowledge and cater for its non-human inhabitants (Plate 7 shows an eco-housing project, Ekolonia, at Alphen aan Rijn in The Netherlands – another watery landscape).

3   Minimise the need for travel, and maximise low-energy modes of transport (pedestrian, bike and public transport), to enable people to connect easily with the local neighbourhood and the wider city.

4   Allow people to enter, leave and move through the site easily. Keep space public and, as far as possible, occupied. Allow no privatised public space or 'gated communities'. In a word, design for 'permeability' and inclusiveness. (Let's not forget that security landscapes with their walls, bars, armed guards and night lighting are also wasteful landscapes.)

5   Design public space for personal safety. This means that places where people walk should be open to view, overlooked, and well occupied. Putting up gates on housing estates and surrounding them with walls is nothing more than a symbolic gesture. It does not provide safety; in fact, the international evidence shows that 'gated communities' can become targets for burglars, who regard the costly defences as an easy challenge.

6   Insist on affordability and inclusiveness. Housing of different price ranges may be developed, but housing should include everybody and be delivered to everybody, whatever their budget, or physical capacities. This includes the special housing needs of the disabled, older people, immigrants and people of different cultures.

In chapter 1 we talked about the twin threats – to the atmosphere and the biosphere – that the green city is designed to overcome. These threats are different in kind. The first is currently the better understood. It is the more horrifying in its implications, but also the more easily remedied. Using energy to construct houses and live in them comfortably is not in any way problematic in itself. It is the source of energy that creates problems for the environment. If the source of energy is fossil fuel – coal, oil or natural gas – burning it puts carbon that was formerly buried and inert back into the atmosphere.[18] Even though alternative sources of energy that do not use fossil fuels are growing quite fast, fossil fuel is still by far the largest energy source almost everywhere in the developed world, especially in Australia. It is this use of the atmosphere as a dump (or sink) for waste carbonic gases that causes the greenhouse effect and global warming.

In Australia, annual greenhouse emissions from the 'residential sector' in 1990 amounted to 49.5 megatonnes (million tonnes), or about 8.8 per cent of Australia's total emissions. This is expected to rise to 58.1 megatonnes by 2010. Overall emissions are expected to grow in this period (1990–2010) by 11 per cent, but the residential sector is a stand-out bad performer. Its contribution is increasing at a rate of about 0.8 per cent per year. If what has happened over the last 12 years continues for the next 50 years, greenhouse emissions from the residential sector will *grow* by about 60 per cent. Yet a global *reduction* of at least 60 per cent on the 1990 level is necessary to stabilise the climate. The longer the start of serious concerted governmental action is postponed (as is occurring at present), the greater the change that will have to be made.[19]

The threat to the biosphere is much more complex. In investigating the behaviour of the atmosphere, scientists had to include in their theoretical models both the circulation of water in the oceans and the exchange of carbon between the land, the seas and the air. Climate science began to produce global models of evolution of the planet. But these models cannot capture the fine detail of evolution of species, the Earth's biodiversity. They do, however, raise the two-way question. What are we doing to the climate? And what is the climate doing to us? They therefore also raise the question of the relationship between humans and the rest of nature. This question surfaces again in worries about species extinction and the threat to the biosphere. What is the relationship between humans and nature? How does this question play out in the specific micro-environments of cities? We have already seen that in sustainable homes and suburbs, greenspace plays an important role. It provides habitat for the more than human, and it is also vital to human wellbeing. The urban landscape – its function for humanity and its ecosystems – is the subject of the next chapter.

FURTHER READING

Ecohouse 2 provides a detailed, expert and highly readable guide to the design of the 'green house'. This book is really more than just a design guide; it delves into some of the philosophy of living well with nature: Susan Roaf, Manuel Fuentes & Stephanie Thomas, *Ecohouse 2, A Design Guide* (Architectural Press, London, 2003). Michael Mobbs's book describes in straightforward, well-illustrated text, how he and his family designed and converted their inner-Sydney house to ecological principles: Michael Mobbs, *Sustainable House* (Choice Books, Sydney, 1998). *Factor Four* is essential reading. 'In a nutshell,' the introduction says, 'Factor Four means that resource productivity can and should grow fourfold. The amount of wealth extracted from one unit of natural resources can quadruple. Thus we can live twice as well yet use half as much': L. Hunter Lovins, Ernst von Weizsäcker & Amory B. Lovins, *Factor Four: Doubling Wealth, Halving Resource Use* (Earthscan, London, 1998). This book, first published in the 1980s, is still a very practical guidebook, and contains numerous examples applicable to sustainable homes and suburbs. Jonathon Porritt (chairman of the United Kingdom's Sustainable Development Commission) writes, on the Earthscan website: 'This book should make you spit with rage at the mainstream engineers, scientists, economists and politicians who still stand between us and achievement of a genuinely sustainable future for all the Earth's people.'

CHAPTER 3

NATURE IN THE CITY

In the course of day-to-day life in Australian cities, it is possible – indeed easy – to forget that our cities have in the past been responsible for rapidly and dramatically changing the landscape, and are still doing so. As the historian Geoffrey Bolton has observed, our hardworking ancestors were a mixture of honest 'toilers' and aggressive 'spoilers' who left a mixed environmental legacy, especially in our most intensely settled areas, the cities.[1] Trees were cut down, the earth reshaped, grasslands ploughed up, creeks and rivers redirected. And the original inhabitants – both human and non-human – were driven out while brick, steel and concrete structures were erected and the earth was paved over. The air over cities, the water that flows through cities and the lives of the flora and fauna that find their home in the city have all been massively altered in the relatively short time since Europeans settled Australia. Before European contact, the Aboriginal peoples had only minimally modified the Australian landscape.

Today, there is no going back, but there is much to be learned from the deep respect for and understanding of the natural world that is so characteristic of Aboriginal cultures. This love of nature ('biophilia'), it has been argued, may not in fact be culturally specific; it may be inherent in all humans.[2] In some cultures it emerges as a central element, while in others it is suppressed or transformed. It may, in the latter cases, be an impulse beneath the surface of everyday life that can be harnessed to help us address the environmental challenges the world now faces.

In this chapter we discuss the importance of integrating nature in to the city and the benefits that might be gained by increasing opportunities for city people to have encounters with the natural world in urban environments. The concept of nature in general will be discussed first; discussion of the benefits of contact with nature in the city will follow. Ideas are then presented about conservation of urban nature, and principles are drawn from the study of urban and landscape ecology that may be useful for guiding the design of urban open space. Finally we consider why we seem to like certain types of landscape more than others and how this understanding can be used to inform the design of open spaces in the city.

WHAT IS NATURE?

Before we can talk about nature in the city we must first define what we mean by 'nature'. Not many people today would deny that humans are an evolutionary product of nature. However, some would argue that because we are capable of radically and consciously modifying the Earth and its biological systems with our technology, we should be viewed as somehow distinct from and superior to the rest of the natural world.

Most people would also agree that cities are predominantly human creations. But where does the influence of humans on the natural environment stop: at the edge of the city, at the edge of the suburbs, at the edge of agricultural lands? It can be argued that because manufactured chemicals are now found everywhere on Earth – in water, air and soil – there really are no true natural environments left. While this may make sense from a scientific and philosophical perspective, it makes it very difficult to deal with the problem at hand, namely how better to integrate elements of the natural environment (non-human organisms and organic matter) with the urban landscape. A useful, yet simple definition of the concept of the natural world is:

> the vast domain of organic and inorganic matter that is not a product of human activity or intervention … It deals with the landscape rather than with the built environment. It includes the world of rock and sand, of shoreline, desert, woods, mountains, and the diverse manifestations of plant and animal life that are encountered there.[3]

Nature figures prominently in value systems across all human cultures, and it can be seen as both positive and negative. Stephen Kellert, a Yale University psychologist, suggests that the attitudes people have towards animals may reflect attitudes they hold about the natural world in general. From his research he has developed a classification of attitudes in which he identifies no fewer than nine value categories:

Aesthetic: Physical attraction and appeal of nature.

Dominionistic: Mastery and control of nature.

Humanistic: Emotional bonding with nature.

Moralistic: Ethical and spiritual relation to nature.

Naturalistic: Exploration and discovery of nature.

Negativistic: Fear of and aversion to nature.

Scientific: Knowledge and understanding of nature.

Symbolic: Nature as a source of language and imagination.

Utilitarian: Nature as a source of material and physical reward.[4]

This typology helps to explain the present relationship of humans to the more than human world by providing insights into why, and how, urban dwellers might value nature in the city. An interesting finding of Kellert's research is that having a university education, regardless of the discipline studied, seems to increase interest in and concern for animals, and perhaps, by extension, concern for nature in general. This finding suggests that through education, and perhaps not just formal tertiary education, appreciation of nature can be heightened. As we argued in chapter 1, remoteness breeds unawareness, and unawareness is leading to the future welfare of the planet being frittered away. However, the suggestion that people may need to be educated about nature in order to appreciate it runs somewhat contrary to the proposition that we have an innate affiliation with the natural world, so the matter is far from settled.

Our view is that in the green city nature matters: the impact of humans on nature and the impact of nature on humans both matter. Level of education, age, gender, cultural background, and income level are unimportant here; everyone living in an urban society needs access to, and should be afforded the benefits of, contact with nature in the city. If people gain even slight physical or psychological benefits from exposure to nature in the city, they may also grow to be more concerned about nature as it exists outside cities, and want to conserve nature – for its own sake – for future generations to enjoy.

So in addition to the direct physical and psychological benefits that people may derive from having contact with urban nature, exposure to and enjoyment of nature in the city may indirectly result in benefiting the health of the planet. It will do so by helping to encourage the view that all species share the world in partnership (an 'ecocentric' view of the world), as opposed to the view that humans are the centre of the universe (an 'anthropocentric' perspective).

THE BENEFITS OF URBAN NATURE

Today the very form of Australian suburbs is essentially a response to the need for contact with the natural world: *rus in urbe* – the countryside in the city. Look at the marketing of residential estates: open space and natural features are promoted as among the biggest pluses of living in such environments. Think for a moment where the most desirable (in many cases the highest priced) residential properties in your city are located. Are they located in, or near, areas of natural open space? Do they have commanding views over surrounding natural landscapes or water? Aren't all of these places where the natural world dominates the built environment?

Throughout history, urban planners and environmental designers have intuitively incorporated elements of the natural world and areas of green open space into their designs for cities in an effort to moderate the stress of urban life. Some of the world's most famous urban parks, such as Central Park in New York,[5] were designed specifically to help alleviate stress and provide health-giving contact with nature for people who were economically trapped in the city.

People seem to think of natural places in the city as different from the other types of places in which they spend their time, such as work, home and shopping environments. Because of this, areas of urban nature, whether they are parks or one's private garden, become places for people to escape their personal concerns and obligations and get away from it all. At the same time, these places can provide habitat for the animals and plants that also make the city their home.

Royal Park in Melbourne, the city's oldest and largest park (188 hectares), is one of several parklands close to the city's central area (Plates 8 and 9). Royal Park's landscape contains scattered clumps of mature eucalypts and other native trees, expanses of indigenous grasslands and wildflowers and water bodies reminiscent of a 'savanna'-type landscape. Even though the city skyline is clearly visible from the park, in some spots one can have the feeling of being in the bush, far from the city. In some places within the park one can even feel as if one is in the wilderness. As well as being a great place for people to make contact with the natural world, the park also provides a home for small mammals, birds, reptiles and insects. More wildlife habitat areas – a wetland and an adjacent rocky area (specially designed for a particular small type of skink) – are also being created within the park. Several hectares of exotic turf grass have also recently been removed and replanted with indigenous grasses and wildflowers. However, the park is under continued threat from the demands of urban growth. Part of the original park once used for a hospital is being developed as an athletes' village for the 2006 Commonwealth Games; this will afterwards be used as housing.

A more dramatic example of such loss of urban parkland can be found in Melbourne's Albert Park, where the construction of a range of sporting facilities, including temporary ones for the annual Formula 1 Grand Prix, has steadily encroached on the more natural areas of the park.

Perth's Kings Park, like Royal Park, is a grand and diverse green space that for many people helps to define what is 'urban' about this beautiful city (Plate 10). Locals and tourists alike gaze down from its heights upon the CBD's spires and the snarled roads below. Somehow, from this perspective, nature seems triumphant. Of course this is not true, sadly, but Kings Park at least reminds us that great natural urban spaces can become part of the very definition of a city, and can remind us of our own innate natural qualities.

Toohey Forest is a large (640 hectares) area of glorious natural bushland only 9 kilometres from the city centre of Brisbane (Plate 11). The forest exists in apparently peaceful harmony with a range of important institutional uses, including a major cemetery, a football stadium and Griffith University. This urban treasure was the gift of a 19th century landowner, James Toohey, whose generosity spared it from urban development. This natural 'island' in the extensive southeast Queensland conurbation acts as a storehouse of biodiversity and a staging ground for some of Australia's most effective environmental education programs. Easily accessible from the city centre by public transport, Toohey Forest is an example of how nature can exist as part of the urban process rather than in splendid isolation from cities and their human populations.

Another natural 'work in progress' is Sydney Park (Plate 12). This 44 hectare park is located in the gritty inner-city suburb of St Peters. It has been rescued from industrial rubble by public authorities, most recently South Sydney City Council, and rehabilitated. Unlike Toohey Forest, Sydney Park was cleared by early settlers; for nearly two centuries the area hosted a brickworks and a waste tip, both of which eventually became redundant. Over the past two decades this derelict urban space has been impressively rehabilitated. It now hosts large revegetated areas of bush, a range of community facilities, walkways, bikeways and carefully preserved remnant industrial structures. The local community has also played an active role here, planting nearly 12,000 new trees and shrubs. A wetlands scheme, covering 8 hectares, will, when completed, retain 75 per cent of the park's rainfall and provide an important new habitat for birds and insects. The park is a triumph of natural rehabilitation in a city setting, fusing urban life and history with a revitalised natural environment.

Brisbane's Northey Street urban organic farm is a small tract of working landscape in the heart of the city (Plate 13). The 1.6 hectare farm, adjacent to Brisbane's Breakfast Creek, maintains more than 1500 exotic and native fruit trees and bush tucker plants. While the farm is by no means a natural landscape, it serves an important social function by providing a place for individuals, schoolchildren and community groups to learn about organic gardening and permaculture, and being a model of ways in which communities can produce some of their own food while still living in cities.

THE IMPORTANCE OF VEGETATION

Vegetation in the landscape, particularly trees, should not be thought of as a frivolous cosmetic embellishment to city life – it is basic infrastructure that makes tremendous contributions to the city aesthetically and ecologically, as well as to community pride, public health and quality of life. Street trees, for example, are important not just because they absorb air pollution and provide a habitat for birds and other wildlife, but also because they can be used to enhance a community's image: trees grown along streets can visually tie a neighbourhood or development together.

There is evidence to suggest that people may derive the greatest psychological benefits from having contact with nature in the city when their place of residence is in close proximity to natural vegetated areas, particularly areas that contain trees. Studies have shown that natural treed areas in close proximity to one's home can result in lower levels of stress. Even having views of trees from one's home – compared with having views dominated by buildings – has been associated with significantly increased neighbourhood satisfaction. This body of research also found that people tend to categorise urban open space into three types; yards, recreation spaces (such as sports fields) and natural settings. When questioned about what it was they liked about natural settings, most frequently mentioned were their natural beauty and the fact that they provide space for activities such as walking.[6]

On a more mundane level, trees provide shade, and with rising maximum daily temperatures (thanks to global warming), on some days city dwellers are going to need all the shade they can get. Summer maximums can be 1–3°C higher in cities than in rural areas because of the heat bank effect of buildings.[7] This difference will be even greater if the residential density of suburbs is increased through 'urban consolidation': the process of increasing dwelling densities through both the redevelopment of older areas and the use of smaller lot sizes in new fringe developments. Trees and shrubs shade the walls of houses and working buildings, helping to reduce indoor temperatures and thus the load on air-conditioning (on the occasions when it may be considered necessary). In many cities, open space around the home is used essentially as an outdoor room, as is the public space of streets and squares – and even car parks and public transport locations; they can all gain significant benefits from the addition of shade from trees.

When governments or businesses put forward proposals that will result in destroying parts of the natural environment, whether that means cutting down trees or building a freeway down a creekbed, they almost invariably meet strong resistance from local residents. No one fights more fiercely to protect and restore open space, and views of it, than the householder who lives nearby. Deriding such struggles as NIMBY ('not in my back yard') battles, fought merely to protect property values, is unfair: these actions often reflect the public's strong desire to conserve the natural world. More importantly, in a world made insecure by policies that leave more and more to be determined by market forces, and made dangerous by polluting technologies, can we really blame people for wanting to preserve and protect their 'patch' of nature?

While many urban ecosystems are vulnerable to human impact and remain threatened, there have also been some notable success stories in restoring nature in Australian cities. A recent front page article in the Melbourne *Sunday Age* proclaims that:

> The platypus has returned to the eastern suburbs, swimming happily under some of the city's busiest streets. Native fish stocks are improving. Murray cod have been caught near Heidelberg … In the inner suburbs it [the Yarra River] is now probably in better condition than at any time since the gold rush.[8]

Restoration of Merri Creek, also in Melbourne, is another example of a degraded waterway being brought back to an ecologically healthy condition after many years of neglect and abuse. By the end of the 1970s, Merri Creek had become infested with weeds, indigenous flora and fauna were rapidly disappearing, water quality had significantly diminished and rubbish dumped along the creek was piling up. Through the actions of government, prompted by community groups, the creek and its surroundings have now been restored, and a century of environmental degradation has been reversed (Plate 14).

POTENTIAL HEALTH BENEFITS

Most urban dwellers would agree that they like experiencing the natural world, even if this simply means walking in a local park or driving to the coast on weekends. Even in the heart of the busiest city, this desire to connect with nature seems to be strong, as witnessed by the high demand for urban parks and nature reserves. A large body of research exploring people's preferences for different types of landscapes has consistently demonstrated that most people – people of different ages, socio-economic class, education, cultural background – prefer natural environments, such as treed parks, over built-up urban environments.[9] This suggests, at the very least, that inclusion of natural areas in cities and suburbs can increase their aesthetic appeal and provide diversity of experience in people's everyday life. But there is more than aesthetic enjoyment at stake: having contact with nature in the city may even help us to live longer and in better health.

There is growing evidence that having direct contact with nature – animals and plants – in the city may impart definite psychological and physical health benefits that we are only now beginning to understand. In the words of one doctor writing in the *American Journal of Preventive Medicine*:

> There is evidence … that contact with the natural world – with animals, plants, landscapes, and wilderness – may offer health benefits. Perhaps this reflects ancient learning habits, preferences, and tastes, which may be echoes of our origins as creatures of the wild. Satisfying these preferences – taking seriously our affiliation with the natural world – may be an effective way to enhance health. If so, then … health professions will need to articulate a broad vision of environmental health, one that stretches from urban planning to landscape architecture, from interior design to forestry, from botany to veterinary medicine.[10]

Despite the likely benefits associated with having contact with natural environments, opportunities for experiencing nature still remain limited within most cities. If increasing such opportunities is to be successful, deliberate and careful urban planning and environmental design is required, based on firm research evidence. In planning sustainable cities, we need to concern ourselves not just with minimising environmental dangers, such as pollution, important though this objective is; we also need to plan and design cities in ways that will allow us to reap the health benefits that having contact with nature can bestow on us.

Although there has not yet been much research exploring the possible health benefits that may come with having contact with nature, what has been done suggests that merely being exposed to vegetation has some real, measurable benefits. For example, the findings of studies by Roger Ulrich at Texas A&M University suggest that merely viewing natural landscapes can have a positive effect on people's sense of physical and psychological wellbeing. In one study Ulrich showed people scenes of natural, vegetated landscapes and scenes of urban, built environments. When viewing the natural scenes, participants in the study exhibited measurably lower stress responses – physiologically apparent through measurement of their brainwave activity – and they expressed increased feelings of wellbeing.[11]

In another study, published in the prestigious international journal *Science*, Ulrich found that viewing natural, vegetated landscapes reduced healing time required after surgery. In this seminal study, which analysed 10 years' worth of data, patients in an American hospital whose rooms looked out on to a grove of trees were found to have significantly higher rates of post-surgical recovery and shorter hospital stays than patients whose rooms had views of an adjacent brick building, with no trees. The patients with the vegetated view also needed less painkilling and anxiety medication and had fewer minor post-operative complications.[12] Another American study, this one in a large prison, found that prisoners whose cells looked out to an internal courtyard were sick significantly more times (24 per cent more) than prisoners who had views of treed rolling hills and farmlands from their cells.[13]

We have all heard people say they can be 'restored' simply by being exposed to wilderness environments – as one might experience through a visit to a national park. Emotions most often associated with such experiences are a sense of inspiration, tranquillity and peace, and sometimes an almost spiritual feeling of being part of nature.[14] Even though true wilderness landscapes are not found in cities, some of the restorative effects associated with these types of environments may still be possible in cities. Natural places that are neither pristine nor isolated, even those with visible evidence of human influence, have been found to evoke emotional responses more usually engendered by wilderness landscapes, provided people *perceive* the landscape as wilderness.[15] Such a perception is likely when people have a sense that the landscape is functioning according to its own laws, thus providing a small glimpse of 'the sublime'.

Although the feeling of being connected with nature will seldom be as strong in the city as it is in more remote wilderness areas, where a sense of vastness, and of the interrelatedness of natural elements is more obvious, even small natural settings, such as neighbourhood parks, can be planned and designed so that they replicate, in a smaller way, perhaps, this experience. Experiences of urban wilderness can be encouraged through conservation of remnant natural areas, particularly woodlands, and by designing open spaces so that they feel and look bigger and more remote than they really are.

Designing urban open spaces so that they will actually appear larger in size than they really are is certainly possible: witness the miniature landscapes in Japanese gardens (such landscapes are subject to constant and careful human intervention, of course). This feeling of being connected to the natural world, even if the natural settings are small in scale and close to civilisation (literally, in the realm of cities: *cives*), is something many people welcome as a contrast to the pressures and frantic pace of their everyday urban life.

In planning green cities, then, we need to think about how the natural world can be integrated with daily life. But planning needs to be based on deeper knowledge. Questions such as the following need to be addressed:

- What benefits, if any, do people derive from having contact with urban nature?
- How can these benefits be optimised through the design of cities and their open space networks?
- What health hazards (if any), both physical and psychological, may result from *not* having nature in the city?
- Are there ways in which the health hazards associated with living in urban environments, for both humans and other animals, might be reduced through expanding natural environments within cities?
- What (if any) are the ecological benefits to plants and animals of integrating

elements of the natural world with the urban environment, and how can these benefits be maximised through skilled urban management, planning and design?

INTEGRATING NATURE INTO THE CITY

One of the pleasures of walking in the English countryside – or anywhere in Europe, for that matter – is finding 'rare' plants or animals. People can go out with a small pocket guide and identify most of the countryside plants they encounter. In Australia this is much more difficult. There are simply many more different species here. In many places one would need a much fatter volume, and it might be too heavy to take on a 'nature walk'!

Australia is a continent of astonishing biodiversity, and it contains a significant number of the world's species: approximately 8 per cent – not bad for one country! But for a variety of reasons, including the growth of urban areas, these species are not adequately protected. Despite this, many of Australia's indigenous creatures can be seen around our cities: kangaroos and wallabies, koalas, possums of various kinds, wombats and platypus. Birds abound. It is not uncommon to view an eagle soaring overhead in the suburbs or hear hawk moths beating against our windows at night. Many beautiful bird species, such as parrots and wrens, inhabit city trees and airways, and a great range of lizards can be found even in the inner suburbs of major cities. We may not all be fond of them, but the different species of snakes that make their home close to areas of housing are also indicative of Australia's immense biodiversity. And most importantly, near and within urban areas there are a large number of small plant, fungi, insect, reptile and bird species that are not so noticeable but from the perspective of biodiversity are just as important.

While humans can, in the short run, insulate themselves from the natural ecologies on which they ultimately depend, many other species cannot. If the environment that provides food and shelter for different species ('habitat') disappears, so do they. It is true that some species can adapt well to changed habitats within cities, but others cannot. By world standards, Australian cities have been able to preserve a reasonably large amount of habitat – and ecosystems – that pre-date urban development. For example, in the inner, older suburbs of Melbourne, somewhere between 2 and 10 per cent of the total land area contains remnants of natural habitat; many developing outer suburbs contain even larger patches. Still, in the Greater Melbourne region alone some 70 plant species have already become locally extinct – unless areas of remnant habitat are protected, many more will soon be lost.

Many species of plants found in and around Melbourne are also listed as rare or threatened at both the national and state level. In many cases these patches of remnant vegetation represent the last remaining examples of the types of habitat that existed before the establishment of the city.[16] Although most of these areas are currently preserved, they are threatened by future development and by public pressure for increased access to open space. The preservation, restoration and sound management of areas of remnant natural habitat can make a real contribution to maintaining and even increasing local, regional and global biodiversity; at the same time, if these areas are managed properly, they can provide people with places where they can reap the psychological and physical benefits of experiencing nature in the city.

Conservation and restoration of remnant ecosystems, and establishing new areas of quality habitat, can also provide significant ecological benefits to the animals and plants that inhabit the city. Currently, however, urban open spaces are rarely designed to cater for the needs of the more than human populations that rely on them for shelter and food. Providing opportunities for nature to exist and thrive in the city and protecting, enhancing and nurturing natural environments that have remained as remnants are worthwhile and meaningful planning objectives. Neighbourhood parks have an important role to play in this regard but they are often poorly located, or designed in ways that do not fully allow people (and animals) to reap the benefits these places can offer. Many urban parks have also been neglected, many are disused and some have become places of fear due to the threat of crime. Their decline reflects in many instances the wider neglect of the urban public realm that has characterised urban management in Australia and other English-speaking countries, particularly during the reign of 'economic rationalism'.

There are many ways of increasing, shaping and restoring urban open space networks. A key issue is whether the many small patches of remnant habitat can be linked up so that the creatures that inhabit them do not become isolated from one another and thus prevented from breeding or finding alternative territory to live in if they need it. Careful development of natural open space patches and corridors will allow plant and animal habitats to be connected in ways that increase biodiversity and enhance ecological health.

There are excellent examples from all over Australia of local governments understanding, protecting and enlarging existing plant and animal habitats. For example, the City of Manningham (Melbourne) has been restoring Mullum Mullum Creek: there has been a prolonged program of weed elimination and planting of indigenous riparian plant species (species that live alongside rivers), plus a program to manage urban stormwater and thus improve the creek's water quality. As a result, the ecological health of the creek has been significantly improved, and even platypus have returned. Restored areas along the creek also provide residents with opportunities to experience nature close up. In a similar way, the inner-city suburb of Leichhardt in Sydney has recently restored a tidal wetland that will provide a new home for a multitude of plants and animals.

Urban community groups are also working independently of government to maintain and restore the integrity of local ecosystems. The 'Osborne peninsula', for instance, is an area of land occupied by houses and gardens between two stretches of the Yarra River in outer Melbourne. There are several groups of 'friends' ('Friends of Wombat Creek', for example) who work in this area, in their spare time, growing and reintroducing indigenous plants and reducing the impact of invasive species – for example, keeping rabbits from destroying local flora. The groups publish a regular newsletter (*Osborne Peninsula Landcare*) recording their activities and inviting participation.

There are many such initiatives happening all over the world. Although these attempts to restore ecological function within predominantly urban environments are welcome, more needs to be done if the massive environmental degradation that has resulted from urbanisation is to be reversed and the benefits associated with weaving nature into the urban fabric are to be available for all.

URBAN AND LANDSCAPE ECOLOGY

Ecologists study the interaction between organisms and their environment at all scales, from small patches of habitat to entire bioregions. Landscape ecology deals with ecological interactions at the scale of the landscape, encompassing the entire complex mosaic of all local ecosystems and land uses.[17] The study of urban ecology, which looks at the complex interactions between humans, their artefacts and other organisms within cities, is a growing and important area of research. Scientists who study the messy ecologies of cities are helping to determine the best ways of integrating nature into the city.

The task of integrating and encouraging nature to thrive in the city means that we have to look simultaneously at the big picture (the scale of the entire landscape) and the small picture (the scale of neighbourhoods and individual developments). Principles of landscape and urban ecology can, and should, be applied to the siting and design of individual developments, larger areas such as parks and, indeed, entire cities. In all cases these principles operate in essentially the same way. Thus one can predict outcomes from their application at any scale and within the context of any landscape type. For example, if the continuity of a habitat corridor is disrupted, animals cannot travel between the patches connected by the corridor, which denies them necessary resources such as food or shelter; this applies whether the animal species is large or small.

In addition to considering the effects of land use changes over space, we also need to consider how places change over time, focusing not just on immediate effects but also on long-term changes. In contemplating any land use change, one must consider how changes in the structural pattern of the landscape – the arrangement of vegetation, rivers, ridgelines and so forth – will later affect the functioning of habitat within the broader landscape, because by changing landscape structure in one small place we will be changing the way the entire landscape of which it forms a part functions. The goal is to make changes now that will result in positive results later. To do this, it is important that we consider the larger ecological context – at the scale of the region and the city – as well as the site of the specific proposed change. A range of questions need to be asked, including how will the proposed modification affect the movement of animals along corridors? And how will the modification reduce the size, or change the shape, of habitat patches, thus affecting the value of habitat areas for particular plant and animal species?

Imagine you are a bird flying high above the land. As you look down you can see the structure of the landscape. These structural elements have been categorised by ecologists into patches, corridors, edges and matrices. Ecological functioning is primarily determined by the arrangement of these basic elements. Patches of natural open space come in all sizes and shapes, and can be found clustered together, more dispersed, or isolated. Corridors are linear arrangements of natural areas, and likewise come in many forms: long or short, wide or skinny, straight or curvy. Landscape matrices, the larger patterns formed by patches and corridors, can be relatively uniform and homogeneous in character or highly heterogeneous and varied over space. These basic landscape elements can be observed at any scale of the landscape, from large bioregions to neighbourhoods, down to one's home garden. By viewing the urban landscape in terms of these basic structural elements we can better understand how any change we make to one part of the landscape might affect other parts.[18]

PATCHES

Patches of urban nature are either remnants of once larger natural areas or newly introduced and established areas. They vary in size and shape. They can be large, such as a nature reserve along a major river, or as small as one's home garden. Each animal and plant species will function best in habitat that has particular physical attributes, particular species composition in particular configurations, and particular ranges in size. When creating new patches, the idea is to match species to habitat and habitat to species.

Generally, larger patches are better than smaller ones because they support larger and more diverse populations of plants and animals. Having large patches in cities is also important for protecting aquifers and surface water quality. Along with increased urbanisation, habitat areas can become fragmented, with adverse effects on ecological functioning. For example, if a large patch is divided, it will generally result in reducing the size of the population of species that live in the interior parts of the patch, but it may also increase the number of other species, species that like to live at the edge of a patch.

Fragmentation of larger patches into smaller ones always presents the possibility of species becoming locally extinct. Some species can survive using a number of smaller patches, but the creation of small and isolated patches should generally be avoided. However, if smaller patches are to be created, it is best to cluster several such patches in relatively close proximity to one another (it is impossible to be precise here about the distance, because it depends on many variables); this at least encourages colonisation by a greater diversity of species. It is sometimes a better idea to have a mixture of large and smaller patch areas, as this can cater better for the requirements of those species that can use or adapt to many different habitats.

Some animals are specialists and others are generalists in terms of habitat: some species require very specific types of habitat while others, generalist species, benefit most from having a variety of habitats and connections between habitats. Specialist species are more susceptible to disturbances at the local scale; generalist species are more susceptible to changes at the larger scale.

EDGES

The edge of a patch is qualitatively different from the interior, as can be seen by the structure of vegetation and the types and number of animals found at the edge compared with those found at the centre. Many patches in cities have edges that have been determined through other than natural processes – as a result of road construction, for example. Such imposed edges tend to be straight and linear, with abrupt transitions from one area to another. In contrast, natural edges tend to be curvilinear, complex and diffuse in form.

The treatment of edges is critical to ecological functioning and the health of the organisms that inhabit them. Juxtaposing straight, hard, human-created edges with the more fluid, curving and diffuse edges that result from natural processes is a good technique for softening the interface between natural and built spaces. As a rule, the more edge area there is, the better. The idea is to create edges that have a lot of vertical and horizontal structural diversity in the vegetation, because such diversity will attract a greater variety of animals. By creating patches that have convoluted edges, with a variety of indents and projections, more overall edge habitat can be created.

While a convoluted patch edge will result in the patch being home to more species that favour the edge habitat, it will tend to limit space for those species that favour the interior of the patch for their habitat. When we urbanise city fringe areas, the ecology of natural open space will often be under threat because of the invasion of exotic plant species as well as because of domestic pets, which can quickly become feral animals. In these situations wide edges can be useful: they can be used as buffers to prevent the spread of exotic species into the interior of a habitat patch.

CORRIDORS

As a result of land use change and urban development, habitat patches in urban areas are continually under threat of being lost, fragmented, dissected and/or reduced in size. This process leads to loss of biodiversity. One of the best ways to safeguard biodiversity is to provide connections between habitat patches through environmental corridors and networks of corridors. Such corridors allow animals to move from one area to another, thereby increasing the likelihood of their survival and reproduction.

Corridors can also be used to control wildlife movement in places where there are potential conflicts between wildlife habitat, human activities and other land uses. The overall objective is to create habitat networks that contain patches and corridors that have a high degree of interrelatedness (connectivity) and that allow a wide range of movement patterns for animals (circuitry).

One of the best opportunities for creating useful environmental corridors in the city is along river and stream courses. Such riparian environments naturally attract and support a wide range of wildlife. They also attract people, who seek out these areas for recreation or enjoyment of nature. Water in the landscape attracts people like no other natural feature. Think of how many dockland or riverside neighbourhoods have been redeveloped for luxury apartments since industry abandoned the sites, and how many new developments feature canals and lakes. Numerous landscape preference studies have identified water as being very important to landscape attractiveness. As always, though, in designing environmental corridors, potential conflicts between people and animals need to be considered.

The most important characteristics of a successful watercourse corridor (or any corridor) are its width and its connectivity (ability to connect areas of habitat). Wider corridors and those with a greater degree of connectivity typically allow better-functioning corridors. Wide and densely vegetated watercourse corridors also provide the greatest protection from pollutants entering the water system because they act as filters for water draining from developed areas into the watercourse. It is also important to incorporate some smaller habitat patches along corridors: animals need places to rest and find shelter as they travel. Places where corridors meet are likely to contain more species than any other part of the corridor – the location and design of these areas need to be carefully planned so that these areas do not produce conflicts between animals and people. It is also important that river corridors be continuous, without gaps (wherever possible), because more continuous corridors help to keep water temperature lower, and cooler water has a greater ability to support aquatic animal species (such as the many types of fish that require a constant cool water temperature to survive).

An excellent example of an environmental corridor which successfully merges high quality ecological habitat and recreational opportunities in the heart of a major Australian city is in the River Torrens Linear Park in Adelaide (Plates 15 and 16). The River Torrens Linear Park now stretches for 50 kilometres, from Mt Lofty Ranges to the Gulf St Vincent. During the layout of Adelaide in 1837, areas along the river (riparian zones) were initially set aside as open space. However, due to a variety of activities – such as mining, agricultural use and waste disposal – along the river's banks, and changes made to the river to help control flooding, the ecology of the river and its surrounds had been severely degraded, with considerable loss of indigenous flora and fauna (both terrestrial and aquatic).

As early as 1912 the local community was working actively to have derelict riparian areas along the River Torrens restored. Because of the area's rich natural biodiversity and the river's proximity to the city, restoration was seen as an ideal opportunity to provide Adelaide residents with direct and nearby links with nature. In the 1970s, plans for the entire 50 kilometre greenway were developed, and they were incrementally implemented between 1982 and 1998.[19] Efforts were made to conserve what remnant vegetation was left and a large amount of indigenous vegetation was planted, with the aim of restoring habitat for all sorts of native animals – birds, small mammals, reptiles, fish, and insects. While indigenous plants were being introduced, weed species were also being eliminated. To cater for the recreational needs of the community, a number of walking tracks and bridges were designed – they were strategically located so as to allow human access to the area while preserving the corridor's ecological function.

Built features in cities, such as roads, railway lines, powerline easements and the like, can also serve as corridors for wildlife movement. However, such corridors tend to occur in straight linear configurations and to be more prone to human disturbance and interference than natural features such as rivers. For example, for animals that move along roadsides, as many do, the likelihood of being killed by passing cars is high; witness the carnage we see even in the heart of the busiest cities.

THE VALUE OF INDIGENOUS PLANTS

From an ecological point of view it is important that locally indigenous plants be used as much as possible when urban areas of habitat are established, because native fauna and flora have evolved together: local animals need local plants for food and shelter. Using locally indigenous plants also helps conserve the flora of the area, and such plants are generally easier and less expensive to grow and maintain. And they often need less water and fertilisers than do exotic plants or plants that are native to other parts of Australia.

Australia needs to conserve water in any way possible, and the use of vegetation that has adapted to survive with limited water, as indigenous plants in many parts of Australia have, is an excellent way of conserving precious water. There are, however, differences in what people think looks best. Some people prefer the lush look of water-consuming exotic plants to that of native Australian plants. Let's hope that through education, people can be made more aware of not only the subtle beauty of Australian flora, but also the water-saving benefits of using indigenous and native vegetation judiciously in areas of urban open space. In a nutshell, using indigenous plants in the landscape can help increase both the ecological and aesthetic quality of urban areas. Ideally, only indigenous plants that have evolved in the specific area where they are to be planted should be used: this helps to conserve the genetic stock of the local flora and simultaneously minimises the risk that the same species, but from another area, and with different genetic characteristics, will hybridise – this results in loss of genetic variation, thus reducing biodiversity.

Integration of nature into the city cuts two ways. The human impact on the more than human environment needs to be considered, but so too does the impact of nature on us humans. If we like or dislike certain landscapes, what exactly does this mean and where do these preferences come from?

LANDSCAPE PREFERENCE

Knowing which attributes of the natural world are associated with the landscapes people like best, and how these attributes can be incorporated into the design of urban open space, is important. If people do not like the look of the natural open spaces designed for them, they may well be less inclined to use or value them. This results in such habitats not being properly cared for. Within natural landscapes, certain elements, such as the presence of water, topographic variation and vegetation, have repeatedly been associated with a high landscape preference and good scenic value; built features and degraded landscapes have consistently been associated with low preference and poor scenic evaluations.

For example, in one study, scenes of forested landscapes in Western Australia were rated for preference by three groups; university students from Western Australia, university students from the United States and members of a West Australian wildflower society. There was strong agreement in preference across all three groups. All respondents liked a scene of a mature forest with visible water and moderate topographic variation best; a bauxite-mining site was rated lowest by all groups.[20] In another study exploring landscape preferences in the small coastal town of Lorne, Victoria, a high correlation was found between the landscape preferences of permanent and seasonal residents of the town and American landscape architecture students.[21] The findings of these studies suggest that many people in Australia do indeed share preferences for landscapes, liking undisturbed natural settings much more than they do built or degraded landscapes.

We do know that certain landscape attributes seem to have a clear influence on the way people appreciate and use open spaces. For instance, people seem to prefer:

- landscapes that have obvious focal points;
- landscapes with clear spatial definition;
- treed landscapes that lack thick underbrush, thus making them seem relatively open; and
- wooded areas that have scattered clearings.

A sense of mystery has also been found to be strongly associated with highly preferred landscapes.[22] In contrast, more familiar natural environments, such as one's back garden or other nearby natural places, have also been identified as valued parts of the landscape. Such small-scale natural places can provide a focus for what has been termed 'soft fascination' – a heightened interest in simple everyday natural phenomena (such as the sound of birds or the movement of leaves in the breeze) that can result in a reflective state of mind and heightened aesthetic experience.[23] The integration of the natural landscape into the new suburbs of Västra Hamnen in Sweden and Kronsberg in Germany (described in chapter 2) are just two instances where planners have made deliberate efforts to encourage this sense of 'soft fascination'. This quality is present too in all the examples of 'ecohouses' described. Providing opportunities for people to experience natural environmental stimuli of this sort may be particularly important in the city, as cities often have limited room where open space can be created. What is created needs to be valued by its users.

Conversely, perceived threat or danger in the landscape also seems to be an important component of negative appraisals of landscape.[24] In rural Australia, snakes, particularly in high grass, are a definite source of fear and danger; this fear could be expected to decrease landscape preference for this type of environment for many people. In the urban context, fear of crime is partly responsible for reducing people's liking for and use of certain areas of open space.

While we are beginning to understand which features may be associated with preferred landscapes (at least within certain cultures), reasons for these predispositions is the subject of a great deal of speculation and debate. Some researchers have tried to explain landscape preferences by linking them to human evolutionary predispositions. For most of human evolution, it is argued by the vast majority of anthropologists, early human beings occupied an African savanna-type landscape, a landscape of relatively open grasslands with scattered groups of trees, and denser forested areas near rivers and lakes; this is a landscape similar in form to that of many contemporary parks (for instance Melbourne's Royal Park, Plates 8 and 9, or Perth's Kings Park, Plate 10). Humans, it is claimed, may retain an inbuilt liking for such landscapes.[25]

The findings of one seminal North American study suggest that people, and children in particular, do seem innately to prefer these savanna-type landscapes, even over those landscapes they are most familiar with.[26] In support of this 'habitat selection theory', the eminent biologist E.O. Wilson suggests:

> It would ... be quite extraordinary to find that all learning rules related to that world (natural) would have been erased in a few thousand years, even for the tiny minority of peoples who have existed for more than one or two generations in wholly urban environments.[27]

While people seem generally to have strong affection for trees in the landscape, the form of trees may also play a significant role in these preferences, with some forms being preferred to others. British geographer Jay Appleton's 'prospect refuge theory' predicts that trees with large canopies would have offered protection and refuge opportunities for our distant ancestors by providing sheltering places from which to obtain unobserved views over the landscape. A tall-trunked tree would provide a good advantage in terms of gaining a view (prospect), as would one that is easy to climb (has a low branching habit). On the other hand, 'habitat selection theory' predicts that humans will prefer tree forms associated with savanna landscapes. Savanna landscapes are typically composed of trees that have short trunks (relative to their height), are more broad than tall, and have wide, spreading canopies and fine-textured foliage – various species of *Acacia* are prime examples.

This predilection for savanna-like landscapes is not confined to European landscape traditions. It is also reflected in the design of

Japanese gardens. The cultivated trees traditionally chosen for Japanese gardens, such as maples, oaks and pines, vary in form from the same species found in nature in that they tend to be broader, with relatively shorter trunks and leaves that are smaller and more divided (Plate 17). Trees used in Japanese gardens are also frequently modified – through pruning – so that they have a layered appearance that is reminiscent of trees typical of savanna lands (such as *Acacias*).

Other researchers believe there is a direct relationship between the ecological functioning of the landscape and perceived scenic beauty. If this is true it means that those environments that are highly diverse ecologically will be seen as more beautiful than those that are not. Aldo Leopold, an important early US ecologist and forest manager, first proposed this notion in his initial writings, including his insightful 1949 book *A Sand Country Almanac*.[28] More recently, Paul Gobster, a researcher with the US Forest Service, has argued for such an 'ecological aesthetic', which he sees as the integration of aesthetic and biodiversity values.[29]

In contrast, British geographer Dennis Cosgrove suggests that people's aesthetic responses to the landscape are laden with symbolic meanings that have been formed in the relatively recent past, and that such meanings are purely a product of our cultural heritage.[30] He and his colleagues propose that human responses to these landscape symbols can only be understood with reference to cultural history, and for people from Europe, the Americas and Australia, that means predominantly European cultural history. Those who subscribe to this belief suggest that current Western notions of 'natural' landscapes are strongly coloured by European traditions of landscape painting dating back to the 17th century, and the 'picturesque' conventions promulgated in paintings.[31] These scholars maintain that gardens and parks designed in the tradition of the picturesque have been treated like landscape paintings, and essentially represent an artificial view of nature. Indeed, parks designed with this picturesque notion in mind are often in sharp opposition to ecological reality.

There may in fact be something of a clash between aesthetic preference defined by culture and ecological function. For example, wetlands are some of the most biologically diverse and ecologically important ecosystems on Earth, yet they are often untidy-looking places. Returning from Europe, the traveller is struck by the messiness of Australian landscapes. Eucalypts calmly drop their limbs and strew bark over paddocks and grasslands. At ground level, forests in Australia, like highly diverse forests anywhere on Earth, are a tangle of dead branches that both make ideal fuel for wildfires and create slowly rotting mulch, teeming with insect and fungal life. Fallen tree limbs themselves make food for insects, while holes left in trees provide essential nesting places for birds and other arboreal animals.

Conflicts between people's aesthetic values and ecological values need to be resolved if urban open spaces are to cater effectively for the needs of both human and more than human urban dwellers. American researcher Joan Nassauer suggests that visible signs of human intervention in a landscape can increase our preference for that landscape if such intervention signifies a degree of human care for the environment: in her words, if the landscape exhibits 'cues to care'.[32] This means, again, that we prefer landscapes that appear neat and tidy to those that look messy or not well tended, as many natural and diverse ecosystems do.

People are more likely to accept and understand nature in cities when it is presented in a way that conforms to their cultural expectations. In the case of urban open spaces that have high *ecological* value yet are seen as having low *scenic* value (remnant urban scrub, for example), Nassauer suggests that the landscape can be modified without greatly disturbing its ecological integrity simply by creating the impression that the place is being cared for, and that this is likely to increase public aesthetic appreciation of the space. So, following Nassauer's ideas, the degree to which we value messy ecosystems – and pristine and intact ecosystems are often messy – may be increased by placing such areas in what she has termed 'orderly frames'. If the aesthetic value of the space has been increased, it is more likely that the space will be protected.

The idea of using 'cues to care' in landscape design to introduce indigenous plant communities to people within an urban context was skilfully employed in the design of a constructed wetland in a park in St Paul, Minnesota – the Phalan Wetland Amenity Park (Plate 18). On the site of a shopping centre which had been a natural wetland 40 years before, a new wetland was created by Nassauer and her colleagues. They used bands of wet-loving indigenous meadow plants and prairie grasses to 'frame' the wetland. The aim was to introduce people to a highly diverse, healthy, functioning ecosystem within a highly urban environment yet present it in a way that people would appreciate aesthetically.

The aesthetic value people place on urban open spaces must be taken into account if people are to be expected to accept ecologically valuable landscapes, because many of these are not considered beautiful in the more traditional sense of the word. Urban open spaces come in many forms: parks, back gardens, nature reserves and sometimes parcels of vacant land that have simply been left over after development. These seemingly derelict places are sometimes perceived as 'natural' in contrast to the purely built environments that dominate cities, and they are often highly valued by local residents. Such natural-looking, yet derelict, places may even cater well for the needs of animals. However, they may often appear messier than – and hence not as aesthetically attractive to the public as – more manicured open spaces such as well-treed parks. In the green city, conflicts can be expected between aesthetic values and the actual appearance of ecosystems. The aim is to resolve such conflicts so that nature in the city can maintain its ecological functions while still being aesthetically acceptable to the general public.

CONCLUSION

We began this book with an image of the city as a vortex of consumption. There is truth in this image, but it is not the whole story. Nature exists in and flows through cities. Cities are themselves patches of nature that have been severely modified by humans. They are the places where human society and the societies of the more than human world interact most vigorously. The result need not be disastrous for urban nature. On the contrary, cities often already contain more biodiversity than their surrounding agricultural regions. They offer considerable resources for non-human species. This chapter has presented a range of ideas about how we might reinforce nature in the city, with two aims: to provide urban dwellers with opportunities for greater contact with the natural world and to provide the plants and animals that live in the city with improved habitat.

We maintain that sustainable urban environments need to be – and can be – places where people can interact with nature, and gain the physical and psychological benefits such contact imparts, and places where the animals and plants that live in the city can be protected and thrive.

In order to achieve this it is important that we design natural open space areas – such as nature reserves and parks – that people will appreciate. If areas of urban nature are not in a form that people like, they are much less likely to be used and cared for. That is why the findings of research on landscape preferences need to be matched with the environmental planning and design principles drawn from the study of urban ecology when creating public open spaces. Bringing these two bodies of scientific understanding together provides us with the best means of integrating elements of the natural world into the city.

So far we have been discussing living space, but the integration of nature is just as important in the working space of the city. Consideration of workplaces, however, introduces some important new elements into the design of the green city. These are the subject of the next chapter.

FURTHER READING

Rene Dubos's seminal book *So Human an Animal* (Charles Scribner's Sons, New York, 1968) was one of the first books to alert society to how cities and the increasing use of technology were fostering an environmental crisis. Likewise, Paul Shepard's *Nature and Madness* (University of Georgia Press, Athens AL, 1982) presents a profound environmental philosophical insight. Those who want to explore the biophilia hypothesis further should look at the collected essays presented in the book *The Biophilia Hypothesis* (S. Kellert & E.O. Wilson (eds), Island Press, Washington DC, 1993). Evolutionary theories are explored in J. Appleton, *The Experience of Landscape* (John Wiley & Sons, New York, 1975), and Rachel & Stephen Kaplan, *The Experience of Nature* (Cambridge University Press, Cambridge, 1989). *Urban Biophysical Environments*, by Howard Bridgeman, Robin Warner & John Dodson (Oxford University Press, Melbourne, 1995) is a useful and readable introduction to the biophysical context of Australian cities.

New Lives, New Landscapes, by Nan Fairbrother, provides a discussion of the social dimension of landscape in urban Britain (The Architectural Press, London, 1970). The relations between animals and humans in cities is discussed in a provocative essay by Steve Hinchliffe in *Unsettling Cities* (J. Allen, D. Massey & M. Pryke (eds), Routledge, London & New York, 1999). Tim Low provides a racy and thought-provoking discussion of wild nature – often in urban settings – in *The New Nature: Winners and Losers in Wild Australia* (Penguin Books, Melbourne, 2003). *Placing Nature: Culture and Landscape Ecology*, edited by Joan Nassauer (Island Press, Washington DC, 1997), is a wonderful collection of essays that explores how contemporary culture shapes our landscape preferences. Finally, Richard Foreman's *Land Mosaics: The Ecology of Landscapes and Regions* (Cambridge University Press, Cambridge, 1995) is a very readable text on landscape ecology.

CHAPTER 4

SUSTAINABLE WORKPLACES

The city is a place of work. People congregate in order to work together. And their capacity to work together brings people together to live. So work is at the core of social life. As work has become more and more specialised, and at the same time more densely interconnected, so cities have grown in size and complexity. Cities are fundamentally places where ideas, goods and services are produced and exchanged. The Latin word 'forum' originally meant both a place of public deliberation and a marketplace for goods. With so many cities occupied today with the 'knowledge economy' and the 'network society', the market and the forum are again beginning to merge.

The modern state, the politics of 'liberalism', and democratic government grew up around city life: the life of the forum. The work-place can (of course) be a place of production – a factory, a place where goods and machinery are manufactured. The factory is characteristic of the industrial age, and factories and warehouses are still important work-places to which green principles should be applied. For industrial cities, especially those of the new industrial regions of China, the Asia Pacific rim, South America and India, the 'green factory' will figure promi-nently in green cities. But factories, those 'satanic mills' belching smoke, are no longer the defining element of cities of the rich post-industrial world or of many cities of the 'developing' world. Places where ideas are generated, and information and goods are exchanged, are more typical. In an important sense, the workplace is a forum, a public place of social gathering and a marketplace for ideas.

The idea of 'sustainable work' opens up a broad vista of questions and potential lines of inquiry: for instance, how can work in cities draw less on the resources of the environment? How will concern for nature change the nature of work? How can we better measure the value of work when the money measure of work reported – gross national or domestic product (GNP, GDP) – does not account for its real social or environmental value? How can work be made more safe and satisfying? In this book there is not space to pursue these questions. Our present concern is with the built environment, essentially the *container* of the workplace, and how that container caters for the relationship between humans and nature, and represents the meaning of that relationship. This concern brings us face to face with architecture. Up to now we have not said much about architecture, but moving the discussion to buildings of larger scale and complexity, which workplaces mostly are, means that architectural concerns must be addressed.

Architecture is about the expression of meaning in buildings as much as it is about meeting functional and technical demands. Sustainable buildings of all shapes and sizes can meet energy-saving requirements, provide a healthy and comfortable environment in which to work, and allow contact with nature. But viewed as architecture, as cultural artefacts, buildings also express something about the human–nature relationship. This is not just a matter of aesthetic style — different styles can express a human–nature relationship in different ways. It is something more fundamental. The main focus of this chapter is workplaces as sustainable architecture. Some examples from around the world will be discussed. But first we will set the broader scene of the workplace as a forum.

THE WORKPLACE AS A FORUM

The workplace is a public place, a place of public exchange, or at least a place where the domain of purely domestic work gradually yields to the domain of public work. In fact there is something like a continuum between private and public. At one end of the spectrum, the home can also be a workplace – the place of outwork or telework, for example. If the home office is connected to email and the internet, at least some part of the homespace becomes in some senses public. Then there are workplaces such as doctors' consulting rooms and barristers' chambers, which have an important air of privacy. Perhaps the offices of chief executives and government ministers have this too, though official secrecy has limits. Beyond that, all forms of shops and markets, schools, universities and colleges, hospitals, libraries, entertainment venues, cafés and restaurants, offices, churches, warehouses, factories and production plants (including energy production plants) are in some way public workplaces, places where individuals congregate to manufacture or exchange goods, services and information. The buildings that house these places are subject to norms of sustainability similar to the buildings that house the domestic sphere. They are just generally larger in scale. We discuss some specific examples of such buildings below. But there are three wider issues with the sustainability of workplaces that should be mentioned briefly: the question of 'greener production', the possibility of green food markets, and the potential of telework to reduce travel.

Many companies are adopting 'green factory' programs. The Sharp electronics corporation of Japan, for example, has developed a ten-point program 'to attain high-level production, maintain harmony with the local community and nature, and reduce the environmental burden'.[1] Environmental management and performance are to be in accordance with the International Standards Organization's ISO 14001 (see Box 4.1). The ten points include: 'to minimise emission of greenhouse gas, energy consumption, resource consumption, discharge of waste, the risk of environmental pollution and accidents caused by chemical substances, and the environmental burden on the atmosphere, water and soil'. The plan also includes 'endeavouring to preserve nature on and off the site, encouraging harmony with the local community, raising environmental awareness among employees', and, importantly, 'disclosing information on the environment'. These are good intentions, but it is impossible to judge what the practical result will be without regular environmental audits and full public disclosure.

The Sharp Kameyama Plant, expected to commence production in 2004, aims to be a model of economic efficiency, 'social mindedness' and environmental conservation. The plant will eliminate the transport of LCD panels between factories, thus reducing packaging, and reducing greenhouse and toxic emissions from vehicles. A co-generation system will supply the plant with about one-third of its annual electricity and will

---

Box 4.1 ISO 14001, OF THE INTERNATIONAL STANDARDS ORGANIZATION

The International Standards Organization is one of a number of national and international organisations that develop standard codes of performance for the management of production. The ISO 14001 standard aims to provide guidance to companies and governments on the requirements of an effective plan to manage the environmental impact of the production agency's operations. Under ISO 14001 the company must adopt a policy 'relevant to the scale and nature of the organization's activities and must include commitments to continual improvement, the prevention of pollution and compliance with relevant environmental legislation and regulations. The policy must be communicated to all employees and must be publicly available.'[1]

The first step is for the company to identify with some precision the environmental impacts of its activities, products and services. The company must identify the legal and other obligations that apply to its activities. Training needs should be identified for all staff whose work may have an environmental impact. Then an environmental management system should be put in place. The system should address six key questions:

- What are the broad outcomes, or benefits to the organization, that are required from environmental management?
- What are the environmental impacts associated with the organization's activities, products and services that will affect those outcomes?
- What is the organization's policy with regard to environmental issues?
- What are the organization's objectives and targets for environmental management?
- What systems and procedures need to be implemented in order to achieve the policy objectives and targets?
- How is the performance of the system to be evaluated?[2]

The most critical parts of the process are quantifying the targets, making sure that the organisation has the capacity (by training, etc) to implement the plan, evaluating performance and making the evaluation public. ISO 14001 does not guarantee any particular level of environmental performance. It certainly does not guarantee sustainability, but it does describe a process of improving environmental efficiency.

1 Rory Sullivan & Hugh Wyndham, *Effective Environmental Management: Principles and Case Studies*, Allen & Unwin, Sydney, 2001, p. 83.
2 Sullivan & Wyndham, *Effective Environmental Management*, pp. 17–18.

utilise waste heat for air-conditioning. This will reduce current CO_2 emissions by about 40 per cent. Natural gas will be supplied through pipelines, eliminating the CO_2 and nitrogen oxides caused by tanker truck transportation. The plant will collect all the wastewater from the production process (up to 9000 tonnes per day) and recycle it via water purification techniques using micro-organism treatment. The factory itself is designed to be a zero emission facility from the start of operations, reusing and recycling as much waste as possible. The walls of the plant will have about 600 photovoltaic modules. The company says that it is actively working towards the preservation of natural surroundings and the establishment of a natural park in collaboration with government, industry and local residents, so that all parties will appreciate the value of the plant. To this end the company moved some of the trees at the construction site to another place and will replant them around the facility after construction has been completed. Other trees that had to be cut down were processed into wood chips to be used as mulch for the surrounding green space. There is a plan to release indigenous fish caught by local volunteers into an artificial pond in the centre of the park.

Every work process consumes energy and materials and emits waste. Greener production means reducing the energy inputs and waste outputs from factories and production plant. Big savings in production costs can be made by reducing energy and waste, so in a competitive world there is a strong incentive for firms to do so. In this respect the market is environmentally benign. For instance, the factories where cars and trucks are produced burn prodigious amounts of energy – the energy bill for a large manufacturing plant can be between US$10 million and US$50 million per year. According to one internet source, General Motors claims that it has reduced energy consumption in its North American plant by 18 per cent since 1995 and is continuing to save energy.[2] Reducing the size of a production facility can also bring reductions in energy use. Several car manufacturers are investing in smaller, more energy-efficient production plants (the new Toyota plant in Valenciennes in France is one example).

To reduce heating and cooling loads, Ford's redeveloped 'Rouge' production complex at Dearborn, Missouri (in the United States) has a roof with a covering of plants similar to the sedum roofs of some of the housing developments discussed in chapter 2. Natural lighting is provided by thirty-five huge skylights. Trellises for climbing plants shade and cool the office buildings on the site. The Dearborn redevelopment was designed by eco-architect William McDonough. A factory for Rolls

Royce in southern England will be built half underground (using thermal mass), and will have a living moss roof. This information is backed up by figures from the International Energy Agency that show that between 1990 and 1999 the United States greatly improved its carbon efficiency of production – that is, it reduced the amount of greenhouse emissions per dollar of product (GDP).

The problem is that total production across all industry sectors is growing even faster than this kind of change, and some sectors, such as transport, showed little improvement in carbon efficiency over that time. So the total amount of greenhouse gas emitted from the United States increased from 1.3 billion to 1.5 billion tonnes in those years.[3] In this respect the competitive market is far from benign. Markets encourage efficiency, and efficiency in the use of energy and materials is highly desirable from the environmental point of view. But markets also stimulate growth, and (so far) cannot be expected to limit that growth to the planet's environmental capacity. To set and maintain limits requires political action: the regulation of markets.

As the above examples indicate, information is critically important in the public forum. Another workplace where information is literally vital is the supermarket. The food products supplied in supermarkets are destined for a very personal form of consumption – eating. Many people, perhaps most, would like to know more about what they eat. And even if some don't really want to know, perhaps it would be better for them if they did. The problem of 'remoteness' mentioned in chapter 1 distances the consumer of food from the living creatures that become food.

The sort of questions one might ask in this context include: how far has the food travelled? A survey of how far a typical shopping basket of goods had travelled showed that the total distance travelled was 100,943 miles (161,500 kilometres) to get all the goods from the supplier into the shopping basket![4] How much greenhouse gas has been generated en route? And this is just the start of what could be a long list of questions. How much collateral damage has been done to other animals and other species in order to provide the food? In what conditions are the animals kept before being slaughtered or while they are providing food? What additives does the food contain? Has the food been genetically tampered with? Our need for information goes much further than accurate labelling of packaged produce. Could we conceive of a supermarket in which the connection with more than human life is made more apparent? With modern information technology it should be quite possible for supermarkets to show real-time displays of the origins of products: farmcam, fishcam. It should be possible for the buyer of a jar of instant coffee to press a button and bring up a live display of the coffee plantations. What are the working conditions like there? This is a little fanciful – but the first supermarket to try it might find that it had stolen a marketing march on its competitors. And there are developments that reflect something of the same concern: the revival of 'farmers' markets, the growth of community-supported agriculture and the increasing popularity of 'organic' produce (food grown without the use of synthetic pesticides and fertilizers and not subject to genetic engineering) (see Box 4.2).

Farmers' markets are really nothing more than a tradition that is beginning to be revived: a regular event at which local farmers sell from market stalls direct to the public. Locally grown fresh produce is put on sale. The consumers have a chance to talk to the producers and find out about the food they are buying and the conditions under which it was grown. Even though France started the idea of the hypermarket (Carrefour), 'farmers' markets' never really lost their popularity in France – and, as anyone who has visited French country towns knows, at local markets country people and townspeople mingle around the great French obsession with the beauty of food.

Community-supported agriculture (CSA) is a different idea. It started in the 1960s in Switzerland and Japan. CSA means a partnership in which members of a local community cover all or part of a farmer's annual operating costs by purchasing a share in the season's harvest. Individual subscribers to the co-operative commit a sum each year, in

Box 4.2 ORGANIC FOOD PRODUCTION AND SUSTAINABLE AGRICULTURE

In April 1995 the National Organic Standards Board of the United States defined 'organic' as follows:

> Organic agriculture is an ecological production management system that promotes and enhances biodiversity, biological cycles and soil biological activity. It is based on minimal use of off-farm inputs and on management practices that restore, maintain and enhance ecological harmony.

'Organic' is a labeling term that denotes products produced under the authority of the Organic Foods Production Act. The principal guidelines for organic production are to use materials and practices that enhance the ecological balance of natural systems and that integrate the parts of the farming system into an ecological whole.

Organic agriculture practices cannot ensure that products are completely free of residues; however, methods are used to minimize pollution from air, soil and water.

Organic food handlers, processors and retailers adhere to standards that maintain the integrity of organic agricultural products. The primary goal of organic agriculture is to optimize the health and productivity of interdependent communities of soil life, plants, animals and people (http://www.nal.usda.gov/afsic/ofp/#intro).

According to British agro-ecologists Jules Pretty and Rachel Hine, sustainable agriculture also contributes to a range of public goods other than food production: clean water, protection of wildlife, carbon sequestration in the soil, flood protection and landscape quality. It also contributes to ground water recharge, reverse migration (urban to rural) and social cohesion (Jules Pretty & Rachel Hine, *Reducing Food Poverty with Sustainable Agriculture: A Summary of New Evidence*, University of Essex, 2001).

Food producers may apply to have their agricultural practices certified 'organic'. Organic certification in Australia is governed by no fewer than seven recognised non-government agencies, each of which is accredited by the Commonwealth Government: the Bio-Dynamic Research Institute, Biological Farmers of Australia, the National Association for Sustainable Agriculture Australia, the Organic Food Chain, Organic Herb Growers of Australia, the Organic Vignerons Association of Australia, and the Tasmanian Organic-Dynamic Producers. Consumption of organic produce is growing fast – estimates suggest by between 20 per cent and 50 per cent per year. The Australian organics industry is worth $250–300 million per year and generates about $50 million in exports (Friends of the Earth, *Towards a Community Supported Agriculture*, Friends of the Earth, Brisbane, 2001, p. 11).

return for which they are provided regularly with seasonal produce. Thus the risks of production are shared between the food producers and consumers, so there is a much more direct link between the public and the environment.[5]

The American economist Paul Krugman applauds globalisation for putting fresh vegetables from Zimbabwe on the tables of Londoners, thus providing the farmers of Zimbabwe with a living. Yes, that is good, but it depends, as Krugman acknowledges, on cheap air transport ('beat-up old Boeings') – that is, air transport whose long-term global warming costs are not taken into account.[6] Colin Hines, in his book *Localization, A Global Manifesto*,[7] argues for local consumption of whatever can be produced locally. In an interview with the UK newspaper *The Financial Times*, he says: 'It's what I call protecting the global, locally. This means getting into a process of "better your neighbour" rather than beggar your neighbour. It means trading locally as far as is possible, helping to protect and rebuild local economies.'[8] When the long-term environmental costs of transport are eventually included in the price of transport, as they must be, Hines's arguments are going to make increasing economic as well as ecological sense.

The biggest English supermarket chains, Tesco and Sainsbury, both market a wide range of organic food products: fruit and vegetables, milk, tea, coffee, baby foods, flour, bread, biscuits, cider, wine, chocolate and some kinds of meat. Sainsbury has used its power as a food retailer to implement procurement policies designed to reduce waste, conserve resources, minimise energy use, and reduce transport. One-quarter of all food sold in Sainsbury supermarkets is organic produce.[9]

Finally, will public workplaces eventually disappear altogether as more and more people work at home? Will the 'forum' of the workplace become entirely virtual, via the internet? From the ecological point of view this may seem a good idea, because it would reduce urban travel. From the viewpoint of the workplace as a forum, though, it seems a diminution of face-to-face sociality. There is no doubt that people who work largely at processing information can do the job anywhere – in cafés as easily as at home (see Plate 19). Phone technology and email provide for instant exchange of messages, which is often all that is necessary by way of communication between workers. Experiments carried out in California suggest that commuting trips of office workers could be greatly reduced by telework. However, email and the internet are not substitutes for subtle, unmediated, multifaceted, and much desired face-to-face communication. For example, university lecturers may do more work at home now than before, and keep in touch with students and staff by email, but they also attend more international conferences, which are facilitated by the internet. Email greatly simplifies the organisation of a conference by bringing large numbers of people into easy, recorded and instant remote communication. These connections lead to increased demands for face-to-face contact.

Certain kinds of travel may be reduced in future because of sophisticated remote communication, but it seems highly unlikely that the gross amount of work travel will diminish unless its real price greatly increases. If as a result of looming ecological catastrophe this does in fact happen, telecommunications will come to play an even more crucial role in holding a global society together.

THE SUSTAINABLE ARCHITECTURE OF THE WORKPLACE

Some of the examples of green housing discussed in chapter 2 were designed by architects, but we have not discussed the buildings from the architectural viewpoint, and in fact architects in many countries play only a small part in the making of homes and suburbs. But with workplaces the situation is different. The level of complexity, the size and interdisciplinary character of the skills needed and used during the design and construction of a responsibly conceived workplace building make architectural skill and design indispensable. That is why an explanation of the sustainable workplace must present both the designers' and the users' side of the story.

In successful projects, architects and users form a partnership that lasts throughout the process of conception and construction – and even later, during occupation – of the buildings. Passive solar buildings need active occupants. And there are ways of use that make buildings perform well. Those ways are taken account of in the building design, and their complexity varies from straightforward, commonsense routines to complex instructions that may require detailed guidelines and even professional building management. The appropriate level of sophistication in use – the ability of users to get the best from the designed potential of the building – can contribute significantly both to measurable environmental performance and to the quality of life of the occupants.

Historically, the concern for the health and safety of the workplace followed hard on the heels of the rise of factories and the growth of the trade union movement. The concern for the *ecological sustainability* of the workplace followed a widespread rise in environmental awareness reinforced by the oil shocks and energy crisis of the 1970s. So the first attempts at development of sustainable office buildings dealt primarily, if not exclusively, with reducing the energy bill. In many instances, and in particular in projects led by mechanical engineers, that remains the key focus.

Energy-orientated design approaches are highly dependent on the climatic context of the workplace concerned. Passive, active and hybrid solar strategies are central to what architects call 'bioclimatic design' – designing for the climate of a particular place. As the climate changes with global warming, adaptation of buildings to local climate, not only without increasing energy consumption but with significant reductions, will become an essential requirement for all new work buildings. But bioclimatic design can do much more than just provide measurable energy savings. It can also improve non-measurable things like the quality of working life, which goes far beyond the numerically expressed features of the building. Energy saving in climatically responsive buildings grows into a sense of wellbeing. Bioclimatic design results in buildings which, spatially and formally, express the values not only of their designers, but also of their owners. The resulting place-specific, regional flavour of architectural form has broad cultural consequences. The quality of vernacular architecture to a large degree comes from how attuned buildings are to both the natural forces and the human cultures that define the place.

Over the last two or three decades, the spectrum of environmentally responsible approaches to workplace design has evolved and broadened – both at the level of technological solutions and at the level of ideas. During the last decade of the 20th century, many issues that were not considered in the brave 1980s emerged, and they now dominate an increasingly sustainability-sensitive property market. Sustainable design is among the liveliest spheres of architectural research and innovation. The most recent trends strive to combine environmental sustainability with cultural sensitivity.

In the discussion that follows we look at office architecture, simply because this kind of workplace provides some of the best examples of the holistic (bioclimatic) approach to design, not because there is any less need for the same principles to be applied to other kinds of building. We discuss ways in which the future users and the design team interact to create sustainable patterns of use that make the most of the built-in capacity of the building. We also discuss some of the often neglected, non-measurable qualities of sustainable workplaces. Significant to the discussion will be the issue of values and philosophical positions embedded in the architecture; these are critical ingredients that frame the technological aspects of the buildings.

We start with two Australian examples, both from Melbourne (Victoria), that illustrate the importance of the conception phase and show how users view the result. These are the recently completed renovation of number 60 Leicester Street, '60L', and Melbourne's new City Hall Building, or 'CH2', which is currently under construction. After that, we return to what is still a classic sustainable office building – the ING Bank building in Amsterdam. As well as mentioning the basic performance of the buildings, we use each case to emphasise different important aspects of design: the process of designing (60L), the projection of the environmental message (CH2), and the building's experiential quality (ING).

THE DESIGN, CONSTRUCTION AND USE OF 60 LEICESTER STREET

The Australian Conservation Foundation (ACF) is a major Australian environmental NGO (non-government organisation). In 1998 it initiated and supported the development of an exemplary 'green' building. The project was distinctive because of its emphasis on behavioural aspects of use. An early insistence on architecture and its potential to express sustainable practices was also important. Crucial steps at the start were the development of a detailed design brief and selection of the appropriate design team. Those cautious steps well illustrate the need to change the current practice of separating the clients from the design team, of viewing the building only as hardware. Instead, the building design emerged from the work of a client–designer team (see Figure 4.1).

The program for 60L included all the traditional elements of architectural practice – a precise account of areas, rooms and their use, functional links and connections. But the program also provided a number of detailed, performance-based design assessment criteria demanding high environmental performance. Performance meant 'the application of environmental principles to the modelling of occupancy, ownership and site selection options; the use of building materials and techniques that minimise embodied energy and toxic wastes arising from manufacture, transport or construction; and building management, use and operation following construction that minimise resource inputs (energy, water and other materials) and waste outputs'.[10]

Figure 4.1 The 'green building', 60L, plan and section

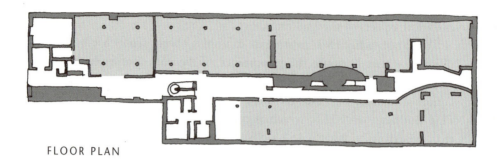

FLOOR PLAN

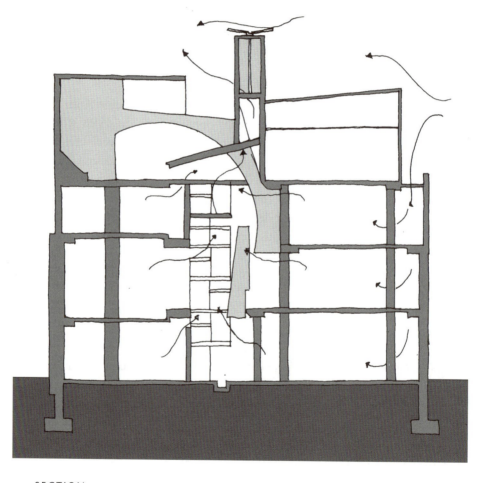

SECTION

Preparation of the brief included discussion of the expressive potential of architecture. The intention of at least some of the team members was to facilitate the emergence of distinctive 'green' architecture: architecture that clearly expresses a sustainable relationship with its natural context (through use of energy and water saving technologies and design forms, for example). The discussion followed questions such as: What does the client stand for? What is the client's position regarding current developments in eco-philosophy? What is the client's position in relation to the place of technology in solving environmental problems? Is the client inclined towards low-technology, 'vernacular' solutions, or does it prefer to be seen as a forerunner in the quest for high-tech responses? What position does the client hold with regard to other questions arising from an urban environmental agenda, such as public versus private transport access, urbanity versus sustainable suburbia? The client–designer team addressed questions that are quite controversial within the architecture profession. Should green architecture look different or recognisable? Is improved environmental performance a quite separate matter from its architectural expression?

Two early exercises were of critical importance in terms of defining the design concept. In the first exercise, representatives of the client, the employees and the visitors to the ACF were encouraged to discuss broad sustainability-related values. In this instance the client was unusually well informed, and its representatives were thus able to provide very useful leads for the design team. The emphasis of the debate was on values which the client wanted to see expressed through the new building. Some of the more detailed and searching questions addressed are shown in Box 4.3. Those or similar questions are crucial for the opening, conceptual stage of design of any buildings that aim to justify the term *sustainable*.

In the second part of the preliminary explorations for the 60L building, the focus shifted to thinking about architectural interpretations of the discussed themes. This phase, again, meant a serious, and much deeper than usual, involvement of the both the client (through its representatives) and the representatives of likely future users (that is, tenants). These preliminary exercises helped produce some critical early decisions of considerable environmental significance. The refurbishment of an existing office or warehouse building was chosen over creating a new building, for one. An inner urban location was selected, and a distinctly 'green' architectural brief was developed, focused on sustainability considerations rather than simply on engineering, functionality and/or a 'pure aesthetic'.

Box 4.3 INITIAL QUESTIONS DISCUSSED AT THE DESIGN STAGE OF 60L

- What is most important to you about the new building?
- What do you think are the key criteria for the selection of the site?
- Should your environmental philosophy be expressed in the architecture of the new building?
- Should soft-tech or high-tech environmental solutions prevail in the architecture?
- Should the building be on a contextually prominent site or a contextually low-key site?
- Do you have views regarding implementation of environmentally appropriate high-performance technology?
- Should natural ventilation or mechanical ventilation dominate?
- What about high-performance lighting technology versus natural lighting?
- Should electronic technology (smart technologies) be used for environmental control or efficient user-operated manual controls?
- Do you want a 'long life, loose-fit' building or a temporary, highly flexible spatial solution?
- How do you think the building might be designed to tell the story of good environmental design and encourage visits by the public without disruption to the work of the staff?
- How do you judge the importance of:
  - the use of local materials for the building?
  - the active use of the building for the local community?
  - the local architectural contextual references for the project?
  - architectural references to Aboriginality in the architecture of the building?
- What word would you use to describe your preferred essence of the building?
- Do you have feelings about materials or colour for the new building?
- Should the building be a single-use office building? If not,

what would be acceptable secondary uses (for example, residential, commercial/exhibition, commercial/recreation, etc)?

- Do you have views regarding the presence of greenery in interior spaces of the building?

- Would you consider culturally specific procedures (for example, Feng Shui) as appropriate for siting and other important design decisions?

- Would you accept significant changes in your own lifestyle (seasonably changeable work hours, lower levels of cooling or heating) to make a fuller contribution to the environmental performance of the building?

- Do you think the building should be designed as a repeatable 'model' building?

Questionnaire devised by Darko Radović.

From the earliest discussions, the process, project management and other aspects of delivery of the building were under close scrutiny by the client. The selection of the design team became one of the critical decisions. It was decided that the market should not be scared off by unnecessary divergence from established business practice. This meant that the design team had to be chosen through a tendering process. The client identified ten key criteria for selection of the designer, including a design philosophy compatible with the brief and proven technical ability to deliver environmentally superior outcomes.

The position statements offered by competitors for the 60L project ranged from fairly wide statements with which nobody could really disagree[11] to very precisely defined statements about the intended features and the performance goals. The analysis of design intentions and philosophical statements exposed two prevailing ideologies: one that put strong emphasis on the qualitative, and another that emphasised the quantitative aspects of sustainable architecture. The few teams that focused on the non-measurable and experiential aspects of the built environment, on the *sense* of wellbeing, the *sense* of health and the psychological impact of the building, belonged to the first group. These teams were expressing the intangible aspects of space. The second group, which typically had a strong engineering core, focused on measurable qualities – and even on *measurability* itself being a desirable quality. The methods of measuring and proving ecologically superior performance were key parts of their strategy. Some teams also made an effort to define the complex synergy between the qualitative and quantitative spheres of ecological sustainability.

The concept of 'life-cycle analysis' – that is, evaluation of the building's performance over its whole lifespan, from construction to obsolescence – ranked high among the themes proposed by the shortlisted architects. It is also interesting to note the prominent place given to the selection of building materials. As expected, energy saving, in its many forms, was the most frequent theme.

The proposition was to transform a three-storey, inner-urban office building constructed in 1876 into 'a 21st century four-storey integrated office using existing, recycled and new sustainable materials'. During the early stages of design – conducted by the winning team, Spowers Architects, from Melbourne – the following key targets were established. The comparisons relate to an average commercial office building of similar volume and levels of activity:

- Energy savings of over 65 per cent;
- Lighting costs reduced by over 80 per cent;
- Equipment, ventilation, heating and cooling costs reduced by over 60 per cent;
- Savings of 90 per cent in average annual potable water consumption (water normally used for all purposes is of drinking water – potable – quality); and
- Zero CO_2 emissions from operation of the building: electricity for daily use is generated onsite (using photovoltaic arrays) or 'green energy' purchased from the electricity retailer using wind power. However, this calculation excludes energy used in transport to and from the building and emissions associated with tenant activity outside the building.

Two years into 60L's operation, the above targets have been met, and research into many aspects of the use of 60L is in progress. The building now boasts large improvements, compared with an average commercial building, in recycling, use of daylight, solar control and natural ventilation, use of thermal mass, and reduction in greenhouse gas emissions. It saves water by recycling and harvesting rainwater.

In order to achieve their full potential, buildings with a sophisticated built-in environmental agenda demand informed and knowledgeable occupants. Most of the occupants of 60L are exceptionally well informed about their building. They know that 60L is almost free of volatile organic compounds; these were rigorously eliminated. They breathe less recycled air, because the building is open to the outside. They also feel better in an environment which is naturally lit. Sun penetrates their work-spaces, and nature is integrated into internal spaces. Even though full evaluation results are yet to come, the building's users generally perceive it to be a healthy workplace. Anecdotally, the productivity of the main occupant of the building is believed to have increased significantly.

The temperature in the building is automatically controlled. In the comfort zone, defined as 19–26°C, the building is in its passive mode (Plate 20). When the external temperature is within that range, the inte-rior of the building interacts freely with the external environment. Below or above that temperature range the system goes into its active mode, shielding the occupants from the excessive heat or from the uncomfortably cold air. Importantly, though, individual users have the capacity to override those controls. Most of the windows are manually operable, and all rooms have their own individual reverse-cycle air-conditioning. All employees can see themselves as a part of 60L, and part of an environment which includes both the mechanical system and the fellow humans who occupy the space. The users are expected to react individually, first by choosing the proper clothing, and then by finetun-ing their local, individualised environment to their needs.

The building manager has a very special role. It is more complex than that of managers of ordinary office blocks, because keeping the building operating in a sustainable way is a requirement, and a process, that is unfamiliar to many tenants. It seems that a significant part of the manager's everyday work includes mediation: this emphasises the social role of the workplace. Tenants' activities can impinge on one another, and the manager's task is to keep most of the employees happy most of the time. The character of the building requires mutual consideration from all tenants – a sophisticated urbanity. In an environment where each individual has the ability to override the system and take control of environmental performance, awareness of the needs of others becomes paramount, and the building manager sometimes has to explain why certain practices go beyond the acceptable.

It is easy to imagine where misunderstandings might occur. The sense of hot and cold varies significantly among individuals, for instance. So in a building that is mostly open to the outside and where air flows freely, temperature is likely to soon become an issue. Noise levels are kept within acceptable limits by carpets with acoustic backing, a ceiling surface composed of 50 per cent acoustic tiles, and staircase steps covered with rubber pads. But where offices do not have the usual soundproof walls shielding workspaces from the common space, noise can also become an issue. In both these cases, however, some reliance can be placed on the occupants becoming accustomed to behaving with mutual consideration.

As the building has numerous tenants (currently fifteen), the fit-out of individual office spaces within 60L is also somewhat contentious. New tenants bring along their own architects, and it is critical to make sure that each of them conforms to the high overall environmental standards. 60L is relatively new, and experiences with new tenants are as yet few. The management is keen to encourage re-use of the furniture and layouts left by previous users, as well as to recycle the furniture the new tenants used in their previous premises.

Some important lessons have already been learned from 60L. For instance, it now seems clear from the experience of inhabiting the building that it is necessary to put an even stronger emphasis on bioclimatic design. A single automatic climate control system does not have the flexibility which some situations demand. Direct sunlight for some users might mean glare for others. Catching a breeze on one side can be chilling at the other end of the building. Individuals sometimes have conflicting needs, some of which are themselves created by detectable local differences in comfort in different parts of the building. The key lesson here is that not only the building as a whole, but also its various parts should be responsive to climate – for the users, the internal climate the building creates is as important as its climatic relationship with the outside world.

Despite some deficiencies, 60L makes a fine contribution to the emerging trend towards sustainability in the office space market in Melbourne. As those in charge of the project modestly stress, 60L is only *significantly more sustainable* than the usual office building. But they add proudly that this quality has not passed unnoticed. Spaces in 60L are in great demand. Many prospective tenants are attracted by the reputation of the building, which has spread by word of mouth. Those who know the building well see it as a pleasant place to work in. In the commercial sense, 'green sells'.

60L is a recycled building, and its only street frontage, on Leicester Street, tells little about its environmental quality. From a strategic point of view, from the point of view of promoting the sustainability agenda, we believe that buildings should not only perform well, but should also in some way announce themselves as 'green'. We now turn to another Melbourne building that does just this.

THE GREEN TOWN HALL:
MELBOURNE CITY COUNCIL OFFICES (CH2)

CH2 is a new office building, and is larger than 60L. At the time of publication of this book, the project is under construction.[12] The project, by Design Inc. architects, is being marketed as revolutionary, not only in a functional and environmental sense, but also in the sense that it is a formal expression of environmental sensitivity (Figure 4.2).

The ten-storey building will use solar energy and natural light and air during the day, cool night air for cooling, wind energy and rainwater. Ten air extraction ducts, which are the main feature of the north façade, will absorb heat and facilitate efficient ventilation. The air movement will be assisted by roof wind turbines, which will also send a visual message about the character of the building. The vertical gardens reinforce that message – they are prominently present on the façade and remind the passer-by that the building is different from its neighbours.

The design of the southern façade is influenced by its sun-less orientation. The five 'shower towers' will let water cascade down to the glass canopy above street level. The recycled timber louvres will make a statement on the western façade. They will be powered by solar energy generated by the building's own photovoltaic panels (on the roof). The louvres will follow the sun-path, reminding passers-by of our world's seasonal and daily rhythms. The effort to tell the sustainability story will be supported by the art program of the Council. Artists will be invited to express their attitudes towards ecological sustainability, and to address the environmental sensibility announced by the building itself.

A number of environmental themes are integrated into the project. Special attention has been paid to the selection of building materials. The careful life-cycle analysis considered embodied energy, embodied water (the energy and water expended in building the structure), potential toxic emissions, the impact of products used in the building on ozone depletion, emission of greenhouse gases, and the building's impact on biodiversity. Importantly, the materials were also assessed for ease of maintenance, and long-life and low-maintenance options were always chosen.

Modelling of environmental performance (done before construction) shows that CH2 will consume only half of the water such a building

Figure 4.2 Melbourne City Council building, CH2, plan and section

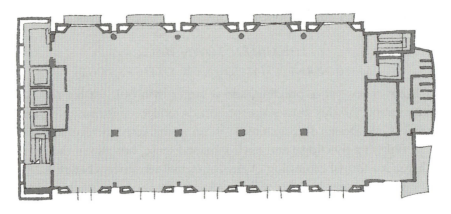

FLOOR PLAN

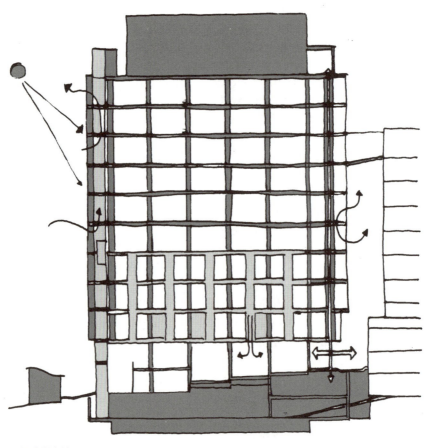

SECTION

would normally require. The other half will come from locally treated recycled water and rain. Energy consumption, compared with a business-as-usual office block, will be reduced by an excellent 85 per cent, while the use of gas will drop by 93 per cent. Thus the expected overall consumption of energy in this building stands at only 13 per cent of the energy consumed by the existing Council office – close to a tenfold improvement. The energy-saving measures significantly contribute to this dramatic improvement, but they are combined with a number of other techniques:

- Night-purge windows (a process by which, during the night, windows on the north and south façades allow fresh cool air to enter the offices, and thus flush out warm air. At the CH2 building, night purging will be regulated by sensors, which will operate the windows in relation to the speed of winds, rain or temperatures);

- Natural ventilation, use of thermal mass (heavy internal construction to absorb heat and release it slowly);

- Shower towers (tubes of lightweight fabric, less than 1.5 metres in diameter. The air within the tower is cooled by evaporation from the shower of water);

- Phase-change heat recovery ('phase changing' is the process whereby a material changes from a liquid to a solid, or vice versa – and thus stores heat, or cold. The best known phase-changing material is water, which freezes at 0°C. The phase-changing material to be used in the CH2 system will freeze at 15°C);

- A fresh air system with heat recovery (heat is recovered from the used air before it gets extracted from the offices. That energy is used to help heat or cool the fresh air);

- Heat from co-generation and wind turbines;

- A lighting system with daylight sensors (sensors will be used to adjust the amount of artificial light in relation to the available daylight);

- Low-energy ambient lighting and individual task lighting (all lamps will be individually controlled by the occupants, ensuring that the level of lighting reflects the level of activity, and thus the need for energy);

- Shading powered by photovoltaic solar panels;

- Using LCD computer monitors (LCD – liquid crystal digital – monitors consume 77 per cent less energy than older monitors. They also provide better conditions for work, because their surfaces do not glare, flicker, or emit radiation. Also, the production process of the LCD monitors pollutes the environment significantly less than production of the older monitors); and

- A hot water system that uses solar hot water collectors.

Box 4.4 GREEN STAR RATING FOR BUILDINGS, developed by the
Green Building Council of Australia (http://www.gbcaus.org)

The green star rating system has been developed by the Green
Building Council to help designers evaluate the environmental
performance of office buildings. The evaluation covers the
following nine categories. In each category credit points are
awarded for compliance with a particular criterion. Below, one
example of a rating criterion is shown for each category.

1 *Management (7 criteria, 12 credits available):* 2 credits
   awarded if a green star-accredited professional is engaged to
   provide sustainability advice throughout the design.

2 *Indoor environment quality (14 criteria, 27 credits available):* 3
   credits awarded if 90 per cent of building is naturally
   ventilated.

3 *Energy (9 criteria, 27 credits available):* 1 credit awarded for
   provision of a solar hot water system (must be gas boosted
   if gas is available onsite) for at least 75 per cent of annual
   hot water.

4 *Transport (4 criteria, 10 credits available):* 2 credits awarded if
   50 per cent less car parking is provided onsite than the maximum local planning allowance. (Up to 5 credits awarded
   depending on the building's proximity to public transport,
   frequency of service and number of routes served.)

5 *Water (4 criteria, 13 credits available):* up to 5 credits awarded
   where building's potable water consumption is reduced
   through efficient use of, or avoidance of, evaporative or
   water cooling towers.

6 *Materials (8 criteria, 20 credits available):* up to 2 credits
   awarded where the total PVC content cost for major services
   (pipes, conduits, cables) is reduced by replacing with other
   materials.

7 *Land use and ecology (4 criteria, 8 credits available):* 1 credit
   awarded where the site has previously been built on or used
   for industrial purposes.

8 *Pollution (9 criteria, 13 credits available):* Up to 4 credits awarded where outflows to the sewerage system are reduced or where sewage is treated onsite.

9 *Innovation (1 criterion, 5 credits available):* up to 5 credits awarded on the basis of innovativeness, environmental benefit of the innovation, and how many credits the innovation has already been assessed as achieving during the above credit assessment.

The overall rating – from one to five stars – is arrived at via the total number of credit points awarded. This system allows designers to choose which aspects of sustainability they wish to claim. If a building is weak in certain areas it may be strong in others. The above gives some indication of the values inherent in the rating system itself.

CH2 emissions will be 60 per cent less than demanded by the strictest green star rating in Australia (see Box 4.4). At the same time, it will produce only one-fifth of the emissions generated by the current Council office. The employees of the Council will breathe fresh air drawn from the roof level. They will be able to individually control their own air intake. All service spaces, such as toilets, will have openable windows and exclusively natural ventilation.

Even though Melbourne has a temperate climate, the summers can produce some very hot days (up to a daytime maximum of 43°C) when the hot north wind blows. Much research has gone into selecting the best cooling strategy. Fresh air will be drawn into the shower towers on the southern façade. Cooled by evaporation, that air will serve the ground-floor retail spaces. The rest will be preserved in the phase-change material batteries (batteries that accumulate thermal energy), to be used for the rest of the building when required. The office space will be cooled by water running through the chilled panels fixed to the ceilings. Natural ventilation will cool the building down overnight. During night-purging, a system of built-in sensors will operate the windows and preserve the interior from possible high winds, rain or other environmental risks. Melbourne's temperate climate also demands heating in winter, so convection heaters will be positioned to create a barrier of warmth around the external walls, to prevent cold air coming in, and to increase the sense of comfort.

An important feature of CH2 is that it extends urbanity, which is the essence of behaviour *within* the sustainable building, out into the surrounding space of the city. Together with the art program, that gesture contributes to the symbolic capital of the project by drawing passers-by in and inconspicuously telling them about the environmental and experiential advantages of a green building. That is a field in which our third example has a proven track record.

THE ING (INTERNATIONAL NETHERLANDS GROUP) HEADQUARTERS BUILDING, AMSTERDAM

Since 1987, when the ING building was completed, it has contributed enormously to the much-needed promotion of the idea of the sustainable business building. Its relaxed environments and integration with the outside world question the usual business mantra that isolation of employees brings better performance (see Plates 21, 22, 23).

The best way to describe the ING building is to explain how one *feels* in its spaces, but first some history and facts about its performance. The ING headquarters was conceived by the bank's management as part of a new image (along with a change of name), but also in full awareness of the insecurity of energy prices following the oil shocks of 1974 and 1979. The building was designed to save money, but it was also designed to provide the best possible working environment for its employees, incorporating visual art, landscape, natural materials, greenery, sunlight penetrating the building, and views to the outside world.

The site area is large – about 43,000 square metres. It accommodates some 2500 workers and provides about 50,000 square metres of office space and 28,000 square metres of car parking space. Back in the 1980s, cars still ruled, and even a building with good ecological credentials had to provide for them. However, the building is also extremely well connected to the railway network. Two different rail lines connect Bijlmemeer station with central Amsterdam and the rest of the city. The walking path from the station through the shopping centre to the ING building is an easy one. Giving instructions for a visit to the site, the guide said, 'You can't miss it.' In fact, although the building is enormous, it is quite easy to miss, because it recedes into the suburb rather than standing out screaming about itself. But when you do discover the building, its impact is all the greater.

The building makes use of an integrated system of heating and lighting: there are internal towers directing natural light to the interior, plus co-generation of heat and power, heat recovery from lift motors and computer rooms, and air-to-air heat exchangers to capture the heat from air that is vented out of the building. This system delivers massive savings in operational energy. The bank's former headquarters building consumed 422,801 btu (British Thermal Units) of energy per square foot annually. The new building consumes 35,246 btu per square foot – less than one-tenth the energy drain of the old building. A comparable conventional building constructed nearby at the same time consumes five times more energy than the ING building. The additional construction and installation costs that were required so that these operational energy savings could be made were found to be about US$700,000. The building saved US$2.6 million in its first year of operation.

There are ten linked towers, each between three and six storeys high (Figure 4.3 shows the plan of the buildings). Their façades are designed to shed, rather than reflect, noise from the busy street, and in the plan and elevation of the building there are almost no right angles. Many of the organic features and unusual building geometries were drawn from the teachings of Austrian philosopher Rudolph Steiner, whose ideas you would hardly expect to find in a commercial office space. The building does not use conventional air-conditioning – a feat virtually unheard of for a building of this size. It relies instead on passive cooling with backup absorption chillers. Yet the building sits comfortably in the surrounding urban fabric. On one side is a marketplace; when the market is in session, it quite obscures the bank's front entrance. This is quite in keeping with the Dutch sense of urbanity. The royal palace in the middle of Amsterdam fronts right up to Dam Square. There is no ceremonial separation like that of Buckingham Palace in London, for example, or the royal palace in Stockholm.

But impressive energy bills and direct financial savings are only one aspect of the huge success of the ING Bank building. Its architects, the firm Alberts and van Huut, were among the first designers to understand that sustainability of built environments depends not only on the building itself, on what we could call *the hardware*, but even more on *the software*, on the way people inhabit those spaces and conduct their everyday business, on their satisfaction with space and willingness to use it in the best possible way. Thus the old saying from the early days of ecologically responsible architecture – that a passive solar building encourages active inhabitants– finds its fuller and richer expression in new, more complex ecologically responsible design of the early 21st century.

Nick Low was taken on a tour of the building and so had an opportunity to experience part of it at first hand. The generosity of public space is the first thing one notices. There is never a feeling of corridors; rather, one seems to move from room to room as in a domestic building. The experience is punctuated by the light towers. In each tower daylight enters through a dome. Walking through the building, one moves from one daylighted space to another. Odd-shaped mirrors at floor level reflect the daylight across the horizontal spaces. Around these spaces are clustered public facilities such as libraries, lecture theatres, conference rooms and cafés. Each facility has its own distinctive art display. It is quite a surprise to walk into a lecture theatre and find large openable windows. Another surprise is the water cascading down through sculpted channels along the handrails of staircases. Bank security prevents the visitor from wandering around the office space, but it is clear that every desk has an external window. The plan of each block – resembling a cow's head, it was pointed out – is designed to provide external views and daylighting for all (see Figure 4.3 and Plate 24).

The landscaped gardens surrounding the building are meant to be both looked at from inside and lingered in (Plate 23). Nick did not see many people wandering in them, though this could be a pleasant activity; the workers just looked too busy. Each garden is designed on a different national theme – there are Japanese, English and Finnish land-

Figure 4.3 The ING Bank building, plan of the towers

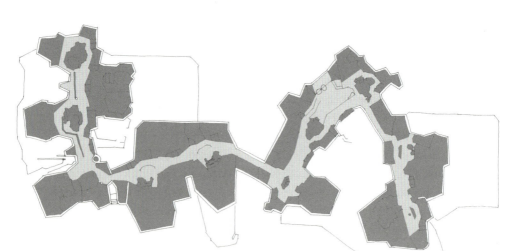

scapes. It is a fantasy, but a pleasant one. There is a real sense of profusion in these gardens, of plants, birds and insects. The more than human world is everywhere present and visible.

The process of construction of the building was important, just as it was in the 60L building. The bank's governing board assembled a multidisciplinary team to design the building. This team included architects, building engineers, landscape architects, energy experts and artists. The team worked for three years designing the building. The process required that each step of the design be understood by every member of the team – so, for example, if the artists didn't understand the natural ventilation system, its operation would be explained. There was frequent input from bank employees throughout this process.

As the planning proceeded, the board's vision was refined by the planning and design team against the following three criteria: first, the building must be thoroughly functional using the latest technology, including a specially designed security system and options for individual climate control. Second, the building had to be flexible, able to respond to the changes in space needs that would inevitably occur over time. Third, the building had to be energy efficient, yet not cost 'one gilder more' than conventional construction. When Nick somewhat naively expressed surprise that the energy-saving conception pre-dated knowledge of climate change, the guide remarked, 'They're canny Dutch businessmen. They like to save money!'

Employee input was used to determine where the new facility would be built. Construction began in 1983, and the building was completed in 1987 – within budget. The bank building has not only been a tremendous success financially, but productivity has risen and employee absenteeism has dropped significantly. The bold new image of the bank – resulting from the building – is credited with elevating International Netherlands Group from No. 4 to No. 2 among Dutch banks, and helping give the bank a high profile internationally.

CULTURE AND CLIMATE

The ING building is essentially Dutch. Anyone who has visited central Amsterdam will recognise its form, scale, stolid character and brick construction as being very much in the Dutch tradition. Essential to green workplaces, like green housing, is sensitivity to local culture and local climate. Turning from the more mundane world of the post-industrial Australian and European city, we now look at three examples of green workplaces that reflect these sensitivities in much more exotic settings. They each also demonstrate a kind of intercultural potential, since the architects are all of European origin. Does this internationalism represent a new 'colonisation'? We don't think so. It is more like an older tradition of cultural exchange in which ideas from different cultures are both imported and exported with mutual respect. We believe that the power of those examples now influences global trends in architecture, and thus provides the host cultures with much-needed recognition. These examples developed out of local conditions and are specifically fitted to those conditions; they are very different from the more usual export of technologies from America and Europe with little or no consideration of local needs, cultures or climatic conditions.

The first example is the glamorous cultural centre of Jean-Marie Thibaud in Noumea, designed by the prominent Italian architect Renzo Piano (who has also designed a major building in Amsterdam). Drawing upon the beautiful forms of indigenous architecture, but also learning from the tropical forms of traditional huts, Piano designed the building complex to be attuned to the local climate and to represent new reaches of the Kanak culture (Figure 4.4 and Plate 25).

Traditional construction principles were followed, which means the building provides valuable shade and captures cooling breezes. It can also withstand the violent cyclones that sometimes sweep through the island, without opposing their irresistible power. In the way proven by centuries of indigenous construction, the external surfaces of the half-cones are designed so that the strongest winds simply blow through them; they bend to the superior force but at the same time avoid destruction. The pleasant work environments both inside and outside the centre are obviously inspired by the past, but are confidently oriented towards the future. The built environment of the island was enhanced by the introduction of this subtle reinterpretation of traditional architectural themes of the hut, and by the brave, cutting-edge technological features employed to execute the project.

A project by another significant contemporary architect exemplifies a different kind of blending of local wisdom and the technology of the 'developed world'. The French architect Jean Nouvel, in his proposed office block for Guadalajara, Mexico, questions the traditional building layout of business blocks. His design begins from answers to critical questions about local climate. The result is an architecture well adapted to the locality.

In the climate of south-central Mexico, a sense of comfort demands good cross-ventilation. The most appropriate architectural forms are

Figure 4.4 The Cultural Centre, Noumea, plan and section

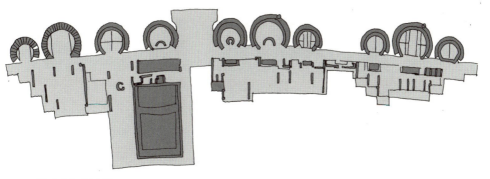

FLOOR PLAN

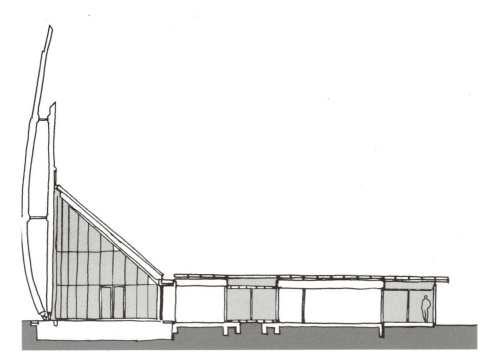

SECTION

narrow, elongated volumes without internal partitions. That is why rather than creating a bulky building that would demand costly mechanical air-conditioning, Nouvel has chosen a solution of diagrammatic simplicity: small, narrow individual units open to cross-ventilation, to deal with the excessive heat, and a huge, umbrella-like roof structure, to keep the rain out. This building is conceptually coherent and a spatially refined response to the particular demands of the client (Figure 4.5).

Figure 4.5 Office block, Guadalajara, Mexico, plan and section

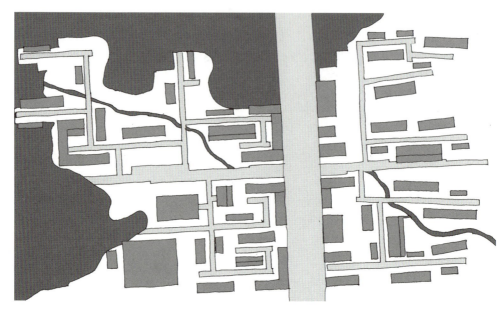

GROUND PLAN

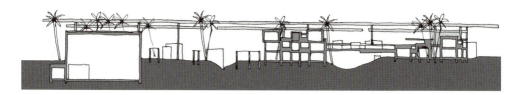

SECTION

What these examples clearly show is that environmental awareness affects all aspects of production and use of the built environment – and thus of our workspaces. The process, the product itself and cultural and climatic sensitivity are all significantly different from the 'business as usual' approach which has been spread indiscriminately from America and Europe all over the planet.

Our concluding example is a design that will not be built because it was an entry to a competition, and was not in the end selected. Nevertheless it illustrates what we see as a key principle of the sustainable workplace: the conscious integration of culture and environment.

Plate 1 *right*
The Mobbs family's
house in Sydney
(photograph courtesy of
Michael Mobbs)

Plate 2 *below*
Professor Susan
Roaf's house in
Oxford, England
(photograph by Nick Low)

Plate 3 *above*
BedZed, London Borough
of Sutton, UK
(photograph by Nick Low)

Plate 4 *left*
BedZed, wall construction,
showing the thickness of
rockwool insulation, light
timber weatherboard outer
skin and heavy internal
concrete blocks
(photograph by Nick Low)

Plate 5 *right*
Västra Hamnen, Malmö's
sustainable housing development:
the seafront boardwalk
(photograph by Nick Low)

Plate 6 *below*
Västra Hamnen: low-rise housing
(photograph by Nick Low)

Plate 7 *below*
Ekolonia, eco-housing
at Alphen aan Rijn,
The Netherlands
(photograph by Nick Low)

Plate 8 *above*
Royal Park, Melbourne offers opportunities for people to have contact with nature in close proximity to the CBD
(photograph by Elahna Green)

Plate 9 *below*
Royal Park, Melbourne contains scattered clumps of mature eucalypts, reminiscent of a savanna-type landscape
(photograph by Elahna Green)

Plate 10 *right*
Kings Park, Perth
(photograph by Nick Low)

Plate 11 *below*
Brisbane's Toohey Forest,
surrounding Griffith
University
(photograph by Nick Low)

Plate 12 *above*
Sydney Park, in inner Sydney
(photograph by Patrick Fensham)

Plate 13 *left*
Brisbane's Northey Street urban
farm *(photograph by Nick Low)*

Plate 14 *right*
Melbourne's Merri Creek: formerly
a degraded waterway, but now
restored to a more ecologically
healthy condition
(photograph by Elahna Green)

Plate 15 *right*
River Torrens Linear Park, Adelaide:
a riparian corridor in close
proximity to Adelaide's city centre
(photograph by Elahna Green)

Plate 16 *below*
Adelaide's River Torrens Linear
Park contains both aquatic and
terrestrial ecosystems that have
been restored to preserve ecological function and to allow access
to nature for city residents
(photograph by Elahna Green)

Plate 17 *left*
Ginkaku-ji temple
grounds, Kyoto, Japan
*(photograph by
Elizabeth Low)*

Plate 20 *opposite page*
The 'green building'
(60L), interior: the
Atrium at 2nd floor
level, showing the
glazed roof and thermal
chimneys providing
passive ventilation
*(photograph by the Green
Building Partnership)*

Plate 18 *above*
Phalan Wetland Amenity
Park, in St Paul, Minnesota,
is a place where urban
dwellers can experience
indigenous wetland plant
communities
(photograph by Joan Nassauer)

Plate 19 *right*
Worker at a café in the
Vondelpark, Amsterdam
(photograph by Nick Low)

Plate 21 *left*
The ING Bank,
Amsterdam: interior
(photograph by Nick Low)

Plate 22 *below*
The ING Bank:
landscaping
(photograph by Nick Low)

Plate 23 *above*
The ING Bank:
landscape gardens
(photograph by Nick Low)

Plate 24 *left*
The ING Bank:
office plan
(photograph by Nick Low)

Plate 25 *above*
Cultural Centre, Noumea
(architect: Renzo Piano,
photograph by Rajko Petrović)

Plate 26 *below*
Architects' model of UniverCity,
Shenyang *(Shenyang competition team,*
photograph by Darko Radović)

Plate 27 *above*
Birmingham's city centre, designed for walking
(photograph by Nick Low)

Plate 28 *below*
Place de la Comédie, Montpellier, with tram
(photograph by Nick Low)

Plate 29 *left*
Café in Montpellier's walkable central area
(photograph by Nick Low)

Plate 30 *below*
Grenoble: Rue Félix Poulat in the city centre
(photograph by Nick Low)

Plate 31 *right*
Tram in Grenoble equipped
with roll-on roll-off ramps
(photograph by Nick Low)

Plate 31 *right*
Tram in Grenoble equipped
with roll-on roll-off ramps
(photograph by Nick Low)

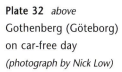

Plate 32 *above*
Gothenberg (Göteborg)
on car-free day
(photograph by Nick Low)

Plate 33 *left & above*
Gothenberg: pedestrian priority crossing connecting the Gothia Conference Centre with the tram interchange
(photographs by Nick Low)

Plate 34 *below*
Brisbane's busway: the Nathan station *(photograph by Nick Low)*

It is a project for an educational complex, the new campus of the Architectural and Civil Engineering University of Shenyang, China, designed by the University of Melbourne design team, led by Radovic, Whitford and Guo. It contains our own ideas about the likely directions of ecologically conscious architectural design. The main aims of the project were derived from the key concept that a new campus of the proposed size actually amounts to a new city. Thus, the university became the *UniverCity*. That conceptual decision provided the grounds for exploration of different aspects of sustainable urban planning and design (Plate 26).

The emphasis was largely on those aspects of urban phenomena that both invoke a sense of being rooted in the culture and yet also look to the future. The built environment of the Imperial Ching city of Shenyang offered interesting challenges, particularly in terms of the critical relationship between local Chinese traditions and Western approaches to city planning, architecture, and spaces for educational activities and living. The design was founded on continuing research into Chinese and other East Asian cultures, and contemporary trends in urban design and architecture – ecological and cultural sustainability, Chinese garden design, and low-cost housing, for instance. The design philosophy represented a complete integration of cultural sensitivity – actually sustaining the cultural tradition – and ecological sustainability. Ecological responsibility requires cultural sensitivity, and cultural sustainability must include ecological awareness.

The university precinct was based on an analysis of the life-cycle of the buildings, assuming continuous efficient, energy-conscious management. The energy needed for construction was to be minimised, with wood-based materials being used wherever appropriate in order to reduce embodied energy (the energy used in the production of the materials used in construction). As far as possible, locally sourced materials were to be used, to reduce the transport load. Maximum use was to be made of daylight inside the teaching and residential blocks. To reduce energy demand further, thermal mass was to be used to trap and absorb heat, and remaining energy needs were to be met from renewable sources.

In construction, use was to be made of long-lasting and recyclable materials. All potentially toxic materials were to be eliminated and the greatest possible use was to be made of natural ventilation. The design aimed to conserve water resources and make use of rainwater falling on the site, and to integrate the local natural landscape into the open space around the buildings. Overall, the design aimed to provide a high quality environment for the occupants visually, acoustically and with respect to air quality. At the same time, the designers were conscious of the need to respect local aesthetic traditions in design and express Chinese cultural values.

The design–research team included eleven architects: there were therefore eleven different approaches to architecture and eleven different attitudes towards the sustainability of the built environment. These architects worked on eleven related architectural projects within the *UniverCity* scheme. Environmentally responsible urban design and sustainability-related codes and guidelines were established on the basis of key principles of ecological and cultural sustainability. These guidelines became a virtual design brief for all the projects, most of which contained major office and workspace elements.

Analysis of the resulting design proposals offers insights into possible design strategies for better integration of green principles into urban and architectural practice. The following are the parameters most often chosen by the designers:

- Passive solar heating, cooling and ventilation;
- Natural lighting;
- Use of local materials;
- Long-life/loose fit (that is, a building whose adaptability to changing needs makes it more likely to be used for longer);
- Integration of vegetation, with possible inclusion of rooftop greenery; and
- Easy building management and maintenance.

All designers accepted the first two parameters, both of which were derived from a bioclimatic awareness. They were rigorously implemented, and had strong influence on the spaces and forms of the *UniverCity*. When one flies north from Beijing towards Shenyang, one can see a gradual, but dramatic, change of architectural layouts – the Beijing quadrangles with almost square courtyards become, as one moves north and the winters get harsher, elongated courts orientated in an east–west direction. The *UniverCity* plan allowed that kind of layout to dominate the city sector.

The urban design of the *UniverCity* project strongly promoted local materials and materials with low embodied energy. The long-life/loose fit approach, and easy building management and maintenance, also ranked high on the list of demands, and had considerable influence on resulting shapes and spaces. The majority of designers agreed that expensive high-technology solutions (sophisticated air-conditioning, for example) do not serve the environmental agenda well when a similar result can be achieved at less cost and without the gadgetry. Integration of vegetation was strongly recommended in the urban design guidelines set out by the design team, and this proved to be popular among the architects of the individual projects. Rooftop greenery contributed significantly to many schemes. The integrated design of green open space with built-up space became an important element of the overall plan.

In conclusion, we want to stress two issues that seem to be vital in the context of emerging trends in sustainable architecture. First, a mature approach to sustainability means acknowledging the dialectics between cultural and ecological sustainability: these two ideas must be addressed as an inseparable complex of related issues. Second, urban design can and should play a critical role in the better integration of sustainability in the built environment. Performance-based urban design guidelines are an important field for further development. The *UniverCity* project showed that environmental themes critically influence urban form and other features of urbanity.

CONCLUSION

Ultimately, the green city will reflect a rather different future for work. On this topic there are some very large questions: can a future of cities competing against one another in world markets be reconciled with a benign future for the environment? What are the limits of competition and how can they be enforced? Does economic growth itself have limits? How can growth be steered into environmentally benign forms of production? What forms of governance are required to regulate world markets in order to guarantee social security and environmental conservation? How do culture, place and climate influence work patterns, and consequently the physical accommodation of work? These questions emerge from discussions of the workplace, but it is way beyond the scope of this book to begin answering them. The focus of this chapter has been the workplace, and how the built environment accommodating work can contribute to environmental conservation. Whatever the future of work, the buildings accommodating it and the practices of their construction and use will be key elements in the green city.

Buildings, however, are just one aspect of the accommodation of working and social life. Another aspect is the accommodation of movement. In both this chapter and the chapter on housing (chapter 2), it is clear that movement and transport are important parts of the life of the green suburb. Journeys between home and work, transport of goods, and the way residential areas and workplaces are linked to transport systems are evidently crucial matters for the green city. Though engineers who specialise in transport systems like to talk about 'sustainable transport' or 'sustainable mobility', transport is not in fact a separate system: it is integral to suburban life and personal health and safety. In the next chapter we turn more directly to the contribution of transport to the green city.

FURTHER READING

Colin Hines's *Localization, A Global Manifesto* (Earthscan, London, 2000) goes beyond simply criticising free trade and globalisation trends. It describes self-reinforcing policies to create local self-sufficiency, and shows clearly that there is an alternative to globalisation – to protect the local, globally. Believing that the best sustainable design builds upon both understanding of timeless principles and awareness about the latest developments in the field, we suggest two sources. One is an all-time classic: Victor Olgyay, *Design with Climate: A Bioclimatic Approach to Architectural Regionalism* (Princeton University Press, Princeton, 1963). The other source offers reliable, annual updates: PLEA (Passive and Low Energy Architecture) Conference Proceedings, published annually since 1981 (for further details and updates, see http://www.plea-arch.org).

CHAPTER 5

SUSTAINABLE TRANSPORT

In the modern city, stepping out of the home often means getting into the car. The private car is more than a convenience. It both symbolises and realises the freedom to move in comfort and security. This is a freedom at the very heart of modern life. Car ownership is also a symbol of success. Advertisements associate buying a car with finding attractive friends, having lovely families, getting rich, or just getting away. There is much exaggerated gloss here, but also more than a little truth. As any teenager knows, a car *is* a major social advantage. Much the same applies to trucking goods. Suppliers like to be able to deliver goods whenever and wherever they are wanted. They don't want to tie up a lot of land in storage space, and they don't want distance or time to separate them from their customers. Consumer patience has diminished over the years – we want things now, not soon. For both personal and freight travel, great expectations therefore come to be placed on the transport system. What is expected is nothing less than perfect freedom of movement.

In Australia, at least in the last fifty years, the aim of increasing freedom of movement in cities has been pursued by governments and industry mainly by building roads and producing private vehicles. But this approach comes at a cost. It overloads the atmosphere with greenhouse gases and local pollution. It chokes the city with traffic, costs many lives and attacks public health. Poorly designed suburbs are built for use with cars; walking around these suburbs becomes difficult and tedious. The choice of transport diminishes. As fewer people use public transport, services are cut back, so public transport becomes less attractive and less safe to use – and therefore fewer people use it. Without anyone really choosing it, a particular kind of 'car-dependent' city grows up around this illusory road to perfect freedom.

It is a city in which a different sort of freedom is being lost, the freedom to enjoy the urban environment on foot and in fresh air. Walking and socialising in urban public space is a healthy and pleasant activity. The rise of street cafés in recent years – even in stinking, congested streets – and the evident delight people take in using them, is testament to the rebirth of a walking culture.

The car is fundamentally not a city vehicle. Almost without exception, car advertisements place cars in an empty, wild landscape, sometimes in unlikely situations: on top of rocky mountains, zooming along the tide line of sandy beaches, surging through swollen rivers and only occasionally on roads – which, however, are always empty. An interesting thesis could be written about the landscape used in the background of car ads. Probably most people do not want traffic congestion on mountain tops or beaches, but that's not the point. The point is that the car brings people into contact with remote nature. It's not just raw nature that is the attraction; it's also people in the landscape – but just a few of them at any one time. Nature, like sex, sells cars. And yet nothing despoils nature like cars! Though some would dispute it, let's accept that car advertisements reflect how people actually want to use cars. They want to *escape* from the city, and to experience nature in the intimate and reassuring company of friends and family.

So let us acknowledge that the car is a rural-recreational vehicle. In contrast, using a car in the city has become a boring, repetitive and, when one stops to think about the statistics, alarmingly dangerous drudgery.[1] Across the whole world, more than a million people are killed every year by motor vehicles. The German sociologist Otto Ullrich writes, 'The most scandalous effect of motorised individual transport is the killing and maiming of people on a warlike scale. Presumably it will remain a puzzle to later generations how a society could come to terms with a technology that demands human sacrifice in such vast numbers.'[2] Unfortunately, when city authorities (particularly in Australian and North American cities, but also to a lesser degree in European, Asian and African cities) do not deliver effective public transport, the public have little real choice but to use their recreational vehicles to get around the city.

Total freedom for the car makes walking a difficult experience. It is also self-defeating, because each individual who exercises his/her personal freedom interferes with the freedom of everyone else, simply by occupying a large amount of what is limited space on the road. And now we have colossal freeways attracting so many journeys that they become jammed. With more and better roads, congestion has not diminished; it has increased. Road transport is today the fastest-growing contributor to greenhouse emissions in Australia, and in most Western countries. Sustainable transport for the green city requires a more conscious attempt at planned compromise – at making the best possible trade-off between freedom of movement and the other qualities desired for the green city.

Just as important as the physical system (the network of lines, routes and roads) is the system by which transport is planned, managed, supplied and funded. And yet when it comes to planning, there is often no system in the real sense of the word: a co-ordinated, integrative mechanism for ensuring urban accessibility. Strangely enough, co-ordinated planning of a whole transport system, including walking and cycling as well as roads, motor vehicles and public transport, is quite rare almost everywhere in the world.

The green city will have a transport system in which there is a network of paths connecting people safely on foot with the places they want to reach from home or from public transport terminals. Space in city centres will be allocated to transport with the primary aim of creating a good environment for human occupation, meaning that a high priority will be given to non-motorised movement. In most suburbs a mixture of workplaces and homes will be provided to increase opportunities for people to live near where they work. People living in green cities will have the benefit of public transport systems that offer a frequent and regular service throughout the city from early morning to late at night, throughout the week and at weekends. Travel on public transport will be fast, and change of mode – changing trains, trams or buses – will be minimised, but where it occurs it will be quick, safe and easy. When people use cars, they will travel in fuel-efficient vehicles emitting not only very little poisonous gas but also little carbon dioxide. Effective demand management will reduce the number of compulsory trips. The priority, in terms of transport system planning, will be foot travel, then cycling, then public transport and finally private motor vehicles.

THE CITY ON FOOT

Travel on foot costs the environment almost nothing. It mainly takes two forms: walking and riding a bicycle. In earlier times we would have had to include riding on horseback. The bike is perhaps today's democratic equivalent of the horse. In some cities of Japan (Kyoto, for example) cyclists are kept off the roads and restricted to the footpaths. But as anyone who has had to share a narrow footpath with bikes knows, cyclists and walkers do not mix comfortably; they should be separated.

If we consider the voluntary movement of human bodies around suburbs and cities, there are general words for the various kinds of activities these bodies do: walk, run, stand or sit. These activities take place whatever the 'mode of transport' used: walking, running, standing and sitting are always components of a journey, whether the journey is made on foot, by car or on public transport. This is just as well, since humans were designed to do these things. The human body is healthiest when using the legs is a normal part of daily life. Arms and wheelchairs can substitute for those without use of legs. If people don't get 'exercise' in their working lives they have to get it in their leisure time, which sometimes means buying time at the gym. Alternatively, they don't get exercise and they put on weight. The city of Johannesburg in South Africa has a growing problem of obesity which has been put down to the fact that travelling in a locked car really does make a person safer from violent crime: more car use plus less walking equals more weight gain.

In Australia, parental anxiety about child safety means that schoolchildren are ferried about by car when once they walked to most daily destinations. This is doubtless contributing to the 'epidemic' of obesity among Australian children that is so concerning public health advocates and authorities. Car dependency is bad for your physique, and therefore bad for your health. A major American study shows that people living in the most car-dependent outer suburbs are on average more obese and more prone to high blood pressure, heart disease and diabetes than those in the inner city, where walking and public transport use are more feasible.[3]

Travel is about various combinations of activities, the states of mind people are in while they are doing them, and the quality of the environments in which they occur. Consider a certain shopping trip. It may start with a person sitting, thinking, and making a list. The person then stands and moves around a bit inside the house preparing for the trip, and then a walk takes place. It may be only as far as the garage. The person gets into the car and sits, activating the controls by movements of the feet and arms, concentrating attention on the road. The immediate environment is a metal capsule occupied (often solitarily) for fifteen or twenty minutes. The person then parks the car in a tarmac or concrete environment, by intensive movements of the feet, hands and neck, and walks from the car park to the place of shopping. The walking environment at this point is often indoors: a supermarket. The person on foot pushes a shopping trolley up and down aisles between shelves of goods. The person then walks back to the car, probably pushing a full trolley, loads the car, drives home (or collects the kids) and then unloads the shopping in the kitchen.

Transport planning in Australia, in terms of the amount of both urban space and taxpayers' money allocated to facilitating the movement of vehicles on roads, places vehicle needs above human needs. Yet the primary facts of travel are bodily facts – movement and stillness, the time taken in these activities, the distance covered, and the environments in which they occur. Reversing the customary order of priorities in favour of walking does not mean *artificially* privileging walking over other modes of transport; it means starting with human activity and attending to human need first, which is surely the correct priority. The trip described above is unexciting. We are entitled to expect more from life in cities than a sequence of monotonous, utilitarian experiences. How then do we increase the delight factor in travel?

We have already seen that green housing developments include walkable open space and path networks both within the housing site itself and connecting the dwelling with the rest of the city and with public transport nodes. It is also clear that providing for personal movement is actually an essential part of the green neighbourhood. If a bus service is essential, there is no reason why it should make money, any more than the service road it runs on should make money. That was the argument for the bus service at Västra Hamnen (see chapter 2). In every society, the role of governments is surely to provide collectively what individuals and businesses cannot provide for themselves. The long-term economic success of a city may well depend on it.

The enormous commercial success of the pedestrian precincts created in the historic centres of many European cities is an example of such collective investment. In these centres the utilitarian activities of shopping and working life have been turned into a varied, delightful and sociable experience. This is so for the local people, without whom the places would be dead, as well as for the many tourists who visit these centres. Those urban centres that lack an organic connection to a lively and sociable local community seem, by contrast, like lifeless stage sets.

In the 1960s, the City of Birmingham in England, at the heart of Britain's motor industry, built a motorway box tightly around the central business district. The traffic managers tried to move traffic flowing to the city efficiently and quickly through the constricted streets of the central business district. The result, by the 1980s, was heavy air and noise pollution, peak-hour traffic jams, and slow vehicle movement. Under these circumstances the historic 19th century core of the city, with its splendid Victorian civic buildings, could not flourish economically. And what was worse was the fact that the motorway tourniquet stopped the expansion of commercial development by cutting off the supply of land in the central area.

In the 1990s the city council decided to turn most of the major streets into walking thoroughfares (Plate 27). A pedestrian priority crossing at street level was established across the motorway. Almost immediately, the area on the other side of the motorway began to be redeveloped. Eventually, Birmingham demolished part of the motorway to allow full pedestrian access to the Eastside district. Most of the city's central core is now a walking precinct. Birmingham is a Victorian city like Melbourne, and supports the arts and music as Melbourne does, but, again like Melbourne, it will never be conventionally beautiful – it is primarily a city of business. But it is making the best of its urban environment, and people flock to work and shop there. New developments around the Bull Ring are further extending the pedestrian area and linking it with New Street railway station. In a Foreword to the city council's 2003 'Locate in Birmingham' brochure, architect Richard Rogers says, 'A well-designed sustainable city will attract people back into its centre ... A sustainable city is compact, polycentric, ecologically aware and based on walking.'

Montpellier, in southern France, is a very different sort of town from Birmingham. Its renaissance city centre occupies a plateau (*L'Écusson*: the escutcheon) rising above the surrounding town. All the streets around the huge Place de la Comédie and the square itself are banned to vehicle traffic except for a tramline that connects the pedestrian centre to the suburbs and flows quietly among the walking traffic (Plate 28 and Figure 5.1). The mixture of trams and walkers seems to be entirely safe and workable, as can also be seen in the pedestrian main shopping street of Zürich, the Bahnhofstrasse, and the Rue Félix Poulat in the city centre of Grenoble in France (Plate 30).

In Grenoble, two tram lines connect the outer suburbs with the city centre. For some of the way these lines run on routes separated from other road traffic, sometimes through busy walking streets, sometimes over grassy lawns. The trams are equipped with small ramps to enable wheelchairs, pushers and trolleys to roll on and off (Plate 31). As a result, the trams are much used by people pushing wheels. The trams have been so successful that a third line is now being built. The city is also served by a fleet of buses (powered by natural gas) that serve an extensive network of 22 routes. Unfortunately, especially for a university town, the bus service is much reduced after 9.00pm. Students and others travelling in the evening have to rely on 'night buses', which run on only four routes and at 30 minute intervals. The planners are using the construction of the tramline as part of their strategy to reduce greenhouse emissions from the city by 75 per cent before the end of the century (according to a public presentation attended by Nick Low in July 2004).

In Europe, the creation of safe zones for walkers and cyclists began in The Netherlands with the *Woonerf* system, where car access in residential streets is allowed but at very low speeds and with physical restrictions. Copenhagen's Strøget was one of the earliest pedestrian shopping streets in Europe, and was pushed through by a strong mayor against massive opposition from retailers. The subsequent popular and commercial success of Strøget and other pioneering examples of walking streets (Cologne in Germany, and York in the United Kingdom, for example)

Figure 5.1 Plan of the centre of Montpellier (L'Écusson), showing the walking district

■ Landmark Buildings

■ Pedestrian Areas

encouraged many other European towns and cities to follow suit. The function of city centres changed from convenience shopping to comparison shopping and 'shopping tourism': a mixture of shopping, socialising, eating and drinking, strolling, and visiting art centres, concert halls, exhibitions and parks (walking is also sometimes about sitting: see Plate 29). From pedestrian streets, European city planning moved on to 'car-free' city centres, as in Montpellier in France and Freiburg and Nuremberg in Germany. 'Car free' is a catchy term, but it does not mean the complete banning of cars from the city; it means the careful management of traffic access, with priority given to people on foot and other slow means of transport, including wheelchairs and bicycles.

The success of pedestrian precincts can sometimes mean that traffic increases around the perimeter. This does not help sustainability or the quality of the environment beyond the precinct. The 'car-free' city limits car access to residents, and to businesses within restricted hours, and encourages much other travel to the centre by public transport. This 'area-wide access control' has been introduced in Bologna and Florence in Italy and Lübeck and Aachen in Germany. In Europe, an annual 'car-free' day has been instituted (in September): on that day, cities actively discourage residents and visitors from using the car and promote walking and cycling activities. Plate 32 shows a shopping street in Gothenberg in Sweden on car-free day 2003.

In European walking precincts, mixed access may sometimes be allowed, with vehicles limited to walking speed and on-street parking banned. Access to business vehicles is allowed for deliveries at certain times. Alternatively, footways and roads may be separated, but the width of the footway greatly increased, and road traffic restricted to 20 km/h or less. In some places of high use by walkers pedestrian crossings are provided where cars have to give way to walkers at all times without traffic light controls (Plate 33). In Sweden, pedestrian priority at such crossings is strictly observed.

Planning for bicycle use requires a step up in spatial scale. Bikes have a comfortable range of 15 to 20 kilometres, so the green city needs a fully connected bicycle network that can provide bike access, on paths separated from road traffic, to destinations over a very large area. In Australia, both Canberra and Melbourne, for example, have some good bike paths, but in neither city are they planned as a network that connects homes and workplaces, and in neither city are they co-ordinated with public transport. Melbourne's Yarra Trail is a beautiful off-road path, but its purpose is primarily recreational, and it meanders with the river. Canberra's sections of bike path frequently just end in a road that has no form of bicycle priority – neither a bike lane painted on the road, nor a separate track.

The City of Copenhagen (population of the metropolitan region 1.5 million) has been developing a bicycle network since the late 1980s. Back in the 1950s, Copenhagen already had 200 kilometres of cycle track, but the popularity of cycling diminished in the 1960s as cyclists found themselves in more and more danger on the roads because of the increase in car traffic. Citizen pressure, however, put cycle tracks back on the political agenda, and the city has built a network of bike paths with special treatment for cyclists at intersections. Today Copenhagen has more than 320 kilometres of cycle track, mostly alongside established roads but separated from them by kerbs. There are 43 kilometres of 'green' (off-road) cycle tracks. One-fifth of all journeys and one-third of journeys to work are made by bicycle – about the same as car journeys to work in Copenhagen. Cyclists ride over a million kilometres every day. This is an immense step towards good urban health and sustainability.

Unfortunately, about 200 cyclists per year are seriously injured – by motor vehicles. The city's aim is to increase the proportion of people cycling to work to 40 per cent and reduce the risk of personal injury by half. Copenhagen provides a stock of free bikes that can be accessed from stands all over the city by a deposit of 20 Danish krona (about $5 Australian). The project started with 1000 bicycles in 1995 and its final goal is to maintain a stock of 5000 bicycles. Currently the aims are to: ensure that cycling is affordable for all residents and visitors, extend bike paths further along main roads, provide more covered and locked bicycle stands (particularly at transport interchanges), reduce stops for cyclists at traffic light-controlled intersections, provide more off-road paths, and link the city's path network with that of the surrounding region.

Many cities around the world are developing connections between bicycle networks and public transport. Vancouver's TransLink transport authority, for instance, is investing in improving safety by building separated bicycle paths along roads and bridges, providing lockers for bikes at railway stations and bike racks on buses so that bikes can be taken on board (some of Brisbane's buses are equipped with bike racks). In the Dutch city of Groningen, more than half of all journeys to work are made by bicycle. The city's aim is to complete a main bicycle network of segregated bike paths along major roads and through open spaces to accommodate the journey to work, a supplementary network to give access to residential and recreational areas, and bicycle parking provision at all main destinations. Supervised parking garages at main railway stations in The Netherlands typically also include bike hire, repair and sales facilities. In The Netherlands, bicycles are not the expensive and highly accessorised style statements they are in Australia. They are simply a mode of transport; they are sturdily built and they often last for many years.

While these initiatives appear to be heading in the right direction from the point of view of sustainability, there is not enough evaluation of the real effect of walking or cycling schemes in reducing car dependence or greenhouse emissions. There may be little effect at all if car parking and use is simply shifted elsewhere – relocated to the periphery of pedestrian zones, for example. Walking zones need to be linked with a public transport network if they are to be effective in the reduction of greenhouse gas emissions. In car-dependent cities (as all Australian metropolitan cities are), policies restricting cars need to be preceded by improvement in the public transport system – the only alternative to the car for moving large numbers of people over the distances a modern metropolis spans.

BETTER PUBLIC TRANSPORT

What makes for better public transport? The answer is simple: service quality (frequency of service, speed of travel, and ease of interchange, as well as a fair expectation of comfort and safety), integrated timetabling and route planning, responsiveness to customer needs and, only then, better vehicles and infrastructure extensions. This is all explained in an influential book by Australian transport activist and planning scholar Paul Mees.[4] Mees has campaigned for years to get this seemingly common-sense view accepted by State planning and transport authorities.

A 'good' public transport journey to work might go like this. You set off from home and walk on a well-maintained footpath down a pleasant suburban street for up to ten minutes to the bus stop. You wait for a bus for no more than five minutes. You have a good expectation of getting a seat and you settle down to a short trip of not more than fifteen minutes, and review a report or read a few pages of a novel, or just listen to your favourite rock music or a Schubert trio – or both read and listen. Maybe you meet a workmate or neighbour and exchange some scuttlebutt. Then comes the change – you step off the bus and walk directly to the train platform wielding your season ticket, which is valid for the whole metropolitan system. The train enters within a minute or so, and you then board and sit down to continue your novel or report, and encounter more acquaintances to chat to if you feel like it. The whole journey to work takes no more than an hour. Of course there are variations: cycling (or wheelchairing or skating) can be combined with a rail trip.[5] In some cases a short tram ride may be added or a longer tram ride substituted for heavy rail. The walked part of the journey may be shorter. For those who cannot walk or cycle, the car can be combined with a rail trip: 'park and ride'. What is important, though, is that every mode of transport plays an effective role in the operation of the whole system, and supports the system.

Public transport in Australian cities is not universally bad. Spread over different cities, it is possible to find many of the individual features of 'world's best practice' public transport. For example, Melbourne has had a single ticketing system for the whole metropolitan area since the 1980s. Melbourne retains its very extensive urban tram network and is extending and improving it. Sydney, Melbourne and Brisbane all have extensive suburban railways. Sydney has a network of over 830 kilometres of suburban rail line, Melbourne 670 kilometres, and Brisbane about 400 kilometres. In 2001 Brisbane opened a 'busway' running from the CBD to the southeastern suburbs. This is a motorway for buses only, with intersections going over the road like bridges, so that vehicles always flow into the busway on the off side – the left-hand side in Australia ('grade-separated interchanges', in engineering jargon). This busway functions as a rapid transit spine, funnelling bus services from the southeastern suburbs into the CBD bus terminal at Queen Street. It has well-designed stations along the route equipped with lifts to move people across the busway (Plate 34).

Following the success of the Brisbane busway, the NSW Government introduced a similar system in Western Sydney, the 'T-way' (transit way) in 2003. Like the busway, the T-way has dedicated road space and 'stations', but without grade-separated overpasses. The T-way buses have driver-activated priority at road intersections. The T-way spine aims to provide a rapid service between suburbs and the CBD, but unlike the Brisbane system, the T-way stations are served by a fleet of feeder buses linking homes with the express route. More than 110 new stations are planned across the T-way network. The new system is expected to reduce some journey times by up to an hour.

Perth has built a new suburban rail line (serving the northern suburbs) which has been very successful in attracting passengers.

Perth's Public Transport Authority (PTA) is mainly a traditional service delivery organisation lacking a long-term planning function. The PTA has separate divisions managing the bus system and the train system, and a division responsible for delivery of the urban rail expansion program: 'New MetroRail'. Within the PTA there is also an operational team planning and managing the 'TransPerth' system, which is responsible for planning and co-ordinating buses and trains across metropolitan Perth.

But in no Australian city do all the features of good public transport come together in a single seamlessly efficient service that is respected and well used by the citizens. Combining all the best features of public transport does not just add advantages; it multiplies them, so that the combined effect is much greater than the mere addition of each small improvement. While Australian city governments have so far failed to reap the benefits that come from planning and managing public transport as a single system, Australian cities do in fact have great potential for major improvements at quite acceptable cost (compared with the cost of massive road projects), and could reduce car use for daily urban travel very significantly. A striking comparison is the number of times (on average) a citizen takes a rail trip each year. In Brisbane the figure is about 20, whereas in metropolitan Zürich, Switzerland, a city region of comparable size, the figure is 530. In neither case was the rail system designed to serve a single metropolitan region. In Zürich, as in Brisbane, the rail system was built to service a collection of surrounding townships and villages and was only later successfully adapted as a metropolitan network. The conclusion must be that Brisbane's infrastructure is being badly wasted. Most North American cities dream of having the extensive urban rail systems that Australia's state capitals possess. We have green capital going to waste!

In the Canton of Zürich, a commercially successful region of 1.1 million people, the essential features of good public transport are combined in a unified system. Zürich is one of the twenty-six confederated Cantons (rather like States) of Switzerland. The city of Zürich is the heart of the Canton, at the top of Lake Zürich, and the suburbs sprawl around the lake. The city is served by a highly visible, attractively liveried (without being mobile billboards) tram and bus network that works on the following principles.[6] Separated routes and busways allow the free run of the vehicles between stops, unimpeded by other road vehicles. This was achieved by a program of improvements by Zürich City Council in the early 1990s: they converted some streets to allow only walking and public transport, removed kerbside car parking along bus and tram routes, provided a raised section for tram tracks, prohibited left turns in streets with trams (since the Swiss drive on the right, the equivalent in Australia would be right turns), built 16 kilometres of bus lanes, and extended the tramlines, including about 8 kilometres of new separated track.

Maximum priority is given to trams and buses at road junctions by enabling the tram and bus drivers to change the traffic lights in their favour. Because the system runs efficiently, without bunching of vehicles, only a short green phase is needed to allow the bus or tram to cross an intersection, but when necessary, the public transport vehicles can cross the intersection without waiting. By 1993, 90 per cent of traffic lights were controlled by public transport vehicles. Information about the whole system is processed by a central computer that constantly relays information to drivers on whether they are ahead of or behind schedule, so that they can adjust their speed accordingly. When public transport vehicles have to drive across several intersections in succession, the computer switches to a 'green wave' for the vehicle. System managers at the control centre are also provided with a constant flow of information on the location of every vehicle and of any bottlenecks or other impediments to the smooth running of the system.

Zürich City Council owns and manages the city's public transport system, but the metropolitan area is much larger, extending out into the suburbs and surrounding villages up to 20 kilometres from the centre. People living and working in this wider area also need to travel regularly within and around it, just as they do in Australia's 'low-density' cities. Switzerland was already well supplied with railway track, and following a referendum in 1981, the Canton Government extended the railways in order to create a suburban rail or 'S-Bahn' system serving the whole metropolitan region. Several new stations were built and a tunnel of 1.2 kilometres was driven under the city centre, connecting suburban lines that formerly terminated on the edge of the centre.

This was a very similar project to the city loop in Melbourne. The gross density of the Canton of Zürich is about 6.4 people per hectare; Melbourne's is about 17 per hectare. The majority live in the Zürich metropolitan region (about half the area of the Canton), which brings the overall metropolitan population density up to something close to Melbourne's – and, incidentally, challenges the proposition that low-density areas cannot be serviced effectively by public transport.

The network of railway lines is denser than Melbourne's, but even so it is clear that a different approach to managing the transport system was required: the more or less constant flow of public transport vehicles at five or ten-minute intervals in the city itself would not suffice. The answer was what Mees calls the 'pulse timetable'.[7] Trains run in 'pulses', at basic intervals of 30 and 60 minutes, from very early to late in the day and at weekends. On the most heavily used sections of line the trains are staggered, resulting in an interval of 15 minutes. Between each station and its catchment area bus services are timed exactly to catch the train pulses. Transport analysts Dieter Apel and Tim Pharoah describe the scene at the suburban station of Wetzikon (which could just as well be any outer metropolitan station in any of Australia's state capitals):

> Wetzikon is a junction of four S-Bahn lines and is the terminus for five shuttle bus services from surrounding smaller communities. Every half hour throughout the day one can observe the following spectacle at Wetzikon station. People who have arrived on foot, by bicycle or by one of the shuttle buses have gathered at the platforms. One after the other, at short intervals, four suburban trains come in, exchange their passengers and move off again about two minutes later. Shortly after that, the shuttle buses, having picked up passengers from the trains, drive off again one after the other. The station is then empty again until the next passengers begin to arrive about 20 minutes later.[8]

That is what is meant by an integrated transport system. Immediately one can see the importance of the station as a node in a network where a person's journey to and from the station is regarded as an integral part of the whole journey. In this journey, it is not only trains and feeder buses that are significant; it is also the network of footpaths and bikeways connecting housing areas with suburban railway stations. Accommodation for bikes is provided at the station, and even on the trains. Like Copenhagen, Zürich has an extensive bicycle network, and planning for footpaths and segregated cycle tracks is given a priority second only to public transport. Interestingly, the idea of a feeder bus service is not unheard of in Australia. The Melbourne Transportation Study of 1969 said, 'In its feeder role the bus network would become an extension of the fixed rail service with the bus schedules closely co-ordinating with rail timetables.'[9]

The necessary co-ordination of timetables, however, can only be achieved by a central transport planning body of a kind that has never existed in Australian cities. The Zürcher Verkehrsverbund (ZVV), variously translated as the Zürich Transport Association or Zürich Transport Community, is responsible for planning the network and timetable, setting fares and co-ordinating routes.[10] This authority, which covers the whole Canton, brings together the interests of 171 municipalities, the Canton Government, Swiss Federal Railways and around 40 transport operators. The ZVV, which has just a small central staff, does the planning, while service delivery is contracted to a variety of agencies: Swiss Railways, the Post Office – running many rural postbus services – and numerous private firms.

This way of operating public transport is now regarded as the preferred model in European cities and intercity networks. Variations can be found throughout what President Bush the younger once dismissively called 'the Old Europe' and even the old New (post-communist) Europe.[11] It combines the efficiency advantages of central network planning with the customer responsiveness and expertise in delivery of a variety of service operators, both public and private. It is, in fact, a very good example of government 'steering' rather than 'rowing'. However, some government agencies, such as the Swiss Post Office, have turned out to be better oarsmen than some private companies![12] Such central planning is essentially a communist notion, but here it is borrowed by a city at the very heart of financial capitalism, simply because, combined with genuinely democratic constraints and sanctioned by popular referendum, it works – wonderfully.

The share of journeys to work in Zürich City by public transport increased from an already high 67.5 per cent in 1980 to 76.1 per cent in 1990 (and from 45.8 per cent in greater metropolitan Zürich to 50.9 per cent). The aim of the ZVV is to offer a seat to all passengers even during peak hours, and a single monthly ticket gives access across the entire public transport network. Compared with the swift running of such a system, a fragmented network operated by agencies in competition with one another, whether they are public or private agencies, merely limps along. Central co-ordination also turns out to be very much in the interests of the private operators, because they profit from the vastly increased passenger flows that the system as a whole is able to attract. This effective public transport system has also stimulated demand for space close to the railway stations in the suburbs, bringing a rise in property prices. So instead of higher densities having to be imposed by planners on the land use system in order to support public transport, a tendency to higher density around rail stations has followed better public transport, and also supported it.

The city of Portland, in Oregon, on the northwest coast of the United States, has had a comprehensive land use and transport plan since the 1970s, when the citizens of Portland and the State of Oregon rebelled against the continuous building of freeways.[13] These new roads were inviting patchy but profitable conversion of rural lands to residential use, resulting in sprawling exurbs, and turning the city centre into a parking precinct, killing off commercial growth. The new plan sought to create a '24 hour downtown' with an emphasis on a high quality public transport service, mixed land use and walking zones, and putting 'a lid on parking'. At the same time a growth boundary was imposed on new residential development at the city's edge – this has been maintained to this day. The harbour freeway was removed in 1976 to make way for a waterfront park, plans for the Mount Hood Freeway were abandoned in favour of the Banfield light rail line (1986), which serves the eastern suburbs, and the money saved from road building was ploughed into multi-modal projects. The Westside light rail project, serving the western suburbs, began operation in 1998.

Planning from 1990 to 2040 moved beyond land use–transport planning, so the new acronym is LUTRAQ: land use/transportation/air quality. As in Zürich and Grenoble, questions of air pollution and global warming are now considered alongside transport and land use planning. The 2040 plan directs most urban growth to compact centres built to human scale and served by good quality public transport. All streets are to be retrofitted to include footpaths and bikeways. Better-connected street systems will allow easier walking and access to public transport, and a frequent service on Portland's tramways will be provided on all major streets. Streets are being redesigned for people's use: there are more and more tree-lined boulevards designed to reduce traffic speed, promote walking, bicycling and public transport, and create 'civic space'. Unlike Zürich and most Australian State capitals, Portland does not have a well-established infrastructure of railways, so it is gradually constructing a new rail network: new tracks are planned across the Columbia River to the north – connecting with the airport – and along three growth corridors to the south.

The real lesson Australia can learn from Portland, however, is not the shaping of the city. Despite occasional regression, Australian cities are already far advanced in planning, and much better equipped with public transport infrastructure. Portland shows how, with strong political leadership, institutional barriers can be overcome – there is more about that in chapter 6.

Public transport offers a variety of personal, social and economic advantages. People of a much wider range of ages and abilities can use public transport, whereas car use is limited to those who can safely drive. Public transport kills and maims a small fraction of those killed and injured by vehicles on roads. Public transport can also allow time for social and personal activities during the trip. Listening is about the only activity that is safe and possible while driving; and even conversation with a passenger reduces concentration on the road conditions. Remote conversation, via mobiles and text messaging, is dangerous (and now illegal). Reading and writing are out of the question. All are possible and widely engaged in by public transport users. Public transport in a well-run system can be a very much less stressful experience than driving. It also guarantees more walking, which is very good for bodily health.

Greater use of public transport also frees up scarce road space for vehicle trips that have to be made by road, particularly freight delivery vehicles. The argument that more roads are needed to accommodate freight vehicles ignores two possibilities that have profound economic consequences. One is that road space can be made available at much less cost by moving a larger proportion of personal trips to public transport. The other is that smart logistical planning can reduce the number of freight collection and delivery trips. No Australian city is short of road space, but all Australian cities at present use that space very poorly. As mentioned above (comparing Brisbane and Zürich), they also use their rail systems poorly, certainly by international standards. Much of the intercity freight 'task' (to employ the unfortunate official jargon) should be shifted from road to rail.

SUSTAINABLE PLANNING FOR ROADS, CARS AND TRUCKS

Green cities are not necessarily ones where people own fewer cars. But they are ones where people *use* cars less. Of course if there are fewer cars the chances are there will also be less car use. But let's go straight to the fundamental point: it is motors burning fossil fuel that cause the greatest threat to the environment. Congestion, road deaths (and injuries) and air pollution are serious negative side effects of the use of cars and trucks. Societies have learned to tolerate these effects, though exactly why remains a complex and largely unanswered question, but global warming cannot be tolerated.[14]

The use of cars and roads designed for high-speed travel is a profoundly social phenomenon in two senses. It is produced by people organised in extraordinarily complex global production chains, and by government agencies acting on behalf of society, and it oils the wheels of society, changing the way people socialise. A motor car, as the English writer Nan Fairbrother pointed out back in 1970, 'is a way of life'.[15] Mobility even infuses the language with metaphors, such as 'oiling the wheels'. The democratisation of mobility is surely one of the great social changes of the 20th century, and it is still spreading throughout the world in the 21st century. Fairbrother continues: 'A car is more than extra mobility: it is also an extra living space, a small room packed with everything we need while away from home (back shelves can be intimately revealing). It is also warm and sheltered, a mobile extension of the indoor environment which transports us through the inclement outside world.' In Australia cars can be a cool respite on a hot day. A truck is also mobile storage space.

But there is no need to waste more time eulogising the car. A Swedish slogan printed on postcards for distribution on European Car-Free Day in 2003 reads (translated): 'Do you love your car? Give it a four-day week!' That is really the point. There are few great social boons in the world (think of alcohol!), which, if used to excess, don't end up killing us. In more general terms, we need to find ways of changing our car-borne society so that it doesn't destroy our health, our cities, our environment and us.

There are always two parts to the car question: vehicles and roads. While the green movement has drawn a lot of attention to the effects of vehicles, this tends to neglect the fact that roads are actually a large part of the problem. Vehicles couldn't run without them. Individuals don't build them, private businesses don't, except with the occasional immense assistance of government. Governments build roads. And seemingly, even though building roads is immensely costly, and drains traffic and funds from public transport, governments just can't stop doing it. To move forward to a greener solution for transport requires a little historical detour. What follows applies to Australian cities, but could be said of most cities of the post-industrial developed world.

There is a theory in modern political economy called 'path dependence'. A series of socially created events begins with a technical solution to a problem.[16] The initial problem in the present case was the difficulty of providing a fast, comfortable ride for people in wheeled vehicles. One solution was the iron rail, hence the railway (*chemin de fer*, path of iron). The other was the tarmac road surface, named after the Scottish engineer Robert Macadam, its inventor. The difference between them was that while any old vehicle could immediately gain access to and travel on a tarred road, only specialist vehicles – trains and trams – could travel on rails.

The popularity of the tarmac led quickly to the mass-produced road vehicle, pioneered in America by Henry Ford. Mass-produced road vehicles in turn led to a new problem that needed to be solved: traffic congestion. It wasn't so much that traffic congestion was a new phenomenon, but that tarmac roads had introduced new elements into the public understanding of the congestion problem. The most important element was the belief that perfect mobility in cities could be achieved, and in fact was just round the corner, if only roads could be designed to accommodate traffic without the vehicles having to stop to cross other roads, or slow down behind slower vehicles. No sooner was that engineering problem defined than the solution was created: the divided highway, in which passing vehicles have their own permanent overtaking lane, and grade-separated interchanges with roads looping over and under one another like spaghetti so that motorists can merge gradually from one stream of traffic to another (moving in a different direction) without stopping. In short, the answer was 'motorways' or 'freeways'. A new branch of engineering specialising in motorway construction was created, responding to the need for better roads. This engineering branch was usually given its own organisation within the public service.

A standard way of calculating the need for roads was to develop a mathematical model that related the patterns of origins and destinations of 'trips' to the pattern of land uses (homes, shops, workplaces and so on). From this model it could be calculated where new or enlarged roads were needed. The vehicle traffic created by roads offered a new source of taxation: vehicle and fuel taxes. So new highways often display signs like 'Your Taxes At Work', and 'Roads to Recovery' (from what? one wonders). The irony of billboards warning that 'Speed Kills' being placed beside motorways designed to permit high speed is unavoidable.

Such was the 'path' taken by the road-building institutions. State organisations, a taxation system, and a branch of the engineering profession combined to deal with the problem of congestion and roads. Once in existence, these institutions deposited a range of arguments, like pearls around a grain of sand in an oyster, justifying more and better roads: people need them, therefore they must be provided; low-density cities can only be served by roads and cars; roads give us economic growth (or conversely, not building roads leads to economic decay), and many other specious arguments. The road–vehicle solution to cities came to be seen in terms of modernisation, meaning of course that all forms of transport invented prior to roads and cars were old-fashioned, obsolete. Walking dropped out of the conception of 'a trip' altogether. A pattern of events could also be seized upon and press-ganged into the argument: history books and some planners who had read them told us that just as 'the railway' had replaced 'the canal', so the road and cars had replaced the railway. 'Path dependence', then, is any persistent pattern that combines a mental map of what the problem is – and what the solution should be – with institutional rules for dealing with the problem and providing the solution.

In fact railways contributed as much to urban sprawl as roads. Meanwhile, even though in some countries many less profitable rural branch lines were excised from the system, as in the UK from the 1960s and in Japan from the 1980s, railways continued to make city life possible by catering for the ebb and flow of mass commuter travel. Cities did not suddenly become low-density 'non-place urban realms'. In Australia the attractiveness of the inner and middle suburbs remained – and probably grew – as a result of the reduced congestion that followed the move of new households to the outer suburbs in the 1970s. In the 1970s, motorway building over the middle of Sydney and Melbourne was halted, because of its enormous financial cost and social destruction. The continued, even if reduced, use of railways, buses and trams kept intolerable traffic congestion in the middle of the city at bay.

Most importantly, the railways and tramways developed a different institutional path, a path that separated them radically from the institutions of road building. First, while road building continued, rail and tram construction (where tram systems were left intact) virtually ceased, which meant that the skill base of roads and railway organisations differed. Second, the problem for rail became the reduction of the deficit. Unlike roads, which generated traffic whose users paid in taxes, rail users were expected to pay for each trip in fares. The difference between the fares collected and the various expenses of running the public transport system was always termed the 'public transport deficit', which implied that it was a burden on the public purse. It was not so much that roads generated a 'surplus' because of the taxes road users paid and the fact that vehicle operating costs were paid privately by individual vehicle owners, but rather that such thinking was simply not applied to roads. More importantly, there was no cross-accounting. No one bothered to inquire how much road building contributed to the 'public transport deficit' by encouraging people to use cars, nor by how much railways, tramways and buses reduced the congestion – and therefore also the costs of congestion – on the roads.

The divergent institutional paths of public transport and roads kept these two vital elements of the transport systems of Australian cities operating in separate compartments even when occasionally they were brought under the umbrella of a single organisation, such as a Ministry of Transport. Meanwhile, the town planning profession has continued to pursue the goal of co-ordinating land use and transport planning. In recent years this goal has meant aiming to make the pattern of population density support the public transport system, in particular by permitting greater numbers (per unit of space: per hectare, say) of residents to live and workers to work close to rail stations and tramlines.

The idea is sensible enough in principle, but has proved extremely difficult to put into practice in Australian cities. It means gradually changing the city's physical structure, but this structure is in the hands of multiple private owners, and urban development is mostly privately initiated and opportunistic. The average property developer has a time horizon of about two years (certainly not more than five), no interest in good urban design and, naturally, an obsession with profits. An easier target than physical structure is institutional structure. As well as, *but prior to*, land use/transport planning must come the integration of all public transport planning, including the planning of the road system, which is, after all, essentially a public good.

Australian cities are exceptionally well provided with roads, and by international standards are exceptionally uncongested. No one is going to take those roads away! But just as the era of railway building came to an end, so today the era of road building must end for Australian cities. What comes next in order to make the green city is not a new marvel of technology but the effective management of the existing transport infrastructure to achieve the results the public wants and needs. The key question to be answered is: how can we manage the vehicle fleet and the path space (not just the road space) to optimum effect in terms of green goals? The answer to this question means taking a new institutional path.

This is not just a matter of road engineers and public transport managers talking together, or a Minister of Transport having oversight over separate agencies or even separate departments within the same agency; it means the creation of a new profession, with a new organisational basis (within government) that is equipped with a new sense of public purpose and new environmental and social goals. What's needed is a new breed of transport planner, someone who plans for access, not mobility. A new form of environmental accounting for infrastructure is also needed. Every new infrastructure project, whether it's tarmac or iron rails, a construction project or a service project (or something that is both, such as doubling up service frequency on a rail line, which might require some track duplication), must be evaluated in terms of its contribution to mitigating *global* warming as well as, and separately from, its *local* environmental impacts. This must be done at the planning stage, not as a kind of *post hoc* justification following publication of the detailed plan, as currently happens with environmental impact assessment procedures.

How then are the economic benefits of different combinations of projects to be weighed against environmental impacts? In other words, how much of the environment and the future are we prepared to trade off for immediate economic returns? Answering this looks like an insurmountable problem until one remembers three things. First, the current method of assessment of economic returns from infrastructure projects is almost completely fictional. Environmental impact assessments typically count additional trips as economic gains on the basis that there must have been someone wanting to make a trip who cannot unless the new project is introduced. Travel is counted as an economic gain whether or not it does anything for the economy or society, positive or negative. Time spent in travel is never counted as time wasted. Outside the curious internal logic of this sort of calculation, there is simply no empirical evidence that new infrastructure projects either promote or discourage growth in a metropolitan economy in any sector other than travel. What politicians see when a new road, for example, attracts new industrial sheds together with some extra jobs in its proximity is merely a shifting of the location of work, not an overall increase.

Second, assuming that a reduction in congestion can be considered an economic gain, most Australian cities are so poorly provided with public transport services that any significant improvement in service is almost certain to reallocate a significant proportion of trips from the existing road space, thereby reducing congestion.[17] Once we abandon the notion that every public transport service has to make a profit, and instead judge it as road projects are judged – according to its contribution to the smooth running of the city and the values citizens wish to promote – the decision to throw resources into public transport instead of roads will not be difficult (at least until the cities are adequately provided with public transport).

Finally, the medium-term risk that global warming poses to the national economy is serious enough to justify making a project's contribution to climate change mitigation the primary economic indicator determining whether or not the project goes ahead. This latter economic revaluation would require national leadership, via the Council of Australian Governments, from a Commonwealth that views the economy as a sustainable organism, not a 'growth machine' that simply chomps through natural resources.

What about the vehicles on the roads? There is no doubt that improved vehicle technology is going to be a major help in reducing the negative environmental impact of cars. Whether it is ultimately the market-imposed oil price or a government-imposed carbon tax that makes fuel more expensive, the simplest response is to use more fuel-efficient vehicles. Fortunately for the rich countries, vehicles with a fuel efficiency ten times better than the average large car are already on the market. Poor countries that use fossil fuel very sparingly will have much greater difficulty adapting to a higher fuel price without economic shock. The first 'oil shock', in 1973 (when the OPEC [the Organization of Petroleum Exporting Countries] oil cartel raised the price of oil four times) stimulated a doubling of fuel efficiency in the United States over the following ten years – from 5.6 to 11.5 kilometres per litre.[18] Today some production models of cars can achieve 100 kilometres per litre.

There are alternative energy sources: electric, fuel cell and hybrid electric vehicles. No technology, however, yet exists that can provide cheap mass private transport comparable with the internal combustion engine using fossil fuel. Electric vehicles have been around since the century before last, and they still suffer from the same problems: the weight of the battery for the energy stored, the slow rate of recharge and the short range of the vehicle. There has been progress, but efficient lightweight energy storage systems for electric cars are still, after 100 years, at the research stage. Hybrid electric cars overcome the problem by using a conventionally fuelled motor to charge a battery continuously, saving the excess energy required for acceleration, and capturing the energy lost in braking. They use fuel more efficiently and thus reduce fuel consumption.

The concept of the fuel cell was discovered in 1839 by Sir William Grove. Since the 1950s, fuel cell technology has developed rapidly –

driven by the US space program.[19] Fuel cell stacks substitute for batteries and produce electricity from the chemical combination of hydrogen and oxygen (electrolysis in reverse). However the components of fuel cells require rare metals such as platinum, and because supply of the metal is very limited, a massive demand for it from the world's vehicle fleets would lead to a steep rise in its price. And pure hydrogen is very difficult to store, because it requires high-pressure containers or very low temperatures. Both making hydrogen and pressurising hydrogen use energy. Instead, methanol, produced from natural gas or coal, which is liquid at room temperature, can be used to carry hydrogen to the fuel cell.[20] A major obstacle to the introduction of hydrogen fuel cell technology is the service station infrastructure necessary for refuelling. Methanol overcomes that difficulty. The US Fuel Cell Council reckons that it would cost about $5 billion to re-equip half of all service stations in the US to provide methanol – by no means a high price to pay (over, say, ten years) for greater fuel efficiency and much-improved greenhouse performance.[21]

Fuel cells are already being used to power larger vehicles. The city of Madrid, for instance, has introduced Mercedes-Benz Citaro city buses with fuel cell drives. The European Union is supporting a test program (to the tune of 21 million euros) within the framework of the Clean Urban Transport for Europe (CUTE) and Ecological City Transport System (ECTOS) projects. The fleet test is being staged in the European cities of Amsterdam, Barcelona, Hamburg, London, Luxembourg, Madrid, Porto, Reykjavik, Stockholm and Stuttgart. The manufacturers claim that vehicle fuel cell technology is 'zero emission', meaning that no carbonic or poisonous gases are emitted from the motor. But hydrogen, or its carrier (methanol or some other compound), has to be produced, and unfortunately the easiest way of producing it is from fossil fuels, in the course of which CO_2 is emitted.

Are there perhaps truly renewable fuels that can keep the vehicle fleet running without loading any carbon into the atmosphere in the course of production? One such fuel is ethanol, which is refined from plant material. Ethanol can be regarded as carbon neutral, because the growth of the plants needed to make ethanol absorbs as much carbon dioxide as is emitted when the ethanol is burned as fuel. The problem here is the land required to grow enough of the plant material. Research at Indiana University in the United States found that if all the wheat, barley, oats, maize (corn), edible dry beans, hay, peanuts, rice, sorghum, soybeans and sunflowers grown in the United States were to be used to make

Box 5.1 EUROPEAN CARSHARING

How it works

When you become a member of a CarSharing service, you pay a deposit and receive your personal key, and a booklet showing the cars available in your town. The use of these cars is as easy as booking a tennis court. You have access to the cars at any time of day. Reservations can be made on the phone any time, any day. You can make reservations in advance or on the spur of the moment. You are free to choose a car at any station. Usually, however, you will order a car close to you.

You will find the CarSharing cars at local sites in reserved parking places. There is a safe, lockable store that contains the car keys at every location. You take the key of the car you've booked. Since there are no staff at the parking place, you need to check the condition of the car and return it in the same state. CarSharing cars usually have a reserved parking space. You fill in a simple receipt showing your mileage and return the car keys and the receipt to the locker. You keep a copy of the receipt to check your monthly bill, which will show every trip.

Some CarSharing services gather data on the use of the cars electronically, so you don't have to fill in forms at all; in these cases, all you need is your key and a phone. Your CarSharing organisation will deal with car maintenance, insurance, and all the other hassles car owners usually have to deal with themselves. Just the driving is left to you. With the cost calculator on the website you are able to calculate the cost of any journey with various organisations.

The program and the price list consider only the basic cost structure for the ordinary type of cars. In addition, the organisations offer special conditions, such as weekend tariffs, night reductions for women, and company tariffs. As well as the costs of a journey, you have to pay low monthly operational costs. In most cases the costs for fuel are included in the costs per unit of distance.

Source: ECS website: www.carsharing.org.

ethanol, it would only be enough to fuel the US vehicle fleet for eight days.[22] Even if everyone driving large cars (sports utility vehicles) were to convert to the most fuel-efficient vehicles available, the ethanol would last for only a little longer, say 32 days. The big problem, though, is that with an ever-increasing population, the world simply cannot afford to sacrifice food-producing land for the production of bio-fuel. The use of ethanol can therefore be regarded as a partial solution only, and makes sense only in tandem with the large improvements in transport efficiency such as might be provided by increased use of public transport.

Finally, a wide range of projects and policies, particularly in Europe, show that the increase in car traffic in cities can be checked. Most have worked by first building an alternative – high quality public transport, cycling and walking systems. Car-sharing schemes in Switzerland and Germany have halved the distance travelled by car annually by participants in the scheme. Liftshare in the UK uses the internet to register people offering and needing transport from place to place. The European CarSharing organisation operating in Germany and Switzerland opens its website with wise words from Aristotle: 'You find wealth much more in use than in ownership.' Car sharing offers convenient use of a car without the costs and worries of owning one. It offers the public a perk that many private firms offer their employees. How the system works is explained in Box 5.1.

THE UNSUSTAINABILITY OF URBAN TRANSPORT TODAY

Urban transport around the world is one of the fastest-growing contributors to greenhouse emissions. In both the developed and the developing worlds emissions from the transport sector are increasing more rapidly than those from housing or most industries. One estimate for Australia is that if current performance continues, by 2010 there will be a 67 per cent increase in emissions in the transport sector above the 1990 level, with by far the largest contribution coming from road use.[23]

The medium-term threat of global warming hangs over all industries dependent on fossil fuel. But road vehicles are dependent on one type of fossil fuel in particular: oil. The so-called oil shocks of 1973 and 1979 triggered powerful responses from governments and businesses around the world. As we saw in chapter 4, the management of what is now the ING Bank in The Netherlands decided that its new headquarters would not be dependent on energy from fossil fuel. Nearer to home, the oil shocks stimulated Peter Newman and Jeffrey Kenworthy to direct their research at Murdoch University in Perth to the task of exploring what makes cities car dependent. In their book *Cities and Automobile Dependence, An International Sourcebook*, they argued for more compact cities with higher-density housing.[24]

Several points need to be made about the sustainability, or otherwise, of urban transport. First, it is not the number of people moving around the city, nor even the number of vehicles, that contributes to fossil fuel use and greenhouse gas emissions; it is the number of motors. Electric engines drawing power from overhead lines or surface rails are in effect linked to a few enormous motors at the power stations supplying electricity. Motors need fuel and, for the most part, what fuels motors creates carbon emissions. So reducing the number of motors per person will help reduce emissions and oil dependence. Most forms of public transport take place in vehicles with the capacity to carry large numbers of people per motor. Of course it is true that a bigger motor emitting more carbon is required to drive a larger vehicle (or a fleet of trams or trains), but in terms of person kilometres travelled per unit of greenhouse emissions, the high-capacity vehicles in public transport fleets are much more efficient than private cars. Car motors are also usually much larger than is necessary to transport what are often sole occupants quickly and safely around cities.

Second, public transport fleets can more easily be equipped with motors with low impact on the environment. It makes good economic sense for bus operators to use fuel-efficient motors, and various inducements can be applied by government to encourage the use of alternative non-greenhouse fuels – as in the case of European cities changing to methanol fuel cell buses. Heavy and light railways (trams) are normally electrically powered, which does away with local air pollution and shifts the emission problem from the vehicle to the remote power station. Here current technology does not offer a substitute for high-voltage power from the electricity supply grid. But the grid can be powered by energy sources that do not emit greenhouse gas: wind turbines, hydropower and various forms of direct solar power. It is important to remember, however, that the problem is shifted, not solved, if electricity is mainly generated by burning coal and transmitted by power lines over long distances – in this scenario, some of the greenhouse efficiency gains of public transport will be lost.[25]

Third, the car and road solution to mass movement in cities tends to sprawl the city patchily out into the surrounding non-urban region, placing stress on agricultural land and wildlife habitat. There is a kind of symbiosis between land developers, who have a large financial interest in converting agricultural land anywhere around the city to urban use, and road builders, who design the means of access by car via massive freeways. Quite simply, cars require a lot of land and infrastructure to accommodate them. There may not be the intractable causal relationship between low population density, car dependence and poor public transport that Newman and Kenworthy imagined, but there is certainly some kind of relationship between those things.

In sprawling cities people have to travel further to reach the services they require, and there are fewer people within walking distance of any form of public transport service. Low density of population translates into low intensity of vehicle use. It does not require sophisticated statistical analysis of large amounts of quantitative data to see that a widely dispersed urban population requires more motors per person to deliver a frequent and reliable transport service – whether that service be provided privately or publicly – than a city whose patterns of settlement are shaped by public transport lines and stops. Higher population densities around public transport stops certainly increase public transport use, but as we saw above, good public transport can also be provided in a moderately 'dispersed' city like metropolitan Zürich or metropolitan Melbourne.

Finally, oil is running out, but to see what this means is quite complex. The 'sceptical environmentalist', Bjørn Lomborg, denies this, believing that there is a more or less infinite supply of oil just waiting to be discovered.[26] In this, Lomborg shows that he doesn't understand the nature of oil geology. Colin Campbell, however, does. Campbell earned his doctorate in geology at Oxford University. In 1958 he joined the oil industry and worked as a field geologist. Ten years later he joined the head office of an oil company in New York, becoming the company's regional geologist for South America. Following two years as chief geologist in Ecuador, he was sent to Norway for ten years as exploration manager, and later became executive vice-president. In the course of his work Campbell became aware of a worrying trend: less and less new oil was being discovered. He began to realise that the discovery of oil fields had peaked around the 1960s, and that the supply of oil would reach a plateau in the early years of the 21st century and then gradually decline. He also realised that the world, especially the economic powerhouse of America, is failing to take note of this fact, and is becoming more and more dependent on oil – especially for transporting goods and people.

Rising demand, not only from the US and Europe, but also now from the future mega-economies of China and India, combined with static or declining supply, can mean only one thing in an open market: rising price. Since cheap transport is a key factor in economic growth, a rising oil price will place a long-lasting dampener on the whole global economy until transport and production systems adapt. Rising oil prices will have particularly pernicious effects on those cities and nations that fail to free their transport systems from oil dependence, and especially on those poorer countries that have little wasted energy to reduce. Campbell therefore helped found the Association for the Study of the Peak of Oil (ASPO: http://www.asponews.org/), a network of concerned scientists (most European countries are represented) which acts as an advisor to European governments and the European Union. Its influence, however, has not reached North America or Australia.

The key premise of the oil problem is that no new oil is being created within the Earth.[27] Disputing that premise is a bit like disputing the theory of evolution. As with 'creation science', faith is contradicted by evidence. The evidence overwhelmingly supports the theory that oil, along with other fossil fuels such as natural gas and coal, originated in vast layers of plant material deposited on the Earth's surface and seabeds at periods of extreme global warming. The last two such periods were around 145 and 90 million years ago. Oil volumes are still rather quaintly measured in barrels. The essential facts are that production was running at an annual rate of 23 gigabarrels (billion barrels) at the turn of the 21st century, 850 gigabarrels had been produced up to that time, and another 850 gigabarrels are held in 'proved and probable' oil reserves – in the language of oil production. What then remains to be found? Campbell argues that only another 150 gigabarrels are yet to be discovered. In total, the world oil industry can produce no more than another 1000 gigabarrels.

The issue is somewhat clouded by three issues that evidently confuse Lomborg: the simple economics of oil search, the 'illusion' of technology, and the politics of oil reporting. There is probably a lot more oil in the ground than will ever be extracted (perhaps another 1850 gigabarrels). That is because as oil becomes scarce it becomes more expensive to find. Oil in a known field, determined by geophysical mapping, does not lie in a convenient natural tank buried beneath the rocks. It lies in fissures and seams interlaced with a very large area of rocky matrix. Extracting the oil is rather like sticking a needle in a human body and hoping to find an artery, but whereas human bodies come in more or less standard forms and the arteries and veins are in much the same locations in each human body, each oil body is different, and the location of the oil-bearing 'arteries' cannot be exactly predicted. Drilling a bore is costly, and oil extraction is, therefore, limited by the number of non-productive bores that have to be sunk before an oil strike is made.

Oil companies want to maximise the financial return they get for the oil they spend so much money finding. When an oil company finds a prospect, it is normal for it to announce an estimate of the oil volume in the 'reserve' on the basis of its initial program for development of the prospect. These 'reserves' find their way into nationally reported statistics. But these initially reported reserves are subject to progressive modification as the company seeks to prolong the production life of the prospect. As work proceeds, the reported reserve estimates are revised upwards. This increase is commonly attributed to advances in technology and managerial skill, but it is actually no more than the increased application of existing technology.

The illusion created, however, is that advances in technology increase the extraction of oil from reserves. Campbell writes: 'The industry has treated reserves from discovery as a form of inventory to be drawn down as best serves financial purposes. No conspiracy is implied: the practice was consistent with prudent management.'[28] Thus *reporting* of oil reserves should not be confused with the realistic scientific estimates of the actual *size* of oil reserves. No more than 40 per cent of the oil in a prospect can be commercially extracted. Just as companies routinely under-report oil reserves, so several countries belonging to OPEC have at times also exaggerated their reserves in order to increase the production quota allowed them by OPEC.

Interestingly, there seems to have been a change in this past pattern of behaviour since Campbell wrote, but it is one that actually tends to support his thesis of the 'peak of oil'. In February 2004 the chairman of the Royal Dutch Shell oil group was forced to admit to *over-reporting* its reserves by 3.9 gigabarrels, thus acknowledging that oil production is set to fall.[29] None of this variety in reporting affects the real size of reserves, of course: these can be estimated by objective geological and statistical techniques.

About half the world's remaining oil reserves are situated in just five Middle East countries (Abu Dhabi, Iran, Iraq, Kuwait and Saudi Arabia). The price of oil is not controlled. It is determined by the behaviour of a large number of actors in the market buying and selling the commodity. And this behaviour is determined by perceptions. These perceptions are in turn influenced by beliefs about what will happen to the price in the future. If most of the world's oil is produced by just a few countries, there is a great likelihood that those countries, through OPEC, will influence the oil price by imposing restrictions on supply – in order to maximise the returns from their oil and for a variety of geopolitical reasons. This is what happened in 1973 and in 1979.

As a result of the nationalisation of oil production by the key Middle East countries, and the testing of their new power in 1973 and 1979, oil companies began opening up new oil provinces outside the Middle East. The Middle East countries took on a 'swing' role, making up the difference between world demand and what the rest of the world could produce within its resource constraints. The 'swing' share dropped from about 35 per cent in the 1970s to about 20 per cent in the 1980s. But because of oil depletion outside the Middle East, the swing share rose to about 30 per cent in 2000 and now stands again at about 35 per cent.

Colin Campbell, writing in 2000 (though published in 2003), predicted what was coming in Iraq two years before the 2003 American invasion: 'Iraq's oil will soon be desperately needed, and with the boot on the other foot, Iraq is unlikely to be sympathetic to Western demands, carrying risks that new pretexts may be found for Western military intervention.'[30] As it turned out, the pretexts – 'weapons of mass destruction' able to be quickly released in acts of terror – have been found to be just that: 'pretext: an ostensible reason, excuse' (*Concise Oxford Dictionary*), without foundation. Whether, now in illegal occupation of the country and supporting a compliant regime, America can turn on the tap of Iraq's oil and thus postpone the coming oil crisis for a few more years remains to be seen. For the somewhat longer run, cities would be wise to reduce the oil dependency of their transport systems.

THE ECOLOGICAL COMBINATION

Transport networks in green cities will be used much more efficiently and healthily. Roads, and especially cars, are overused for journeys that could easily be made by other transport modes, including walking and cycling, while public transport systems that could move people efficiently, comfortably and safely are allowed to languish and go to waste. Dieter Apel and Tim Pharoah, reviewing the European experience, use the term 'the ecological combination' to describe the alternative to private cars and public roads: the combination of rail, bus, bike and walking. They sum up the philosophy of transport for green cities very well:

> The purpose of establishing an attractive local public transport system, or promoting the use of bicycles, is not to get as many people as possible on to one or other means of transport at any price. The aim is, or rather should be, to create a suitable combination of the city and environment-friendly modes of transport to make possible closed chains of trips, i.e. to offer acceptable alternatives to car travel.[31]

Greener transport systems will not cost more; they will probably cost less than the expensive road-based systems of car-dependent cities. A huge amount of time and money is wasted on transport in our affluent cities. Transport is not really a separate item in the green city. It is a key part of the living and working system that a city represents. It is part of the system of home and work, suburb and centre, and absolutely essential to the efficient – and ecologically sustainable – performance of city life.

Australian cities have the infrastructure to run magnificent transport systems. And they don't yet have the kind of fear-fuelled sprawl that so complicates and undermines planning for sustainability in the US. Australian cities also have high 'social capital' – skilled workers and community cohesion – and relatively less social polarisation, though both are under pressure. The main elements in need of change are institutional: the organisations and cultures surrounding transport planning. Changing those, essentially changing minds, costs little. The physical and social facts of Australian cities surely provide a fertile soil in which a major political-economic and institutional transformation may grow. Let's now turn in the next chapter to that and similar issues relating to how the green city can be made to happen.

FURTHER READING

Making Urban Transport Sustainable is a series of essays by transport experts ranging from global issues such as the diminishing supply of oil, reducing CO_2 emissions from vehicle engines, and the impact of e-commerce to local solutions in Europe, America and Asia. The book deals directly with the sustainability and unsustainability of transport: Nicholas Low & Brendan Gleeson (eds), *Making Urban Transport Sustainable*, Palgrave -Macmillan, Basingstoke, 2003. *The Greening of Urban Transport* comprises short readable essays on all aspects of planning for foot traffic, walking and cycling, in cities: Rodney Tolley (ed.), *The Greening of Urban Transport*, 2nd edition, John Wiley & Sons, Chichester, 1997. *Transport Concepts in European Cities*, by Dieter Apel and Tim Pharoah (Avebury, Aldershot, 1995), describes the best examples of the ecological combination of rail, bus, bike and walking in Europe. *A Very Public Solution*, by Paul Mees (Melbourne University Press, Melbourne, 2000), tackles the question of whether or not good public transport can be provided in Australia's 'dispersed cities'. The answer is a resounding 'yes' and Mees shows what should be done.

CHAPTER 6

MAKING
THE GREEN CITY

It has been our thesis throughout this book that green cities are already beginning to emerge. Their further development will need a lot of help, because this welcome emergence now needs to move from experiment to mainstream. The avoidance of catastrophic climate change is not a matter of choice. It is an imperative. Green cities are simply necessary if the human species is to have a long-term future in anything like the environmental abundance with which humanity at large is now fortunately surrounded. It is worth remembering that it is not lack of abundance that is the cause of poverty; it is the inability or unwillingness to share it fairly among the Earth's citizens.

Green cities will not be planned like the 'cities of tomorrow' envisioned by reformers and dreamers at the beginning of the last century. They cannot be built afresh on green fields according to a master plan drawn up by experts. The main task is to transform our existing cities and towns so that their constant building and rebuilding occurs under green principles supported by the public.

Democracy is the political system most likely to succeed with such a transformation.[1] But given the evident weaknesses and vulnerabilities of liberal democracy, it is a puzzle to know how this transformation could possibly occur. The institutions of liberal democracy are designed for the short term. This 'short-termism' places a quite deliberate limit on the exercise of public power. If one person or a number of persons is allowed to hold power over a long period of time, the power they hold increases massively, and their 'accountability' declines. They acquire the freedom to use power not for the public good but for their private purposes. Hence everyone has reason to fear the 'president for life', the single-party state, the thousand-year Reich, even the lying prime minister. Environmentalists may detest the market, with its overwhelming emphasis on what will make a profit now, but the market is a potentially democratic institution designed to serve whatever interests exist today, as long as they can pay. Provided wealth is widely shared, the market is a powerful guarantor of democracy. The question is: can the market's innate short-termism be transformed by new political and institutional rules that place a concern for nature, for human welfare and for the future at the centre of decision making? Without built-in short-termism, governments and companies could give people what those authorities thought was best for the public rather than what the public wants. But democracy is about delivering what the public, the *demos*, wants.

It is often assumed that there is a perfect political mechanism – the market or liberal democracy or government planning, perhaps – that will lead to the best outcome. Unfortunately, however, there is no single perfect political mechanism that will simultaneously deliver ecological sustainability, social justice and economic success while protecting the rights of the individual. We simply have to try to find the best possible combination of imperfect mechanisms. How then can the long-term future and the more than human interest be taken into account in a democratic, market-based society?

Let's put the question another way. It must first be recognised that a globally co-ordinated human society is the dominant force on the planet today: a society of different but interconnected cultures and communities, mostly now in harmony but sometimes in conflict. To be successful in the long term, this human society must arrive at a symbiotic relationship with the rest of the planet: that is, a state of co-operative, mutually supportive coexistence, or 'sustainability'.

Global warming is a signal from Earth that human society has not achieved that symbiotic relationship and is heading for destruction. Somehow the more than human and the long-term interest must be represented within the society of the present. So what elements of this global human society might be the carriers of such an interest?

When the question of the long-term future was put to the Melbourne architect and environmentalist Allan Rodger, the answer he gave was surprisingly vehement: 'It's the community!' He talked about the '200-year present'. All of us can imagine the world of our great-grandparents and that of our great-grandchildren, and perhaps a little beyond. All of us can relate empathically to the more than human world. Most of us love to do so; it is our joy. As we argued in chapter 3, the natural world shapes our consciousness from birth. To ask the unanswerable question – what *is* 'the community'? – is to miss the point, though. The point is that every person, no matter what their function, status or position in the global society, in some way has a profound interest in the long-term future of the planet as a whole. Everyone has some capacity to mobilise the engines of society and steer it towards sustainability.

This is beginning to sound like fundamentalist individualism, as though changing our own behaviour is all that is needed: simple! No, the behaviour of persons is governed, shaped and regulated by social machinery: policies, institutions, taxes and subsidies, interest rates, organisations, markets, companies, groups. These are the means by which human persons act together, and it is these means of *collective* action that have to be grasped and reshaped for the achievement of sustainability. Interestingly, Rodger's observation recalls that of Hungarian socialist anthropologist Karl Polanyi, who was writing in Britain in mid-20th century. In his much-neglected book *The Great Transformation* (1944), Polanyi argued that when, in the 19th and early 20th centuries, the exploitation of labour and the environment by an untrammelled market had become so intense as to endanger society and the land itself, a widespread movement was generated among the public at large to protect the cultural and environmental basis of society. The principal actors in this movement were to be found in many different social positions: in the legal, medical and engineering professions, in politics and the public service, in the church, in factories and trade unions, in community groups of all sorts and in what today would be called non-government organisations (NGOs).

When Polanyi was writing, in the 1940s, the 19th century liberal project of subordinating all human activities to the logic of the market had ground to a halt, because of, first, the Great Depression of the 1930s, and second, the most destructive war in human history. Faced with the task of reconstruction and restarting economic growth, the endangered societies had no choice but to turn to government to regulate the market and re-establish the basis of social security.

Ironically, it was the very economic success of the welfare state which was thus constructed that permitted a new effort on the part of the market enthusiasts to wind back government and extend the scope of the market: the market advocacy we know as neo-liberalism. This pro-market wave, implemented by the Thatcher Government in Britain and the Reagan Administration in the US, swept across the world, resulting in what is now called 'globalisation'. Although

Polanyi's historical analysis was limited to a single nation, Britain, he foresaw what was coming: 'The true implications of economic liberalism can now be taken in at a glance. Nothing less than a self-regulating market on a world scale could ensure the functioning of this stupendous mechanism.'[2]

The dominant thinking today is still harshly averse to what the philosophers of neo-liberalism (or 'economic rationalism') call 'collectivism'. The founding father of neo-liberalism, Austrian Friedrich von Hayek, argued that collectivism was 'the road to serfdom' – imbued as he was with fear of both Nazism and communism, it is easy to see why he believed that. But there is no natural tendency towards slavery that results from creative engagement with the tools of government. Both government and the market are flawed. Today there is at least a real desire in the world of politics to relearn how to use society's collective tools, the tools of government (including markets), without becoming authoritarian and heavy-handedly bureaucratic. This 'third way', pioneered by the Hawke–Keating Governments and later in Britain by the Blair Government, is starting to replace the *laissez-faire* dogma of 'government by market'. Critics have railed against the seemingly feeble results of this new attempt to restrain market short-termism. Nevertheless, third way politics have reinstated a public debate about the perils of ignoring the future. How then can society proceed further along the third way towards the green city?

The order in which knowledge is arranged is important. It is first necessary to know about sustainability, then to know about policy making and its institutional setting, then to be expert in a specialist urban policy field: housing, open space, transport, workplaces, social services, industry, shopping and commerce. It is necessary to have some understanding of how cities work, the geography of urban development, and it is equally important to know how the policy-making system works. Cities by and large develop themselves through multiple interactions among individual developers, public regulators (the town planning profession) and public investors (transport agencies, for example), but it is the *policy system* that must be the immediate target of the builders of green cities.

We can think of the policy system as an extremely elaborate game in constant play. All games have two aspects: the play itself – what actually happens on the field – and the rules of play. In that respect policy making is not much different from football. So we can divide the policy system into policy making (the play) and the policy institutions (the rules). The meaning of these terms will become clearer as we proceed, but it is perhaps worth mentioning one of the many definitions of 'institutions': 'the formal or informal procedures, routines, norms and conventions embedded in the organizational structure of the polity or political economy'.[3] But first to policies: the players are in government, in the professions, in businesses, and in community groups or NGOs – in short, in 'the community'.

GREEN POLICIES: SMALL SCALE, WIDE SCOPE, LONG TERM

Green policies are built up through many small-scale actions heading in the same general direction, as we said in chapter 1. These changes will be made in every sphere of human endeavour: in government policies for housing, transport, open space and workplaces, in how businesses make profits, in the election platforms of political parties, in the activities of community pressure groups.

The Scottish philosopher credited with the foundation of market economics, Adam Smith, believed that under the right institutional rules, the pursuit of self-interest could be socially directed for the good of the whole community. He thought that the market represented one such rule, and indeed in some circumstances it does. But he also thought there were other social rules, the rules of common morality, that were quite separate from the market – rules that suggested that people place themselves in the position of others they have dealings with. And beyond even this social rule there was also a weak but persistent motive: social survival. Like gravity, the social survival force pulls the community towards sustainability. Many people share that motive force, regardless of the position they occupy in society. In any society there is always conflict, because people's opinions differ, but in some respects there is also always a sphere of consensus. It is the business of planning to elicit and express the common interest – the sphere of consensus – and try to work through with the public how best to achieve it.

The environmental planning approach we advocate can be described as 'small scale, wide scope and long term': 'small scale' because small steps in the right direction can add up to big changes over time, 'wide scope' because planners need to think beyond the confines of current town planning institutions, and 'long term' because the environmental crises we confront are themselves unfolding over a long duration. We hasten to add that like all essentially political activities, this approach is imperfect. It does not dispose of the dilemmas of democracy. It is just what reasonable people might do in the ecological, social and economic circumstances in which they find themselves.

We can think of the policy process as having five main components: long-run goals, short-run targets, social barriers, strategies and indicators.

LONG-RUN GOALS

Australian commentators David Yencken and Debra Wilkinson write of the 'compass of sustainability'.[4] Swedish scientists Karl-Henrik Robért, John Holmberg and Göran Broman describe a planning instrument they call 'the compass', that relates individual decisions to their eventual outcome, even into the distant future, the planet's geological timescale.[5] We use a compass to know the direction to move in. These scientists say that planners need to 'think upstream' to the source of a problem rather than just tackling its symptoms. Planning starts, therefore, with the most radical goals to be achieved in the long run. They set the direction.

The City of Manningham in Melbourne's affluent eastern suburbs has adopted a framework for its planning called 'The Natural Step' (TNS), which was created by Robért and Holmberg (Box 6.1). Considering the uncompromising nature of these principles, the TNS website claims a surprising variety of adherents, including Swedish furniture company Ikea, whitegoods manufacturer Electrolux, the fabric and carpet tile manufacturer Interface, Geelong Grammar School, the Canadian energy corporation Ontario Hydro, and even the mining company Billiton QNI (now merged with BHP).

The City of Manningham, in its *Greenprint for a Sustainable City*, says of its 'stretch goals': they 'are designed to be long term, inspirational and challenging. Their purpose is to provide a vision of where an organization or community needs to set its sights in the long term.' Roughly following the TNS principles, the goals are: zero climate damage, zero extinction, zero pollution, zero soil degradation and zero waste.

It is best to be cautious in the applause we give to such long-term directions. After all, a dramatic long-term goal that will only be achieved in 1000 years is a lot less impressive and a lot harder to grasp than a more modest one that can be achieved after 20 years. The *rate* of achievement matters. What does 'zero climate damage' in 1000 years mean when the climate is already being adversely affected by industrial emissions? In Manningham's case these goals are coupled with quantified targets and indicators, and strategies to achieve them. It seems that

Box 6.1 THE NATURAL STEP

The Natural Step (TNS) is a non-profit organisation set up to train practitioners in environmental planning. Four fundamental ecological principles are espoused:

1 *Substances extracted from the lithosphere (Earth's crust) must not systematically accumulate in the ecosphere (the world of living things).*

   This accounts for all pollutants as well as non-toxic substances such carbon dioxide and CFCs (chlorofluorocarbons). The implication is zero emissions, or whatever comes out of the Earth's crust must be put back there.

2 *Society-produced substances must not systematically accumulate in the ecosphere.*

   The principle covers everything that human society may make out of the materials coming out of the Earth's crust. Either don't make it at all or we put it back when it becomes waste.

3 *The physical conditions for production and diversity within the ecosphere must not systematically be deteriorated.*

   The implication is much more efficient and careful use of productive areas in agriculture, forestry and fishing and more careful planning of infrastructure. Presumably it also refers to the very restricted use of rainforest timber.

4 *The use of resources must be efficient and just with respect to meeting human needs.*

   What is wanted here is increased technological and organisational efficiency and a more equitable division of wealth in global society, including more resource-efficient lifestyles amongst the rich part of humankind.

Source: City of Manningham, *Greenprint for a Sustainable City,* Melbourne, 1998.

the long-term goals are really just a reminder of the purpose of the more specific targets and 'milestones' on the way. The uncompromising language of TNS principles is perhaps also a powerful reminder of the enormity of what is at stake.

TARGETS AND POLICIES

The next step is to set intermediate targets to be achieved within a given period, say the next five years. What can practically be changed that will make a difference in terms of the compass of sustainability? A target can be almost anything the planner wants to achieve or change, something as small scale as the introduction of water-saving shower roses into a housing estate, or as large scale as the protection of a species or the transformation of a profession; as technical as a low-energy air-conditioning system or as social as persuading a group of local retailers to give approval to a walking precinct.

The City of Manningham has set itself the target of reducing the amount of greenhouse gas emitted as a result of the council's activities (council's buildings, municipal street lighting, vehicle fleet) by 5 per cent (of the total of 10,100 tonnes in the baseline year, 1997). This is a clear target whose achievement can be measured. The City of Moreland in Melbourne's northern suburbs has set itself the target of reducing greenhouse gas emissions from council operations by 40 per cent (on the baseline year 1995–96). In that year emissions stood at 14,600 tonnes of greenhouse gas; the target is to get this down to 8760 tonnes by 2010. Applause is merited for both targets.

Under Moreland's Greenhouse Action Plan the council has agreed to purchase energy for heating and cooling its main buildings from a private producer offering 'Green Power' – energy produced by non-emitting sources such as water or wind. In addition, the plan lists actions to be taken in phases between 2001 and 2010 to reduce emissions in each of the six branches of the council's organisation. These are actions to reduce energy consumption, and are used as a proxy for emissions. The actions include energy audits of buildings, recycling schemes, implementation of leases containing clauses on energy management, revised specifications for internal and street lighting, sustainable road construction, audits of staff travel, selection criteria for the council vehicle fleet, purchasing policies and education programs.

In another example, the City of Melbourne reports annual greenhouse emissions from the residential, industrial, community and transport sectors within the municipality. Under 'business as usual' conditions the municipality (covering central Melbourne) is expecting a nearly 10 per cent increase in emissions on 1996 by 2010. The increase from light commercial vehicle traffic is expected to be more than 13 per cent. Under the international Cities for Climate Protection program, the city council adopted a target of a 20 per cent reduction on 1996 levels.[6] The city council is now moving further, to achieve zero net greenhouse gas emissions within the municipality by 2020. To reach the target, the council itself plans to purchase only renewable energy (that is, energy that is not generated by fossil fuels). The council hopes to persuade businesses in the city to purchase renewable energy for up to 40 per cent of their energy needs. The plan includes doubling the efficiency of conventional energy, halving the energy demand through increased efficiency and better building design within the commercial sector, a 15 per cent decrease in demand through energy efficiencies in industry, and sequestration projects to offset the remaining emissions.[7] Not yet included are the greenhouse emissions from the transport sector in the municipality. Zero emissions will ultimately have to include transport, but beyond a sequestration program (planting trees to soak up the equivalent CO_2 emissions) for its own vehicles, the city has not begun to consider how the rising level of emissions in this sector can be attacked.

The City of Leichhardt in Sydney has also placed sustainability requirements in its development control plans, supplementing the provisions of the city's environmental plan.[8] The city's 'vision' is 'to conserve and enhance the quality of the natural, living, working and recreational environments of the local area of Leichhardt. The protection of the amenity of residents should be pre-eminent.'[9] Guidelines specify how all housing must comply with the requirements of ecologically sustainable residential development. The energy-saving principles discussed in chapter 2 are included in the guidelines: use of thermal mass, solar control and window shading, insulation, natural ventilation and solar energy.

All new development, including major renovation, must provide solar hot water and rainwater tanks for water conservation. Solar access for dwellings is protected. Acoustic privacy is also protected, as is existing dwellings' access to views (wherever possible). The latter relate to amenity rather than sustainability, but still fall within the broad concept of the green city. Other policies encourage the avoidance, reuse or recycling of waste from the demolition of buildings, and of waste generated during construction. Green waste from food scraps and plant material is to be composted. Development proposals must be accompanied by waste management plans. New development must seek to enhance access rather than mobility, necessitating better land use planning, reducing the need for car travel, maximising the use of public transport facilities, enhancing the opportunity for pedestrian and cycle links, 'identifying and ameliorating adverse impacts of all transport modes on the environment' and improving road safety, particularly for walkers and cyclists.[10]

In earlier chapters we have described many examples of actions involving governments. Here are some other examples of targets and actions by private companies. In 2002 the furniture company Ikea set itself the target of reducing CO_2 emissions by 15 per cent for each cubic metre of goods transported in Europe. Transporting goods by rail reduces carbon emissions by 70 per cent compared with transporting them by road. So the company has organised its own international trains for freight transfer. Five trains per week were reported to be operating by 2003, replacing 50–60 trucks per day. From 1997, Ikea was also operating a solar roof covering its entire furniture centre in Älmhult in Sweden, as well as a south-facing wall of the building (an area of 630 square metres) of photovoltaic cells generating 60 kilowatt hours of electricity.

The American carpet company Interface now offers its European customers a carbon-neutral floor covering, 'cool carpet', for commercial buildings. This carpet is guaranteed 'climate neutral', meaning that in the course of its production and distribution, the net sum of greenhouse gas emitted is zero. This doesn't mean that no greenhouse gas is ever emitted; it means that any gas that is emitted is reabsorbed – by planting trees or by vegetation used in making the carpet. The Body Shop, an international toiletries and cosmetics retailer with outlets in 51 countries, has set itself the target of offsetting 30 per cent of greenhouse gas emissions from its products by 2004, by using and investing in renewable energy. In partnership with the NGO Greenpeace International, The Body Shop has conducted campaigns to persuade its customers to use renewable energy, calling on governments to support the provision of renewable energy to 2 billion people who are at present without access to energy sources at all.[11]

These examples from the private sector are recorded in the reports of a group of six international companies that have formed BLICC (Business Leaders Initiative on Climate Change). BLICC is a voluntary program operating as a network to stimulate action on climate change within industry. Its members regularly report their greenhouse emissions, in terms of direct emissions from sources owned or controlled by the company (*Scope 1*), indirect emissions associated with imported or purchased electricity, heat or steam (*Scope 2*), and other indirect emissions – from, for example, employee business travel, including commuting to and from work, transportation of products, and waste – where the point of emission occurs at sites owned or controlled by another company (*Scope 3*).

In the BLICC Reports of 2002 and 2003 the companies' greenhouse results for 2001 and 2002 are recorded. From the reported figures, it seems that the three companies mentioned above have a major task on their hands to turn their greenhouse performance around, because total reported emissions for the three companies increased by 11 per cent over just one year (2001/2002) and turnover per tonne of greenhouse gas emitted fell by 8.4 per cent – this despite a reduction of 43 per cent in *Scope 2* indirect emissions from energy inputs (Table 6.1).

It must be said immediately that these results do not yet provide strong evidence of performance over time. The figures may also be subject to discrepancies in data collection as the companies learn more about what to include. The existence of the data and the fact that BLICC has been bold enough to report it is a sign that this particular business network is serious about its aims.

The question we have to ask, however, is this: if a network of a few major companies can report greenhouse data in a way that provides valuable feedback to themselves and the public, even saving money in the process, why shouldn't such public reporting be made mandatory for

Table 6.1 Change in greenhouse gas (GHG) production from three leading companies in the Business Leaders Initiative on Climate Change

Ikea, Body Shop and Interface	2001	2002	% +/–
Scope 1 (tonnes GHG)	71,650	122,261	+71%
Scope 2 (tonnes GHG)	662,343	375,567	–43%
Scope 3 (tonnes GHG)	1,234,413	1,680,493	+36%
Total (tonnes GHG)	1,968,406	2,178,321	+11%
Turnover (million euros)	12,263	12,426	+1.3%
Turnover (euros per tonne GHG)	6230	5705	–8.4%

Source: Business Leaders Initiative on Climate Change (BLICC), *BLICC 1, 2002: Establishing a Baseline* and *BLICC 2, 2003: Establishing Priorities*, BLICC, London & Amsterdam.

all companies? Why shouldn't there also be independent auditing to ensure that companies don't cheat? Who could object to a mandatory scheme that saves individual companies money and furthers the cause of sustainability? No doubt such an idea would strike terror into the hearts of the many company boards who have little appreciation of the value of the common interest. Most seek to guard a narrow ideal of pecuniary interest in short-run profits, and would be intensely resistant to such change. Governments would then be quickly threatened with capital flight – companies moving 'offshore', to anywhere in the world that did not impose such a requirement. And that, of course, is why such mandatory reporting should be included in any future international climate protocol.

Government, business and community organisations need to plan for sustainability. Good planning means setting real targets for improvement on key environmental issues, targets that have a reasonable expectation of being met by a given date. Plans must clearly indicate benchmark dates from which the improvement can be measured. Policies governing actions by people over whom the policy maker has authority need to be drawn up, as those people need to change their procedures if the targets are to be reached. This, however, is where barriers to implementation are often encountered.

BARRIERS

Any change means dealing with something that is already embedded in the human systems of production and consumption, ideas, institutional rules, organisations. The policy maker needs to consider the social barriers to action. These systems should be known and described as fully as possible. Interestingly, 'decision theory' relating to planning for ecological systems demands that the ecosystem 'being managed' should be well understood and described before intervention. This may seem like commonsense, but much human 'decision theory' is highly abstract and based upon assumptions about behaviour rather than on empirical knowledge of how humans behave.[12] The same level of understanding should be applied to human systems as is applied to ecosystems. One of these human systems is the organisation to which the policy maker belongs. Where are the rigidities and resistances? The institution itself might have to change before anything else can. Systems can throw up difficult barriers to overcome in the form of conventional wisdoms – 'we've always done it this way', 'it's commonsense', 'it's logical', 'our model says so', 'there is no alternative'.

Despite the City of Manningham's goals and targets, a new section of completely unsustainable freeway was approved for outer east Melbourne, and is currently being dug through the municipality, tunnelling under one of Manningham's most environmentally sensitive creeks (Mullum Mullum Creek). That freeway was in gross violation of all the TNS principles, and Manningham's own environmental goals and targets. Although the freeway was designed and implemented by the State Government of Victoria and not Manningham, the council could have lent its weight to attempts to stop it. It did not. This is an example of the strategies of the planners who were trying to steer the municipality meeting the resistance of entrenched beliefs about the benefits of freeways, plus various sets of interests which were defined by those beliefs. We don't know whether or not a strategy could have been devised to get over those barriers. In the short run probably not, because institutions mostly change slowly. We return to the question of institutions at length below.

We discussed the idea of 'path dependence' in chapter 5 – in the transport context, it is the seemingly entrenched institutional devotion to investment in roads above all other forms of transport. There is a countervailing idea in political science called 'path dislocation', in which these entrenched ways of doing things are suddenly derailed (let's for once mix metaphors!). The most common cause of such a dislocation is an external shock – the sudden realisation that things cannot go on as they are. Examples are the shock discovery of the ozone hole over the Antarctic and the oil shocks of the 1970s. In both cases the 'shock' led to dramatic and widespread policy changes. Prolonged droughts in some parts of Australia (Perth, Canberra and Victoria, for example) have galvanised local authorities into action and helped to make municipalities some of the leading 'change agents' in Australia. It seems possible that a steady increase in oil prices over the next five or ten years will be enough to shock governments into action on transport.

Can such shocks be institutionally induced? Can planners themselves 'create' a shock effect? We must remember that the 'ozone hole' is actually an image, as is 'the peak of oil'. Most people don't know that ozone is naturally much lower over equatorial latitudes, and that, extremely serious though it is, the so-called hole is merely a thinning of ozone where it is normally most concentrated. Likewise, oil will not run out; it will slowly diminish, forcing up the price. The 'hole' and the 'peak' images are designed to provoke action. One of the great difficulties about global warming is that its effects are insidious, and very slow in political time. Recall that British Prime Minister Harold Wilson once said, 'A week is a long time in politics.'

Environmentalists tell the story of the frog placed in a lidless cooking pot which is slowly heated (don't try it at home!). The frog gradually becomes comatose; it fails to jump out of the pot. The point of inducing a shock is to make present what is in reality gradually unfolding, so that the political frog jumps in time. We have to be extremely cautious about this, of course, and also tell the truth. Any lie, when discovered, destroys confidence in the liar ('weapons of mass destruction' leaps to mind as an example). There must be a real longer-term danger. We probably know enough now to sheet home extreme weather events and droughts to global warming even though their proximate cause remains in doubt. Shock images to save the environment should always be accompanied by cushioning programs for rapid economic adjustment and mitigation of social inequity. This question of deliberate institutional change leads us to the next item: strategies.

STRATEGIES

The term 'strategy' is often misunderstood and misused. Planners use the term to mean any large-scale plan, and completely miss the central meaning, which is a means of *winning* an objective. Melbourne's 2030 plan, for example, describes large-scale and admirable goals but lacks strategies for their achievement.[13] The word 'strategy' comes from the Greek, meaning 'to lead an army'. The *Concise Oxford Dictionary* defines 'strategy' as 'the art of war' and no doubt the wars of the 20th century account for its infusion into the language. In fact all political action designed to win *in the face of opposition* involves strategy, and as we just discussed, there *will* be opposition. In planning the green city, therefore, there is a place for strategy.

In the 1970s an American professor of social work at Michigan University, Jack Rothman, carried out a useful research project on 'social change'. Part of his work was concerned with innovation. He drew particularly on the work of Everett Rogers, the seminal thinker on innovation. Rogers' model of innovation posits three main elements in the track an 'innovation' (a new technology, practice, or policy) follows towards its adoption by society: the antecedents (to do with actors' identity and their perception of the situation they face), the process of adoption, from awareness through evaluation and trial to adoption, and the results of the process – some people will continue to accept the innovation, some will later reject it, and others will later come to accept it.

Rogers writes of 'target systems', shorthand for the people and organisations that the social planner wants to adopt a new policy or practice. From his review of 149 reports and articles by over 100 different authors, Rothman derived a series of generalisations and 'action guidelines'. Think of a green policy as an innovation. Then consider the 'action guidelines' that will improve the rate of adoption of an innovation. Box 6.2 shows some of these guidelines, paraphrased. These are strategies designed to win acceptance of an innovation.

These action guidelines do not involve lies and deception. They are legitimate means in a society that expects governments to be effective; that is, to put policies *into action*. The democratic requirement that governments be effective cannot be reconciled completely with the democratic requirement that governments be inclusive and open, with their policies based on consensus. If no policy could be pursued unless it had the total agreement of all the voters, no policy would ever be implemented and the government would be completely ineffective. So there is a time and a place for strategy. But there is also a time and place to drop strategy.

German philosopher Jürgen Habermas has argued that for democracy to be more than a sham, there must be times when the government consults the community openly, with maximum inclusion, and without any form of manipulation in order 'to win'. The only objective on such occasions is for the best argument to emerge and win the day solely on the basis of its own compelling reasons: its innate truth and justice. This proposition may be idealistic, but there is also practical sense as well as ethical aspiration in it. Community support, as Rodger said, is the best guarantee of a long-term policy being sustained. Because individuals are not purely self-interested in a narrow sense, a community view can be

---

Box 6.2 ACTION GUIDELINES PROPOSED BY JACK ROTHMAN,
Professor of Social Work at the University of Michigan

- Approach target systems that have had positive experience with innovations, particularly if these past innovations were similar to the present one.

- Concentrate on those target systems that are discontented and therefore more predisposed in favour of change.

- Contact individuals who are active in formal organizations or voluntary associations.

- Underline the advantage of the particular innovation relative to the status quo. If a crisis situation appears, use it as a lever for introducing an innovation.

- Either introduce innovations compatible with the values of the target system, or work towards the emergence of values within the target system compatible with the innovation, or interpret the innovation to the target system in a manner consistent with its existing values.

- Formulate the innovation in such a way that it can be experienced initially in part, or by a limited portion of the target system.

- Make the innovation as easy as possible to explain or demonstrate.

- Bring the innovation to the target system rather than waiting for the innovation to be discovered by the target.

- Formulate the innovation at a level of complexity that can be accommodated by the target system. (This does not mean just 'make it simple' – if the target can handle complexity, oversimplification is not a virtue; on the other hand, if it can't, simplify).

- Use the means of communication that the target system itself uses.

- Try to gain the support for the innovation of people and organizations the target system respects as equals (gain 'peer support').

- Gain the support of those the target regards as 'opinion leaders'; they tend to be well educated, cosmopolitan and of high social status.

- Present a clear, unified and unambiguous message in favour of the innovation.

Source: Jack Rothman, *Planning and Organizing for Social Change: Action Principles from Social Science Research*, Columbia University Press, New York & London, 1974, pp. 417–83.

formed through argument in a forum in which all parties are asked to listen to argument, be open to persuasion, and thus be guaranteed that the best argument will prevail and be implemented.

The most important thing to be avoided is the government (or any other party) using the time of open and inclusive consultation as a *strategy*. Just as lying becomes ineffective when people stop believing the utterances of the liar, so consultation becomes ineffective once it has been used for strategic purposes: to legitimise an already decided policy, or simply to make a government look 'consultative', for instance. A failed consultation (in this sense) is worse than no consultation at all, because it contaminates all future attempts by that government or agency to engage with the public.

The time for open consultation is when periodic in-depth reappraisals of city policy are being conducted. These should occur at least every ten years, to make sure objectives and current policy settings are on track, and still in line with what the community wants for the city. This idea is discussed later, in relation to the Aarhus Convention. Governments should act as facilitators of such events; they should not expect to enter them with a program already decided. Within the forum, government leaders can act as policy advocates if they have strong beliefs about particular policy lines – and if they do not they should not pretend otherwise simply in order to look 'leaderly'. But the policy program should emerge from the forum. After that, strategy can take over to turn the policy into action.

There is very little public participation at the policy reappraisal stage in Australia on the whole; there is more likely to be lengthy and expensive participation through tribunals, inquiries and courts during the implementation of policy. This is entirely the wrong way around. Large numbers of planning appeals, for example, are an indicator of policy and strategy failure rather than of healthy democratic practice. There must be exhaustive deliberation on policy, and once policy is decided it should be implemented. Sometimes strategy is needed to innovate and overcome institutional resistance.

INDICATORS

Finally, it is essential to know when the target has been reached, or by how much the policy has fallen short. As Einstein is reputed to have once said, 'not all that can be counted counts, and not all that counts can be counted'. But countable, that is quantitative, indicators, such as the speedometer on the car, give the most precise results. It is important to count what can be counted, while remembering Einstein's point and not trying to quantify what does not lend itself to counting but must be included in some other way because it is important. The point is to measure strategy and policy effectiveness *accurately*, using both numbers and other measurement criteria. This practice has been adopted with varying success in the following examples.

The government-owned land development corporation of New South Wales (Landcom) has adopted 30 key indicators to evaluate its progress towards the ecologically sustainable development of housing in the State (see Box 6.3). These indicators include quantitative targets. For example, under Indicator No. 1 *Integrated urban water cycle management* we find: 'Landcom's target is to incorporate in all projects water conservation measures that will reduce the use of potable (drinking) water by up to 40% over the five years to 30 June 2008. The foresight already shown by the Corporation has brought it more than halfway towards this target in its first year of TBL (triple bottom line) reporting, achieving an estimated 22.3% reduction in potable water use during 2002/2003.'[14] We can allow Landcom its boast here. Not quite so good was the result under Indicator No. 8 *Energy efficiency*. The target was to achieve a 40 per cent reduction in greenhouse emissions from all Landcom developments over five years. A 10 per cent reduction was reported up to 2003.

The BedZed development, discussed in chapter 2, has been monitored by the Biffaward Program on Sustainable Resource Use, which provides information about the flow of resources through the UK economy. The Biffaward study used a life-cycle assessment method developed by the UK Building Research Establishment to measure the energy and greenhouse gas emissions embodied in the building materials. In other words, it was the 'ecological footprint' or 'ecological rucksack' of the buildings that was assessed, not their environmental impact in operation.

The main construction materials used at BedZed were assessed against twelve environmental indicators: climate change, fossil fuel depletion, ozone depletion, human toxicity to air, human toxicity to water, waste disposal, water extraction, acid deposition, ecotoxicity, eutrophication (adding nutrients to water), summer smog and minerals extraction. The environmental impact of each BedZed building material was compared with the impact of a comparable conventional material: reclaimed steel with new steel, local oak weatherboarding with preserved softwood timber weatherboarding, timber-framed

Box 6.3 LANDCOM NEW SOUTH WALES: INDICATORS OF SUSTAINABLE HOUSING (main headings)

1   Integrated urban water cycle management.

2   Moderate-income housing provision.

3   Effectiveness of community consultation.

4   Community facilities.

5   Welcome programs to help clients with occupation of new housing.

6   Consumer education on sustainable living.

7   Reuse and recycling of construction and demolition materials.

8   Energy efficiency.

9   Influencing design of building products to improve sustainability.

10   Sustainable or renewable energy supply.

11   Native vegetation management.

12   Riparian corridor management (streams and creeks).

13   Conservation of indigenous heritage.

14   Conservation of non-indigenous heritage.

15   Regulatory compliance with environmental legislation.

16–21   Profitability indicators.

22   Financing capacity.

23   Financial return to government

24   Job creation.

25   Demonstration projects.

26   Internal and external training.

27–28   Supplier pre-qualification (sustainability conditions for suppliers).

29   Stakeholder relationships.

30   Aboriginal employment opportunities.

31   Employee satisfaction.

32   Employee retention rate.

33   Energy use and greenhouse emissions of Landcom itself.

34   Strategic and complex development projects.

Source: Landcom NSW, *The Measures We Take*, Landcom NSW, Sydney, 2003, pp. 26–32.

windows with aluminium windows, recycled aggregate (crushed waste concrete from demolition sites) with 'virgin aggregate' (stone mined and crushed in the United Kingdom), for example. The environmental impacts were also compared with cost and ease of handling. The conclusion was that the life-cycle embodied energy and CO_2 emissions of building materials used in BedZed were at the lower end of the benchmark range for domestic dwellings. This is in addition to the fact that the BedZed buildings will be carbon neutral in operation over a 60 to 120-year period – they will be emitting zero net greenhouse gas into the atmosphere.

The Australian Institute of Urban Studies runs an ongoing project that is the equivalent of a state of the environment report card for metropolitan Melbourne.[15] Although entitled 'Environmental Indicators for Metropolitan Melbourne', the bulletins don't in fact contain much in the way of quantitative indicators; instead, they report hopeful examples (case studies) purporting to show that Melbourne is improving its environmental performance. One such example is the tunnelling of the Eastern Freeway extension under the Mullum Mullum Creek. This is regarded as a win for biodiversity, which it is, of course. But it is also a huge loss for greenhouse emissions. The report is strongest in its reporting of the location of endangered species around Melbourne: 5 mammals, 48 birds, 6 reptiles, 2 amphibians, 6 fish, 2 insects, 7 tree species and some 57 plants. What is really needed is a much more rigorous quantitative assessment for the metropolis of air and water quality, water consumption, waste production and recycling, ozone depletion, eutrophication, and greenhouse emissions by industry sector.

SAVINGS MULTIPLY

The German Wuppertal Institute for Climate, Environment and Energy (www.wupperinst.org) and the Rocky Mountain Institute in the United States (www.rmi.org) are two of the world's foremost independent institutes developing policies for sustainable development. In 1977 the two institutes collaborated to produce a book, *Factor 4, Doubling Wealth, Halving Resource Use*. It has gone through several revisions since (the latest edition was published in Australia in 1997 by Allen & Unwin). The book is a remarkable manifesto for feasible change in the world's technical production systems to reduce consumption of the natural environment. An important message that recurs throughout the book is that sustainability can best be achieved not by single 'big-ticket' changes but by multi-

Table 6.2 How savings in greenhouse gas ghg emissions from the private vehicle fleet could multiply*

*Public transport vehicles still also use fuel; these figures apply only to the private vehicle fleet, not to the transport sector as a whole.

Action	GHG reduction	Cumulative reduction
Reduce travel demand by 10%	0.9	0.9
Shift 10% of journeys to public transport	0.9*	0.9 x 0.9 = 0.81
Improve vehicle ghg emission performance by 10%	0.9	0.9 x 0.9 x 0.9 = 0.73
Improve fuel efficiency by 30%	0.7	0.9 x 0.9 x 0.9 x 0.7= 0.51
Obtain 20% energy from renewable sources	0.8	0.9 x 0.9 x 0.9 x 0.7 x 0.8 = 0.41

ple smaller changes that build on one another. In short, rethinking our everyday decisions and activities is the key to achieving the sort of cumulative changes that will reset our 'urban compass' towards sustainability.

For example, consider the following ways of improving the environmental performance of the private vehicle fleet through greenhouse gas (ghg) reduction (Table 6.2).

Each of the above smaller improvements multiplies to a situation in which greenhouse gas emissions are reduced by nearly 60 per cent. Each action can itself be built by a succession of yet smaller changes that also multiply: say five smaller changes that cumulatively produce a 10 per cent reduction in travel demand.

Savings multiply, and they often span professional domains. Professions are changing, but new trans-boundary professional networks also need to emerge. Such networks would be formed by people working in different spheres who are aware of the environmental imperatives, wish to act effectively to implement them, and are prepared to cross traditional professional lines to do so. The focus should be on solving problems and mustering the professional competencies to do this. Existing professional domains (such as architecture, landscape architecture, town planning, engineering, medicine and law) need to educate their practitioners about how to participate in these networks and provide them with the capacity to 'cross the lines'. The Planning Institute of Australia is leading change in this area, having decided a few years ago to redraw its own professional boundaries to accommodate a range of planning competencies, including social, economic and environmental planning. The narrow traditional approach of the planning profession to land use control has given way to a more inclusive, multi-disciplinary approach that focuses on urban issues and recognises their many causes. The institute is to be commended for this shift to a more reflexive, outward-looking stance (see www.planning.org.au).

Many of the small changes that multiply savings involve business and industry. As we have seen, business can make a major and far-sighted contribution to sustainability. Unfortunately, however, the short-run profit motive may overpower the long-term common interest. And politicians, professionals and businesses can misuse the language of sustainability to project an incomplete and misleading picture of their environmental performance. This can be done without lying, in the strict sense of the word, and is part of their strategy to counteract the demands of real sustainability. This misrepresentation is sometimes called 'greenwash' because it covers up with a 'green' appearance an underlying reality that is environmentally damaging. So while firms that make money from exploiting the environment must be part of the solution, they are also part of the problem.

POLICIES THAT PRETEND, OR 'GREENWASH'

Most firms see themselves as responsible not for shareholders' long-term wellbeing but for delivering short-run financial returns. Change is risky and complex. New technologies represent products that compete with existing ones. Therefore firms that exploit the environment have a considerable stake in continuing to do so in the way they always have. Nevertheless firms still have to cope with changing values in the community: consumers do *not* want the natural environment destroyed. One strategy that is less risky – and cheaper than real industrial change – is for their promotional associations and governments to represent industries as environmentally responsible without doing anything substantively different. Greenwash is not a lie; it's a half-truth. Two examples come to mind.

The timber industry today carries out logging of old-growth forests in just two Australian States: Victoria and Tasmania. The Timber Promotion Council (TPC) exists to promote the exploitation of Victoria's native forests. The TPC has developed a brand called 'ecoSelect' timber taken from these forests. The advertising material says: 'Australia is a world leader in sustainable forestry ... by specifying ecoSelect timber, or by buying the ecoSelect brand, you will be ensuring both the future growth of our forest assets and our continued enjoyment of one of Australia's most beautiful, natural and renewable resources.' The advertisement features a lady in a long white dress playing a cello (made of wood, of course) between two mature eucalypts: 'a beautiful expression of sustainable forestry', gushes the ad.

Native forests grow and decay according to their own life-cycle. Logging replaces a cycle of hundreds of years with one of tens of years. Logging also replaces the messy and diverse habitat of old-growth forests with tidy paddocks of trees and a habitat of reduced diversity. Antichinus, several species of sugar glider, mountain brushtail possums, species of bats, owlet nightjars and a variety of cockatoos, parrots and owls live in the trees. After an area is logged, the 'coupe' is firebombed, and most of the creatures die. Harvesting is the correct word, because wilderness is in the process reduced to farming – silviculture. Creek systems are filled with the muddy run-off from the soil churned up by the bulldozers.[16]

How many cellos are produced each year in Victoria? How many trees need to be felled to keep the whole musical instrument industry in business? Only a tiny proportion of the timber from native forests goes to make fine musical instruments and furniture. Most of it goes for much more mundane purposes, such as woodchips for paper, timber building materials, pallets and garden mulch – for which there exist perfectly adequate substitutes. What really keeps the industry going is woodchip exports. The logging industry could be replaced by plantation timber established on agricultural land. The human and cultural capital embodied in even such a fine instrument as a cello cannot be a substitute for the environmental capital that is destroyed in its making. It is true, of course, that in one sense forestry is a sustainable industry – the *industry* is sustained, the trees regrow. What is not sustained is the forest ecology, and the unique habitat that ancient forests provide for many species of animals, birds, plants, insects and fungi.

The worst logging offender is undoubtedly Tasmania, where the influence of the Green Party, once strong, was eliminated by agreement between the major parties to amend the constitution. As a result, some of the finest untouched forests on the planet, such as the forests of the Styx Valley, are being turned into monocultural paddocks of gum trees for woodchipping.[17]

Another example of greenwash comes from the privatised energy industry in Victoria. Under the Commonwealth Government's voluntary program to reduce the increase in greenhouse emissions, agreements were signed by the five major private producers of electricity in Victoria.[18] Notably absent from the agreements was any plan for demand management. Under the agreements, each producer had to submit to the government its own greenhouse gas inventories and action plans to 'reduce' emissions at each plant. What 'reduction' meant in this case, however, was not the *actual* reduction of emissions compared with the levels at a baseline year (such as 1990), but the *projected* emissions that *would have been* produced if the 'action plan' had not been implemented. In short, the aim was merely to produce electricity by burning coal with greater efficiency.

The Hazelwood Power Station in the Latrobe Valley in Victoria emitted 9.45 million tonnes of CO_2 in 1995–96. By the year 2000 – after the 'action plan' – the emissions were planned to be 15.1 million tonnes. The 'action plan', it was claimed, would save about 0.7 million tonnes, reducing the increase from 67 per cent to 60 per cent.[19] A reduction from a 67 to a 60 per cent *increase* is still a very big increase.

Contrast that performance with the plans of the industry before privatisation. The State Electricity Commission of Victoria (SECV), being accountable to the State Parliament, was required (by the then Labor Government) to make and implement a plan for the reduction of greenhouse gas emissions. In 1989 the SECV published a discussion paper which set out alternative strategies to balance the supply of and *demand for* energy to meet the target agreed at the Toronto conference on global warming, which was a 20 per cent reduction on 1988 levels of carbon dioxide emissions by 2005.[20]

The strategies included 'aggressive demand management' through extensive conservation and co-generation programs, increased use of natural gas, hydro and wind power for electricity generation, deferring construction of new coal-burning plant, reducing energy losses in both generation and transmission of electricity, retiring old plant early (notably the inefficient Hazelwood power station), tree planting (140,000 hectares) and reducing interstate export of electricity.[21] The SECV subsequently (between 1991 and 1995) set annual targets for emissions. The 1991 annual report showed that the 1990/91 target of 42 megatonnes of CO_2 had been exceeded by only 1.3 megatonnes. Important elements of the strategies foreshadowed in the 1989 discussion paper were being implemented. Particularly important was the three-year 'demand management plan', which included 36 programs designed to encourage reduced consumption of electricity by SECV customers.[22] All these encouraging plans were abandoned when the industry was privatised in 1996.

As a result of the prevalence of greenwash, the term 'sustainability' itself has begun to lose its meaning, sadly. Greenwash makes it extremely difficult for firms that are making a real impact in reducing consumption of the environment to distinguish themselves from those that just want you to think they are. If, as Bjørn Lomborg correctly argues, scepticism about the claims of the environmental movement is warranted, how much more sceptical do we need to be about the claims of firms and governments to be engaging in 'sustainable' practices? Scepticism means examining the reality behind the rhetoric, looking for truth. It should never turn into a nihilistic cynicism about the possibility of change.

INSTITUTIONAL LANDSCAPES AND BARRIERS

Institutions are the procedures and routines, norms, beliefs and conventions, organisations and networks that govern collective action in what is sometimes called the 'polity' or 'political economy'. As we said, sometimes policy cannot make headway or is deliberately blocked and resisted. Then it is necessary to look at the rules of the game. The term 'institution' is actually a little misleading, because it suggests an object, or at least a place with an address. It is no such thing, though it may have many addresses, both actual and virtual. It is really something more like a landscape.

Imagine a landscape composed of hills and valleys, vegetation, soils and rocks, flora and fauna. Policy, like water, is the output of this landscape – flowing in a particular direction, around the hills and down the valleys and carving channels as it flows, in fact itself shaping the landscape. So when environmentalist Stephen Dovers writes that 'institutions for sustainability' should be 'adaptive' and display the characteristics of persistence (where policy making is consistent over time), purposefulness (based on the purposes of sustainability), information richness (where the best information is sought), sensitivity to new information, inclusivity of the full range of interests, and flexibility (being prepared to experiment and innovate), that is just the start.[23] All this is needed, but it is essential to remember that it is impossible to design institutions afresh; like cities and landscapes, they are already there.

Green institutions, like green cities, will be reshaped little by little so that the output of the institutional landscape flows in the direction of sustainability. This is a difficult, long-term process that means changing the procedures and routines, norms, beliefs and conventions, organisations and networks that construct the landscape. Institutional landscapes vary from nation to nation, so specifying universal principles for 'green institutions' is not very useful. Every different institutional landscape needs to be surveyed and understood before reshaping it can be attempted. For green cities to be produced in Australia, change is needed across the Australian institutional landscape. Two key regions of that landscape are in particular need of such reform: housing and transport.

HOUSING

The Australian housing system has been shaped over the years since World War II to ensure that enough housing is built to satisfy demand, and that what is built stands up safely and pleases consumers over a reasonably wide range of income. The Australian dream is said to be the detached house and garden – and nothing will shift it! Certainly there is a lot to be said for detached houses and gardens, but it's not consumer preferences that are the problem. In recent years Australians have embraced terrace housing and flats: note the willingness of those who can afford it to pay high prices for these. What they are often paying for is a brand new dwelling that requires less maintenance and offers increased access to urban services: what the press tend to call 'an urban lifestyle'. But this higher-density housing is often no more sustainable than its low-density counterpart, simply because the housing is not built with energy efficiency, noise insulation, public transport access and greenspace preservation in mind.

Four features of the institutional landscape are primarily responsible for the general unsustainability of Australian housing: the central objectives of the housing system that govern policy at Federal and State levels, the dominant system of housing tenure and provision, the structure of the building and land development industries, and the regulation and finance of housing. All these institutional features play on the behaviour of consumers, who are then often unfairly blamed for choosing unsustainable housing.

There have from time to time been inquiries into 'housing affordability', but none so far into housing sustainability. There is no overall objective in the Federal and State policy systems such as this: 'To ensure that the design, construction, maintenance and improvement of all housing in Australia makes progress towards ecological sustainability.'

That said, most of the State development agencies, essentially government-owned development corporations, have taken on the objective of sustainability in the form of the 'triple bottom line': economic growth, social responsibility and environmental sustainability (Box 6.4). For instance, the NSW land corporation, Landcom, asserts on its website that 'Sustainable development and the protection of the environment form our core principles. Landcom is committed to the principles of Ecologically Sustainable Development (ESD) and endeavours to incorporate these principles in all our projects and day-to-day business decision making.'[24] These public realm institutions have the capacity to act as key 'change agents' within the broader urban development industry, demonstrating the possibilities for constant ecological improvements in the design, construction and use of housing and other buildings.

In housing tenure, social housing appears only as welfare housing for the poorest of the poor, and is under-funded. There is never enough public housing to meet demand. Australia, unlike Europe, has almost no social housing for the middle class. Yet it is the social housing sector (such as the Peabody Trust in England and the housing associations of Sweden), strongly influenced if not directly provided by local government, that has made most of the strides towards sustainable housing in Europe. This is partly because the primary aim of the social housing sector is to make affordable and sustainable homes, not to make profits, and partly because it is a large enough and strong enough sector to pursue this aim and survive. The recent creation of the Brisbane Housing Company, a joint initiative of the Brisbane City Council and the Queensland State Government, is a welcome sign that the European social housing model is again receiving support in Australia.

The main problem with Australia's housing industry is that it is frag-

Box 6.4 TRIPLE BOTTOM LINE REPORTING

The 'triple bottom line' is a term coined by author and management consultant John Elkington. The term refers to the three elements of accountability: social, environmental and financial. The notion of reporting against the three components (or 'bottom lines') of economic, environmental and social performance is directly tied to sustainable development. Triple bottom line (TBL) accounting requires measurements of social and environmental success, aiming to provide information to show how sustainable an organisation's or a community's operations are.

The perspective taken is that for an organisation (or a community) to be sustainable (a long-run perspective) it must be financially secure (as evidenced through such measures as profitability), it must minimise (or ideally eliminate) its negative environmental impacts, and it must act 'in conformity with societal expectations'. The last of these seems a rather weak requirement and there is no statement about social justice or equity even though this seems to be implied.

The difficulty is in integrating the three dimensions into a coherent whole. The consensus is that the 'financial' aspects are best established first (what a surprise!), followed by 'environmental', with 'social' bringing up the rear. Integrated TBL accounting and reporting implies that the three measures of value-adding are incorporated into a single measurement. So, for example, economic value-added measures would be adjusted for the environmental and social dimensions.

At the macro level, integration efforts are already in existence – the Index of Sustainable Economic Welfare (ISEW) adjusts normal measures of welfare by subtracting costs such as those associated with unemployment, commuting, automobile accidents, and all forms of environmental pollution. Such approaches imply moving towards a single set of accounts, but there is as yet – and many would argue there is unlikely ever to be – a single 'currency' into which the value added or destroyed in each of these three dimensions can be converted. For the moment, the aim is convergence (towards a single set of accounts), recognising that different indicators will often need to be assessed in different ways, sometimes quantitative, sometimes qualitative. The initial task is to identify a limited set of key *performance indicators* for each bottom line, with a constant eye on the degree to which – and how – progress can be measured and integrated into an overall set of accounts.

Source: John Elkington, *Cannibals with Forks: The Triple Bottom Line of 21st Century Business*, Capstone, Oxford, 1997.

mented and over-competitive. Construction costs are driven down through relentless competition, but little consideration is given to the cost of owning and maintaining poorly insulated and badly sited dwellings. Despite the good examples of sustainable housing provided by a few large builders (such as Lend Lease), and the individual examples of new and renovated housing, the bulk of new housing and renovation is conventional. Most new housing is constructed by small builders. Around 70 per cent of new detached housing is constructed by builders who complete no more than four houses in a year, and 85 per cent by those who construct fewer than ten.[25]

Mostly, builders purchase land from a land development company, rather than buying 'raw land'. What is built is what builders and developers think consumers will buy. This in turn is strongly influenced by the competitive nature of the market and the desire of builders to safeguard their business. The layout and choice of building materials is heavily influenced by what has sold houses in the past. As one American proponent of sustainable housing put it, 'consumers are a rear view mirror'. The building firm's aim is to win a contract ahead of its competitors, so it will tend to choose a design or building material that it can be sure will not price it out of the market or lose it market share. Builders and developers work closely together. The builder's success in marketing a house depends in part on the success of the developer in marketing a housing estate.

The developer has to convince a house buyer to purchase a vacant lot on their estate rather than estates promoted by competing developers. The builder's task is to convince the buyer to contract it to build one of its designs on the vacant lot. The developer controls the design, layout and release of allotments as well as the location of display sites. The success of both depends on the success of each in performing their respective tasks: high sales rates by builders translate into more lot sales. Dwelling sales depend on how many potential buyers visit the estate. These highly competitive circumstances and the division of labour between builders and developers may be good for efficiency, but they are bad for sustainability, because trying out different technologies that may cost a bit more initially is risky. And simply because of the pressure to survive, every small competitor must be averse to such risk.

Very few individual builders or developers within a competitive market will take the steps necessary to guarantee housing sustainability. And the organisations representing the building and development industries may well lobby against 'regulation'. They would prefer as little change as they can get away with. Who can blame them? But in fact the market system can operate perfectly well under different rules, and only the Australian Federal Government (the Commonwealth) can provide these rules of play. No individual developers or builders will be prevented from doing their jobs as long as what they are obliged to do applies to all equally.

The market, as it stands, is threaded with taxes and subsidies, regulations and incentives. Reforming the Building Code of Australia so that it reflects the objectives of sustainability, for example, has been considered for years. But no action has been taken. Instead it has been left to the States to create their own regulatory codes. This makes no sense, and places the States in competition with one another for housing investment.

The Commonwealth State Housing Agreement (CSHA), created after World War II as part of Australia's 'welfare state', is the most important of a range of institutions through which the Commonwealth provides financial assistance to housing consumers. It is mainly concerned with funding public housing (provided by the States), but also provides funding for other types of tenure. The main identified funding priorities of the CSHA are public housing, community housing, crisis accommodation, Aboriginal rental housing, private rental support and home ownership support. Sustainability should become a primary objective of the CSHA.

The full range of regulation, taxation and subsidy in the institutional landscape is far too complex to describe here. Suffice it to say that the principle is that the whole landscape should be carefully examined and subjected to ecological reform. Here we should remember that it is actually not new housing, but existing housing, that creates the greatest problem in terms of unsustainability. New housing never makes up more than 2 per cent of the housing stock in any one year. The greatest challenge is refitting existing housing stock to improve its environmental performance, especially housing located in the ageing 'middle ring' suburbs constructed before and after World War II: in short, we need to focus on doing something about what the institutional landscape of the past has shaped. Targets need to be set to reduce the consumption of fossil-fuelled energy throughout the entire housing stock. Here the housing sector itself begins to overlap with the energy sector. The creation of a renewable energy industry becomes a very high priority. It is no use creating a demand for renewable energy unless the energy industry is equipped to meet it. So the institutional landscape of energy comes into view. We have more to say about the changing institutional landscape of energy in the UK below. And as we saw above, privatisation of the energy industry in Victoria actually moved that State away from sustainability.

TRANSPORT

As we saw in chapter 5, transport policy, even more than housing, is beset with institutional roadblocks. To sum up the discussion set out in chapter 5, the main barriers to green transport in Australia appear to be threefold. First there is the absence of action at Federal level to change funding priorities. Federal governments have continued to pour funds into roads without examining their effect on ecological sustainability. Between 1975 and 2000 the Commonwealth Government spent about $40 billion on roads compared with about $1.9 billion on railways.[26] At State level, the way that road space is paid for (in block payments for vehicle registration and exchange) compared with the way that public transport is paid for (in fares at point of sale) introduces an incentive to use the car wherever the choice between the two is available.

Second, the institutional divisions between road building and public transport agencies and the absence of systemic planning of transport as a whole have combined to prevent integrated solutions to transport problems being developed. In all the metropolitan cities of Australia the road-building agencies have consistently demonstrated their supreme competence (at road building) and command of strategy. They are far-sighted, and are continually developing major motorway projects for the next twenty years and beyond. Whenever a politician has wanted a project to impress the voters, a future motorway, bridge or tunnel can be produced. The agencies share an ethos of public service and an admirable *esprit de corps*. But their professional competence is focused on road engineering, and their foresight extends neither to the conditions of sustainability, nor to the transport system as a whole. Where they have engaged in transport planning, it is from the perspective of road engineering and its techniques, and is heavily biased towards road-building solutions.

The public transport agencies, on the other hand, have traditionally been concerned with reducing the 'public transport deficit' (that is, basically, the excess of annual expenditure over returns in fares) and running trains, trams and buses as more or less independent enterprises.[27] Planning metropolitan public transport as fully integrated systems to compete with the private transport system – cars, trucks and roads – has never been undertaken. In the 1980s in Melbourne, steps in this direction were taken with the creation of the Public Transport Corporation. The decline of patronage across the public transport system was reversed following the introduction of a single ticketing system that is valid for trains, trams and buses. Patronage of the services grew and plans for continuous extension and renewal of infrastructure and rolling stock were drawn up. But in the 1990s this direction was put into reverse following the election of a government that was saturated with market ideology – the Kennett Government. The public transport system was fully privatised in 1999, making integrated planning impossible. By 2003, no improvement in service could be noted over what had already been achieved by the Public Transport Corporation before privatisation.[28]

This was not, of course, how privatisation was supposed to work. On the contrary, the introduction of incentive-based subsidies was meant to spur the private operators to such heights of service quality that patronage of trains and trams would rise rapidly (Swanston Trams by 40 per cent and Bayside Trains by 84 per cent), eventually eliminating the need for subsidies altogether. The transport deficit would finally be conquered. Unfortunately, the anticipated jump in patronage following privatisation did not occur, largely because of the absence of integrated planning and the narrow focus of the operators on maximising short-term profits and reducing their financial risk.[29] The Victorian Government was forced to pump money into the system.

Even so, in 2002 the major private operator, the UK firm National Express, withdrew from the field. The public transport deficit remains the same as – or higher than – before privatisation. In a virtual monopoly situation, private operators can cream funds off the government through implicit threat of withdrawal.[30] Yet the State Government of Victoria remains unwilling to unscramble the system. Having been forced to take over most of the metropolitan public transport system, in 2004 the government decided to re-privatise the operation of the trams and railways and consolidate them in two private monopolies (one for trams and one for trains), at an additional subsidy cost of over $1 billion. This, the government explained, would not be any more expensive than public ownership. But why not, then, continue with public ownership? The promised quality of service is no better than before the first privatisation, strong central planning and co-ordination of the services is more difficult after privatisation than if the system were publicly owned, and there is the near certainty of future rent-seeking by the private monopolists.

Fortunately, in all the State capitals except Melbourne, responsibility for planning public transport still remains in governmental hands, so it is still possible that institutional change towards a fully integrated and planned system along the lines of the Zürich Transport Community (see chapter 5) could, with strong political will, be created. The first city to do so will certainly gain a real economic advantage. The institutional system favoured in Europe involves strong central planning agencies that can capture the advantages of system-wide co-ordination of routes and timetables, with private companies subcontracted to run the services. Adelaide and Perth have both moved in this direction.

The third barrier is in people's minds and public documents. A range of arguments in formal policy documents and procedures supportive of road building have excluded discussion of alternatives. These arguments, which marginalise the problem of sustainability, amount to a common vocabulary knitting together the groups, organisations and agencies that support ever more expenditure on roads. For example, 'balanced transport' is a favourite way of hiding an imbalance of transport expenditure between roads and urban public transport, a true application of 'doublethink' (from George Orwell's horrific vision of the future, portrayed so terrifyingly in his novel *Nineteen Eighty-Four*).[31]

In Perth, 'balanced transport' was a key part of the transport language of the late 1980s, and was the main objective of the Metropolitan Transport Strategy of 1995, but it has been successfully subverted by the road planners. A notable example reported by Carey Curtis (a transport planning scholar at Curtin University) was the justification for duplicating the Narrows Bridge, a major river crossing for north–south traffic travelling to and around the Perth city centre, so that there were twelve road traffic lanes instead of seven. 'Balance' was provided by the addition of a second dedicated bus lane. In another example, publicity by the State road-building agency – Main Roads Western Australia (MRWA) – suggested that the addition of extra traffic lanes on the freeway from the city to the northern suburbs would improve the environment by reducing emissions (by reducing congestion). Always ignored is the obvious and well-established fact that more roads lead to increased road traffic.[32]

Congestion has been consistently presented as if it were an externally inflicted malady of the city that could be overcome through corrective surgery, sometimes radical in scale and dramatic in consequence. Further, it has been asserted that such cures, by clearing the sclerosis of urban arteries, will improve the circulatory capacities and therefore the productivity of cities. Whether investment in new road infrastructure actually improves the economic performance of a city, as opposed to moving economic activities to different locations nearer the road, has never been shown. Even less has the comparison been made with a similar level of investment in public transport infrastructure.

Earlier institutional changes in the direction of environmental reform have seen to it that sustainability must be dealt with when a major road project is proposed. But this has not had the effect of giving sustainability any sort of priority. Projects do have to be subjected to analysis for their 'environmental impact'. The road agencies employ consultants to undertake studies documenting the environmental costs of the scheme. The reports of such studies published for the Sydney Orbital and the Ringwood to Frankston section of the Melbourne Ring Road dispose of sustainability in different ways. In the former, sustainability was taken care of by 'demand management' elsewhere on the road system – without specifying the measures that were to be taken. In the latter it was acknowledged that the proposed motorway was unsustainable, but this was regarded as compensated for by the alleged economic benefits resulting from increased travel on the roads. Increased travel is (implausibly) regarded as an economic benefit rather than an economic cost. The costs of such 'distant' factors as global warming were simply excluded from the cost–benefit calculations.

In a democracy, the public is supposed to blame government ministers for failure, which provides an incentive to promote desirable change. But how realistic is this? There are always powerful interests stridently lobbying government to conduct 'business as usual'. Within government, highly competent agencies equipped with specious arguments constantly advise ministers of the wisdom of the status quo. It takes both deep commitment and specialist knowledge to oppose these arguments. Yet politicians are just ordinary people representing ordinary people. Commitment we might be able to expect, but not specialist knowledge. Ministerial accountability in the short term, so necessary for democracy, can inhibit the holders of public office from radical change.

A passage in *The Discovery of Global Warming*, by Harvard historian Spencer Weart, nicely captures the essence of the process of institutional change:

When a group of citizens (in this case scientists) decides that their government should do more to address some particular concern, they face a hard task. The citizens have only a limited amount of time to spare, and officials are set in their bureaucratic ways. To accomplish anything – to bring about a new government program, for example – people must mount a concerted push. For a few years concerned citizens must hammer at the issue, informing the public and forging alliances with like-minded officials. These inside allies must form committees, draft reports, and shepherd legislation through the administration and legislature. Roadblocks will be put up by special interests that feel threatened by change, and the whole process is liable to fail from exhaustion. Typically such an effort only succeeds when it can seize a special opportunity, usually news events that distress the public and therefore catch the eye of politicians.[33]

Leadership must itself be structured into the institutional system, at a distance from day-to-day politics. The British Royal Commission into Environmental Pollution established in 1970 provides a precedent in warning of the long-term environmental effects of road building.[34] In Australia, institutional reform in pursuit of the ideal market has been conducted by the Industry Commission and the Australian Competition and Consumer Commission (ACCC). What is actually needed to accomplish across-the-board *environmental* reform is an Australian Environment Commission, staffed by a range of specialists, including ecological and institutional economists, and with the power and scope of the ACCC, to examine and audit the environmental effects of all institutions and industry sectors and propose to the government policies to rectify areas of environmental unsustainability.

INSTITUTIONAL CHANGE

The process of institutional landscape building is slow, complex and frequently contested. There is more than one tectonic force at work in any period. Even as the institutional structures of the welfare state and the United Nations were being thrown up in the postwar years (from the 1940s to the 1970s), a new movement reasserting the pre-eminence of the market was stirring. Even as the landscape of environmental protection was being shaped (from the 1960s to the 1990s), the forces for market-style 'reform' were shaking the foundations of social protection and eroding the institutions of environmental conservation. Deliberate institutional landscape building, whether liberalisation, socialisation, or environmentalisation, is beset by political setbacks and bureaucratic roadblocks. Yet there is institutional progress towards sustainability.

For example, evidence of institutional change can be found at the UK Government's website on sustainable development (http://www.sustainable- development.gov.uk/), where a wide range of government and partnership initiatives are reported on. The fact that the government has brought these initiatives together under one heading – 'sustainable development' – is itself significant. But this attempt to co-ordinate sustainability across departments is also backed by sustainability targets the government has set itself and on which its progress can be measured. There are 150 quantitative indicators and fifteen 'headline' indicators covering economic growth, social progress and environmental protection. The headline indicators, the government says on the website, 'are intended to raise public awareness of sustainable development, to focus public attention on what sustainable development means, and to give a broad overview of progress'.

The headline indicator on climate change, for instance, is of course emissions of greenhouse gas. Progress on emissions is easily accessible: it is charted on the internet and backed by quantitative data. The trend is down, and well in line with the country's Kyoto obligations. The stated objective is to 'continue to reduce our emissions of greenhouse gases now, and plan for greater reductions in the longer term'. The British Government's aim is to reduce greenhouse gases to 80 per cent of the baseline year 1990 by 2010 (a 20 per cent reduction). It is expected that this objective will be met – it may even be bettered.

Not all the institutional news is good. Headline indicator number 11 (H 11) is 'road traffic', and here the trend is relentlessly upward. The objective is: 'to improve choice in transport; improve access to education, jobs, leisure and services; and reduce the need to travel'. One must question, given the indicator, why the objective is not simply 'to reduce traffic on the roads'. The answer is obvious. If that were the objective, the government would have failed dismally, so the government has changed the objective to one which bears no relationship at all to the indicator. If this is supposed to be 'spin', it is a feeble attempt that should deceive no one. A much more powerful spin would be to admit failure and promise to do better! Still, the indicator is itself transparent and the government is, in all fairness, to be congratulated for publishing it. The transport field in Britain seems to be just as beset by institutional blockages as its counterpart in Australia is.

As a stimulatory peak in the institutional landscape, the Carbon Trust was created by the Blair Government in March 2001. This is an independent non-profit company, funded by the government and the regions (Scotland and Wales). It was set up on the recommendation of the Advisory Committee on Business and the Environment (ACBE), to take the lead in generating a low-carbon industry in the United Kingdom. The Carbon Trust has three main objectives: i) to ensure that UK businesses and the public sector meet ongoing targets for carbon dioxide emissions; ii) to improve the competitiveness of UK industry through resource efficiency; and iii) to support the development of a UK industry that capitalises on the innovation and commercial value of low-carbon technologies both nationally and internationally.

Acknowledging the real target for climate change mitigation, the CEO of the trust, Tom Delay, said, 'Tackling climate change is a huge challenge for the United Kingdom. We are on target to meet our Kyoto obligation, but Kyoto is just the start. Stabilising CO_2 concentrations in the atmosphere needs global emission cuts of 60 per cent or more over the next 50 years. We need to move quickly to decouple the growth in CO_2 emissions from economic growth.' In February 2003, the Department of Trade and Industry and the Carbon Trust published a report proposing that the UK fuel cell technology industry should become a significant player in the world zero emission fuel cell market.

In the regulatory valleys, the UK Government has established the Renewables Obligation. This is the government's means of encouraging the growth of renewable energy. It requires all licensed electricity suppliers in England and Wales to supply a specified proportion of their electricity from renewables, and provides a number of paths to compliance. Individual suppliers are responsible for demonstrating compliance to the regulator, unattractively titled OFGEM, through a system of Renewables Obligation Certificates (ROCs).

Annual targets – and they increase each year – have been set up to 2010/11. Renewables cover landfill and sewage gas, hydroelectric power, wind energy, co-firing of biomass from energy crops, geothermal, tide and wave power, and photovoltaics.

In a creative use of a governed market, ROCs can be traded, thus allowing those who have surpassed their obligation to sell electricity to those suppliers who have been unable to purchase enough renewables-generated electricity. Individual suppliers can also choose to 'buy out' their obligation. The buy-out price is currently set at £30.51 per megawatt hour. All payments are then recycled to those suppliers who have chosen to demonstrate compliance by presenting ROCs to OFGEM. The aim is that by 2010, 10 per cent of the United Kingdom's electricity should be supplied from renewable sources.

A very different example of institutional change, from a very different part of the world, is the integrated planning of the city of Curitiba in Brazil's Paraná Province.[35] Curitiba, a metropolis of 1.6 million, is internationally known for its sustainable urban development. The best-known feature of the plan is the integration of traffic management, transportation and land use planning, with transport being viewed very much from the perspective of personal movement, as outlined in chapter 5. Most of the central business district has been transformed into walking precincts, including a 24-hour shopping mall, restaurants and cafés, plus a street of flowers with gardens tended by street kids.

Nearly one-fifth of the city is parkland – there are over 80 square kilometres of green space. Volunteers have planted 1.5 million trees along the streets. The city has 200 kilometres of bicycle paths. An all-bus rapid transport network with special bus-only avenues has been created along main roads that also form axes for the city's growth. The 'speedy bus' runs along a direct line and stops only at tubular stations designed to move passengers quickly. Feeder buses bring passengers to transfer stations called 'district terminals', and local urban development and commercial activity has grown up around these.

Economic development has followed in the wake of sustained planning. The citizens can boast an average income per person that is 66 per cent higher than that of Brazil as a whole. The city's 30-year economic growth rate is running at 7.1 per cent, much higher than the national average of 4.2 per cent. Curitiba has one of highest rates of car ownership – a significant indicator of wealth – in Brazil, as well as high population growth. Yet car *use* has fallen. Curitiba has the highest public ridership of any Brazilian city (about 2.14 million passengers a day), and it registers the country's lowest rates of air pollution and per capita petrol consumption.

Curitiba's buses are privately run by ten companies but managed by a quasi-public company. There is public–private collaboration: public sector concerns (safety, accessibility and efficiency) are matched with private sector goals (such as low maintenance and operating costs). The bus companies receive no subsidies; instead, all fares collected go to a central fund and companies are paid on the basis of distance travelled. Curitiba's buses carry 50 times more passengers than they did 20 years ago, but people spend only about 10 per cent of their annual income on transport. An inexpensive 'social fare' promotes equality, benefiting poorer residents settled on the city's periphery. A standard fare is charged for all trips, meaning shorter rides subsidise longer ones. One fare can take a passenger 70 kilometres.

The strategic vision that has informed all aspects of Curitiba's planning since 1965 was stated by its visionary former mayor, Jaime Lerner, who led the city's transformation: 'There is no endeavour more noble than the attempt to achieve a collective dream. When a city accepts as its mandate its quality of life; when it respects the people who live in it; when it respects the environment; when it prepares for future generations, the people share responsibility for that mandate, and this shared cause is the only way to achieve that collective dream.'[36]

Strong political leadership and institutional continuity have been essential to long-term implementation of the city's plan. Lerner, now governor of the State of Paraná, worked as an architect on the city's 1965 Master Plan. A very important ingredient of institutional continuity is the Urban Planning Institute of Curitiba (IPPUC), which Lerner helped found. IPPUC provides a permanent and independent source of ideas. The city's current mayor, Cassio Taniguchi, was a senior IPPUC official for seven years. The combination of core values expressed in the city plan and IPPUC's creation allowed planning for efficiency and sustainability even during the military dictatorship and during times of economic crisis in Brazil, and despite large numbers of poor migrants flowing into the city.

The lessons that can be learned from this example are first, that a plan needs to articulate strong, locally generated core values. The time for participation and debate about these values is while the plan is being made and when it is being reviewed. In this respect it is worth taking note of the principle stated in the Aarhus Convention: 'Each party [to the Convention] shall provide for early public participation, when all options are open and effective public participation shall take place.' Second, there is a need for an independent municipal authority such as IPPUC, to provide continuity and implement plans, as well as to monitor planning and research to improve future efforts. Third, integrated planning across departmental boundaries is needed. Most importantly, the transport system needs to be planned and linked to the land use plan.

Almost certainly, risk-taking political leadership is also needed. A new crop of 'sustainability champions' has recently made inroads into deeply embedded institutional barriers worldwide. London would not have its highly regarded 'congestion charge', which has made the inner city habitable again, without the leadership of an energetic mayor, Ken Livingstone. Portland, in the US State of Oregon, would not have its 'urban growth boundary' and effective public transport, making it one of the more sustainable cities in the United States (though still unsustainable in global terms), without the leadership of its mayor and the State Governor. It seems certain that a requirement of such leadership is a structure of representation and articulation for the metropolis itself. In only one city in Australia does this occur: Brisbane.

It is sometimes said that a representative metropolitan government would necessarily rival the State. This need not be so. The experiment of localising planning power was tried in Britain and failed. London was only given back its metropolitan authority because the city was wallowing in a tangle of committees and quasi-government authorities, and no vision to rival the great cities of Europe – such as Paris – was forthcoming. The great cities of Australia also need a truly metropolitan focus of local government.

THE THIRD WAY

This has been a long and complex chapter, and we will conclude by attempting to sum up. The green city is a working project, not a utopia. New green cities are beginning to emerge in the midst of old brown ones. This movement is being driven by the community to which we all belong. In saying this, however, 'community' has to be understood in the broadest possible sense: not as a distinct entity, different from, say, 'government' or 'the private sector', but as the totality of the individuals and the organisations and cultures through which they act collectively. Government, social action groups and markets are all tools for collective action, which, with other tools, creates a society.

During the 20th century, society learned that it had to abandon growth as its guiding economic principle and find some other principle that would combine an increase in wellbeing and justice with the capacity to extend these values into the future. The clumsy term given to that principle is 'sustainability'. Society also learned that both democratic government and the market were powerful social tools, but that the use of one as a principle to the exclusion of the other led to disaster. There is much to be learned in the 21st century about how to govern better, and how to combine government – regulation – with markets and/or other means for social co-ordination. This groping towards a richer understanding of collective action has been called the 'third way'. This third way is a broad path, and what we see in most societies is a meandering course, heading sometimes towards the market principle and sometimes back again towards government. The third way needs also to revisit a third principle of organisation: democracy. We need to understand that democracy makes contradictory demands: for both *effective* governance and *consultative* governance. Finding creative ways to reconcile those precepts, in fact and not just in words, poses a major challenge for the green city.

The green city will not be created by a 'blueprint plan', or even a planning process dominated by a single profession. It is rather odd, when one comes to think about it, that town planning, or city planning, ever became a profession in the first place, claiming its own special techniques and practices. The best planning will always be integrative, outward-looking and self-critical. Green cities will be created by policy processes and institutional landscapes under the motive force of multiple professional and political actors. So in thinking of the green city it is absolutely necessary to think across traditional boundaries, both spatial and institutional. How to keep these outward connections alive in the mind while engaging in focused action in a particular policy domain or on a particular topic is another challenge for the green city.

If horizontal, outward connections are important, so also are vertical connections: from the small scale to the large. Much change will be incremental, an aggregate of small changes all heading in the same general long-run direction. Occasionally, external fortuitous or even deliberate shocks may trigger an avalanche of change cascading through policy systems. But what has to be appreciated is that a small policy shift may have systemic consequences. Indeed, a number of small changes, if they are coherent, multiply the effects the way laser light does (all the photons moving in parallel). On the other hand, some policy systems cannot be changed without action at the scale of the larger system: urban transport systems would be one example. Without pushing a biophysical analogy too far, it may be helpful sometimes to view a policy system as an ecology, with mutually supporting elements, 'keystone' organisations and ideas, and boundaries that are difficult to define.

There are two tiers of action, reflecting the two elements in the policy system: the game and the rules, policy making and institutions. Effective policy making requires definition of long-term goals, and specific short-term targets. Then there is the hurdle of institutional barriers. Action will meet resistance. Overcoming that resistance demands strategy, plus 'battlers' within institutions and 'sustainability champions' outside the institutional walls. Finally, measurement of progress requires indicators. It is easy to state this sequence, but it is just as important to understand the complexities and subtleties involved in carrying it through. Why should we be surprised or shocked that green ideals can become subverted into greenwash, or that there are contradictory requirements inherent in democracy, or that there is a place for both moments of free and open consultation and moments of decisive strategy? This is the complex and subtle policy world we live in, and only one thing is certain: there are no simple answers. That is what makes building the green city, a living project, interesting.

FURTHER READING

In *Urban Future 21, A Global Agenda for Twenty-First Century Cities* (E. & F.N. Spon, London, 2000), the distinguished English planning scholar Sir Peter Hall and Dr Ulrich Pfeiffer survey the world of cities at the beginning of the third millennium. This is a book of huge scope, encompassing the geographical and the political, the developed and the developing world, description and prescription. The idea of the 'sustainable city' is at the core of their analysis. Two long chapters (4 and 5) address the matter of governance of sustainable cities. For those who want to pursue the question of self-aware and self-critical democracy, Ulrich Beck's book *Democracy Without Enemies* (Polity Press, Cambridge, 1998) is important. He asks: 'What if [industrial] society's necessities, functional principles and fundamental concepts are undermined, broken up and demystified with the same ruthlessness as were supposedly eternal truths of earlier epochs?' For an international take on greenwash, check out *Slow Reckoning, The Ecology of a Divided Planet* by Tom Athanasiou (Vintage, London, 1998). Sharon Beder, in *Global Spin* (Scribe, Melbourne, 2000), tells the story of greenwash in Australia. Finally, those who want to pursue the subject of democratic institutions and ecological sustainability should read Robyn Eckersley's brilliant analysis: *The Green State: Rethinking Democracy and Sovereignty* (MIT Press, Cambridge MA & London, 2004).

CHAPTER 7

GREEN-SHADED CITIES

Let's return to the poem at the start of this book. 'A green thought in a green shade' – Andrew Marvell's image is intriguingly ambiguous. This is both material and metaphysical poetry. It looks beyond human life. The poem is about a garden. A garden is a human artefact, of course, but it is also where we mostly experience the more than human world – nature. The poem conjures delight in the natural wealth a garden provides. Today humanity has the power to make the whole world into a garden. But do we want to? How do we want to relate to the more than human world that, entirely without human intervention, provides immense abundance of life, and support for humanity? Green cities 'in a green shade' would tread less heavily on that natural abundance.

'Green shade' speaks of protection from the heat of the sun, but importantly, and in a quite different sense, it also speaks of the many shades of green that cities of tomorrow will take on. Even though we may talk about the 'green city', there is no one approach to greenness. Every culture will interpret the green city in a different way. Every city will take on a different shade. Green must not be interpreted literally. In Australia, much of the land, for much of the time, is brown and red. The bluey green of the untidy gum tree, shading to pink, is more character-istic of the Australian landscape than the brighter greens of Europe. A dry ecology may be entirely appropriate for Australia – but even in the desert there are oases where one may 'stumble on melons'. Our European urban public gardens and parks are now also part of Australia's culturally diverse heritage.

Principles for green-shaded cities have been announced. The task for this century is to implement them. Our governments can readily develop the practical means to do so. There is no technological or scientific excuse for not acting. Those governments who continue to stall and call for further evidence and more research to justify action are deeply disingenuous: it would be more honest of them simply to repudiate the principles of urban sustainability and accept the consequences.

PRINCIPLES FOR GREEN-SHADED CITIES

Nothing can substitute for action, at the policy and at the institutional level. But there is also a place for rhetoric: the statements that declare ideals, capture the imagination, and fly the banners of sustainability. Green-shaded cities have their charters and principles.

In April 2002, *The Melbourne Principles for Sustainable Cities* were developed at a meeting organised jointly by the United Nations Environment Program and the Environment Protection Authority of Victoria. They articulate the following vision: 'To create environmentally healthy, vibrant and sustainable cities where people respect one another and nature, to the benefit of all.' The principles are stated in the imperative, for example: 'Recognise the intrinsic value of biodiversity and natural ecosystems, and protect and restore them' (Principle 3) (Box 7.1).

The Melbourne Principles build on earlier declarations, such as the important international statements made in Danish cities: the Aalborg Charter of European Cities and Towns Towards Sustainability[1] and the Århus Convention[2] (see Box 7.2). One statement in the Århus Convention stands out: 'Each party shall provide for early public participation, when all options are open and effective public participation shall take place.' All too often, public participation in Australia is either ineffective or too late – after the critical decisions have been made. The chronic conflicts in Australia's land use planning systems caused by high levels of planning appeals are a case in point. The appeal system that exists in each State and Territory is seen by many as a democratic safeguard, but in reality it functions as a costly and time-wasting check on the implementation

---

Box 7.1 THE MELBOURNE PRINCIPLES FOR SUSTAINABLE CITIES

1 Provide a long-term vision for cities based on: sustainability; intergenerational, social, economic and political equity; and their individuality.

2 Achieve long-term economic and social security. The elaboration states: 'Through fair allocation of resources, economic

Box 7.1 continues over page

strategies should seek to meet basic human needs in a just and equitable manner. In particular, economic strategies should guarantee the right to potable water, clean air, food security, shelter and safe sanitation'.

3 Recognise the intrinsic value of biodiversity and natural ecosystems, and protect and restore them.

4 Enable communities to minimise their ecological footprint. 'The ecological footprint of a city is a measure of the load on nature imposed by meeting the needs of its population'.

5 Build on the characteristics of ecosystems in the development and nurturing of healthy and sustainable cities. 'The characteristics of ecosystems include diversity, adaptiveness, interconnectedness, resilience, regenerative capacity and symbiosis'.

6 Recognise and build on the distinctive characteristics of cities, including their human and cultural values, history and natural systems.

7 Empower people and foster participation. 'The journey to sustainability requires broadly based support. Empowering people mobilises local knowledge and resources and enlists the support and active participation of all who need to be involved in all stages, from long term planning to implementation of sustainable development'.

8 Expand and enable cooperative networks to work towards a common sustainable future.

9 Promote sustainable production and consumption, through appropriate use of environmentally sound technologies and effective demand management. 'Demand management, which includes accurate valuations of natural resources and increasing public awareness, is a valuable strategy to support sustainable consumption'.

10 Enable continual improvement, based on accountability, transparency and good governance.

Source: United Nations Environment Programme (UNEP), *The Melbourne Principles for Sustainable Cities*, UNEP, Division of Technology, Industry and Economics, Integrative Management Series No. 1, 2003:
http://www.epa.vic.gov.au/Business_Sustainability/sustainable_cities.asp.

Box 7.2 THE ÅRHUS CONVENTION

The principles of the Århus Convention have now been converted into legislation by the European Commission, with a view to formal adoption by the European Parliament.

The aim of the convention, which was adopted in June 1998 in the Danish city of Århus, is specifically 'environmental justice'. It joins environmental rights to human rights. It acknowledges that people alive today owe an obligation to future generations. Article 1 of the convention, the 'objective', states:

> In order to contribute to the protection of the right of every person of present and future generations to live in an environment adequate to his or her health and wellbeing, each party shall guarantee the rights of access to information, public participation in decision-making, and access to justice in environmental matters in accordance with the provisions of this Convention.

Article 3 contains the general provisions. The main burdens of these are various obligations:

- to give members of the public open access to information without discrimination, to promote public environmental education and awareness as well as the means of obtaining information;

- to provide recognition and support to groups and organisations promoting environmental protection (and to ensure that the groups themselves also comply with the principles of the convention); and

- to ensure that the public have access to 'the possibility to participate' and access to justice in environmental matters without discrimination.

The rest of the articles contain quite specific instructions on *how* to provide for access to information, participation and environmental justice.

Source: United Nations Economic Commission for Europe (UNECE), *Convention on Access to Information, Public Participation in Decision-Making and Access to Justice in Environmental Matters*, UNECE, 1998:
www.unece.org/env/pp/documentse/cep43e.pdf.

of poorly conceived and poorly debated plans. We would do better to undertake much more thoroughgoing consultations as part of the plan-making process, so that we produce strategies and controls that reflect community aspirations (rather than functioning as mere developer roadmaps). These plans should then be rigorously implemented.

Under the Århus Convention, access to information is regarded as crucial for environmental justice, and recourse to a court of law – as a last resort – is allowed only in order to guarantee that the convention's provisions on access to information are upheld. The convention has the great advantage of specificity. It will be hard for signatories to wriggle out of its provisions.

An important threshold of environmental awareness in the architectural profession was reached at the World Congress of Architects held in Chicago in 1993. Architects from all parts of the world adopted a carefully crafted 'Declaration of Interdependence for a Sustainable Future' (the Chicago Declaration).

In that document the participants recognised that 'buildings and the built environment play a major role in the human impact on the natural environment and on the quality of life'. They came forward with a definition that amounts to an action sheet for design practice:

> Sustainable design integrates consideration of resource and energy efficiency, healthy buildings and materials, ecologically and socially sensitive land-use, and an aesthetic sensitivity that inspires, affirms, and ennobles; sustainable design can significantly reduce adverse human impacts on the natural environment while simultaneously improving quality of life and economic well being.[3]

The Chicago Declaration introduced the language of environmentalism into the architectural profession: 'We are ecologically interdependent with the whole natural environment; we are socially, culturally, and economically interdependent with all of humanity; sustainability, in the context of this *interdependence*, requires *partnership*, *equity*, and *balance* among all parties' (emphasis added).[4] In what became a blueprint for action, the International Union of Architects stated:

> We commit ourselves, as members of the world's architectural and building-design professions, individually and through our professional organisations, to:
> - place environmental and social sustainability at the core of our practices and professional responsibilities;

- develop and continually improve practices, procedures, products, curricula, services, and standards that will enable the implementation of sustainable design;
- educate our fellow professionals, the building industry, clients, students, and the general public about the critical importance of and the opportunities for sustainable design;
- establish policies, regulations, and practices in government and business that ensure sustainable design becomes normal practice;
- bring all existing and future elements of the built environment – in their design, production, use, and eventual reuse – up to sustainable design standards.[5]

This was surely evidence of a profession that had taken a 'reflexive turn' by making itself more aware of the natural environment in which it was working. For any self-aware professional, the products of technical knowledge and specialist labour cannot merely be seen as fine artefacts or wondrous machines. Reflexive urban professionals – architects, engineers, planners – are deeply aware that the objects of their labour – buildings, bridges, plans – are the living, *and lived in*, organisms of the green city.

The Chicago Declaration has inspired many local variations around the world. The Royal Australian Institute of Architects, through its Code of Professional Conduct and its Environment Policy, reaffirms the responsibility of the architectural profession to contribute to the quality and sustainability of the natural and built environments. The members of the profession in Australia are asked to:

> … affirm their commitment to the principles of this policy in the buildings they design and are responsible for constructing. The principles are:
> - Contribute to the quality and sustainability of the natural and built environments.
> - Reduce the use of fossil fuels.
> - Maintain or restore biodiversity.
> - Minimise the consumption of resources, especially those which are not renewable.
> - Minimise pollution of soil, air and water.
> - Maximise the health, safety and comfort of building users.
> - Increase general awareness of environmental issues.[6]

Box 7.3 A MANIFESTO FOR GREEN-SHADED CITIES

1 Ratify the Kyoto Protocol and work towards the next round of greenhouse gas reduction with a view to reducing greenhouse emissions by 60 per cent on the 1990 level by 2050.

2 Implement the UN Convention on Biological Diversity in urban settings.

3 Let the Commonwealth Government resume its responsibility to provide national leadership on urban sustainability by supporting ecological and social improvements to cities and suburbs.

4 Develop an Australian program for sustainable housing with a particular emphasis on enlarging the social housing sector.

5 Make housing sustainability a primary objective of the Commonwealth State Housing Agreement.

6 Reform the Building Code of Australia to reflect a priority for ecologically sustainable buildings, respecting the variability of regional ecological conditions across the continent.

7 Where greenfield development is necessary, design new city sectors or new towns that are fully equipped with urban services and public transport and connected to adjoining urban areas.

8 Let every municipality produce 'green structure' plans to connect and protect open space, particularly riparian areas and watercourses, creatively addressing the relationship between humans and the more than human world.

9 Place urban public transport in all Australian cities under fully integrated, publicly accountable planning and management, with a brief to maximise the use of existing rail infrastructure. Recognise that privatised public transport has failed. There is no place for publicly subsidised private monopolies in public transport.

10 Shift the balance of Commonwealth transport funding in favour of urban and regional public transport, cycling and pedestrian access, including assistance to the States to provide higher levels of service at lower prices to the travelling public.

11 Subject all new infrastructure projects to an audit of their contribution to greenhouse emissions, during both construction and use.

12 Facilitate the transition of urban systems to local supply, management and containment of energy, water and waste.

13 Legislate to require environmental labelling of all products and buildings, and environmental audits of all public companies.

14 Reform the planning system so that it requires full, democratic and effective public participation at the review stage, and restrict appeal rights after the adoption of a plan.

In this book we have tried to focus the debate on the environment in Australia on cities. We have shown that an urban lifestyle is not only compatible with global environmental responsibility; it is enhanced by it. The declarations, conventions and principles exhort us to act. We have made some specific proposals for immediate action. These are summarised above in Box 7.3. But such action will only occur if people are purposefully using the collective institutions of society. We now add our final thoughts, in the form of 'green reflections' on cities.

GREEN REFLECTIONS
IF YOU KNOW, YOU CAN ACT

Citizen action can push governments and business corporations to change their ways. Citizen action can sometimes be collective action – in rallies, campaigns and boycotts. There is nothing wrong with organised non-violent action against companies and governments that are damaging the environment. However, such action always takes time and energy that many workers simply don't have. It is hard enough balancing the time demands of paid work, families and leisure. But people can also act individually in the course of working for their family or organisation (government, community or business). To be effective, such action requires knowledge of the origins and environmental impact of products. At the supermarket (to use just one example), the labels of all products should provide clear and accurate information about the product's origin and environmental impact. Environmental labelling cannot be a voluntary matter; it must regulated by law. That is the only way to create the 'level playing field' for all producers. Otherwise the most devious and ingenious – rather than the most honest – will win market share, and the outcome will be determined not by truthful information but by 'spin' (and haven't we had enough of spin?).

SPREAD THE RISK

It is a sensible rule of investment to 'spread the risk'. There is a tendency for governments to put their faith in huge research projects to save the planet. Hundreds of millions of dollars are currently being provided by the Commonwealth Government, for instance, in a bid to develop ways of removing carbon dioxide gas from coal after it is burned (and then burying the carbon at depth in such a way that it will not seep back out into the atmosphere) or using coal to produce clean hydrogen before combustion. Similarly, there is a belief around in transport circles that all that is needed to reduce greenhouse emissions are fuel cell vehicles. Both these concepts may ultimately play a role in achieving sustainability, but they can also become ways of resisting change: they can lead to people believing that we can go on burning fossil fuel as we have been doing, and that we don't need to improve public transport. Many small improvements spread the risk of failure. If one large technical project on which our future is staked fails, or is indefinitely delayed, we are left with the problem – and with a large amount of public money wasted. Environmental damage and global warming continue. But with a broad-based approach, if one smaller change doesn't work, many others will.

DEMOCRACY IS FRAUGHT WITH ANTINOMY

'Antinomy' means that there are two or more desirable aspects of an institution or practice that pull in opposite directions, and neither aspect can be altered at will; both are embedded, like laws of nature, in the practices of the institution. An example would be the idea of the market. There are serious inherent deficiencies in markets (in practice) when it comes to both fair distribution of the benefits of belonging to a society, and respecting the limits of the environment. Yet it is a principle of democracy that people and firms should be allowed to trade goods and services freely.

Likewise, we want governments to be decisive and strong, and to reflect broad-scale social values and priorities. We also want governments to consult the public, to allow the maximum public participation in policy formulation. But taking this idea to extreme lengths just leads to endless consultation – all talk and no action. We need to stop using an either–or sort of logic to analyse things and instead examine the merits of different ways in which our various conflicting requirements can be reconciled. Of course in practice, in most modern societies, they *are* reconciled, but less well than they could be. The great and insufficiently celebrated product of the last century was the democratic welfare state, which reconciled the principle of distribution of benefits by an elected government with the principle of distribution by markets.

CITIES HAVE A STAKE IN 'FOREIGN POLICY'

Cities are made vulnerable by poorly considered policy: foreign as well as domestic. The refusal of the Australian Commonwealth Government to ratify the Kyoto Protocol, for example, will make our cities increasingly vulnerable to the effects of global warming. The so-called war on terror would be more correctly called the war *of* terror, since city dwellers on both sides, whether intentionally or collaterally, become targets. This war is fraught with contradiction: does the end justify the means? Or only sometimes, depending on which side one is on? This war could in future have a profound effect on cities. The Madrid bombings in March 2004 reminded us of how vulnerable to attack urban public transport systems are. Australia's urban scholar and practitioner, Patrick Troy, of the Australian National University, has written in recent years of the increasing vulnerability of the Western city to institutional breakdown (the result of unrestrained market forces) and violent external threat (the result of political and diplomatic failure). The 2003 *Jane's Urban Transport Systems* (it is an annual publication) has a section on the potential effects of a radioactive 'dirty' bomb on London's Underground, and claims that such an event might lead to indefinite closure of sections of this crucial urban arterial network.[7] Such dangers cannot be properly met by local actions such as subjecting travellers to ever more screening – in any case, mass screening of commuters is simply impossible. These matters must be resolved by international diplomacy.

This war of terror is, as yet, a faint echo of the horrific wars of the 20th century between market democracies and what Dutch political economist Kees van der Pijl calls 'Hobbesian' contenders – societies whose governments are empowered to act autocratically in the interests of what they believe to be best for society as a whole.[8] From the experience of these wars the world drew the conclusion that force must only be used to settle disputes between nations (however 'good' or 'evil' the regimes were) as a last resort, and only if sanctioned by a single legitimate world body: the United Nations (UN). Unfortunately, we do not yet have an effective and legitimate world 'police' force under UN control, whose role is to uphold democratic values on which all nations have agreed. While city networks remain vulnerable, part of the work of city governments (not just national governments) must be to confront international problems and participate in international debates about what solutions would be appropriate.

ONLY RECONNECT

One of the effects of the process of city building is that urban dwellers become, to a large extent, disconnected, both physically and psychologically, from the natural world. Yet despite the massive modification the Australian landscape has undergone, people living in cities still encounter elements of the non-human, natural world. Many people cherish these contacts with nature in the city, and it is likely that psychological and physiological benefits result. Cities are built on a foundation of geological, hydrological and biological systems. What remains of these systems after a city is established, plus what has been introduced, provides opportunities for city dwellers to experience nature in the city. People respond to natural phenomena, such as hearing the sound of birds or seeing water in the landscape.

Urbanisation has been responsible for precipitating a great deal of the world's loss of biodiversity, climate change, land, water and air pollution and many other negative environmental changes. As the rate of these changes has increased, many city dwellers have begun to notice changes in their surroundings. A neighbourhood stream may appear to be more polluted than it once was, or there seem to be fewer numbers and fewer types of birds and other small animals in the back garden. Such observations have inspired some Australians to greater concern for the future of their local environment, and in some instances have prompted them to work actively to help stop further environmental degradation. This work inspires our vision for the green city, which is about changing the nature of urbanisation and the *urbanisation of nature* to produce settlements that are ecologically sustainable.

This increased awareness of the local environment has also resulted in people becoming more aware of the environmental problems the entire world now faces. Recent studies exploring public attitudes about the future, conducted in various Asia-Pacific region countries (including Australia), have found that the future health of the environment continues to be a major concern, particularly among young people.[9] It will continue to be important for citizens to keep up pressure on their governments to deliver improvements in the quality of the natural environment both in the city and in the products consumed in the city. If we want to protect our own areas of natural forest – in the Styx Valley of Tasmania, the Otways, the forests of West Gippsland, the rainforests of the north – constant vigilance and community action are needed. Our urban areas exist in antipathy to nature, regarding it as no more than a resource for growth: this is a ruinous course. 'Consuming cities' are machines for resource depletion, environmental pollution and therefore, ultimately, social breakdown.[10] Cities must coexist with, and indeed within, nature. Cities must become resource pools, rather than users of resources, reusing their own energy and resources – both natural and human.

CONFRONT COMPLEXITY BUT DON'T BE BAFFLED BY IT

The idea of sustainability can appear very complex, for two reasons. First, many people have tried to define the term, and consequently there are many different definitions. These definitions overlap significantly: there is a core of agreement, but the residual differences can create confusion. Second, 'sustainability' has been used as a term to cover just about every possible virtue. Ideas like the 'triple bottom line' encourage that usage, insisting that 'sustainability' must include both social responsibility and financial profitability. The 'triple bottom line' is designed to remind business corporations of their ecological and social responsibilities, not to dilute the concept of ecologically sustainable development. Recently, the 'triple' has become 'quadruple': governance has been added to the social, economic and environmental trio. This is a healthy move, reflecting the emphasis in this book on the need to generate institutional change in order to achieve sustainability.

Ecological sustainability is a complex idea, but not for the above reasons. It is complex because achieving it, even approaching it – becoming more ecologically sustainable – requires change in so many different (but interconnected) parts of the economy. Handling the complexity of ecological sustainability requires a conceptual strategy that runs something like what follows.

DISTINCTIONS

Though all three may be desirable for different reasons, ecological sustainability *means* something different from social responsibility and profitability. Whether or not ecological sustainability can be reconciled with social responsibility and profitability is an extremely important question, but it cannot be answered unless the three terms are separated from one another conceptually.

DEPENDENCIES

In the long run, both social responsibility and profitability depend upon ecological sustainability. Society as we know it everywhere, and especially the complex democratic capitalist societies of the developed world, is highly dependent on the continued exploitation of the natural world, the world that evolved over billions of years and which developed nations have learned to exploit so profoundly in just the last two hundred.

INTERESTS

There are powerful interests working to protect profitability. Who can doubt it when the entire capitalist system, with its network of giant corporations, is collectively focused on just that? Social responsibility (or social protection) also has its champions, in community and industrial organisations (such as trade unions), and in the institutions of democracy and the welfare state. But the people who will most benefit from ecological sustainability are not yet born. So ecological sustainability depends heavily on the people in the present, whose material interests are least affected, taking up the struggle on behalf of the people of the future. Ecological sustainability should be pursued for its own compelling reasons, though we must at the same time recognise that there are other important objectives with which it must be reconciled.

MATERIAL REQUIREMENTS

Once we agree that 'ecological sustainability' has meaning and should be pursued, the next step is to identify those material requirements which, if not met, would mean that ecological sustainability has not been achieved. In this book we have referred to the global threats to the atmosphere and the biosphere. One requirement related to those threats appears overwhelmingly important: the stabilisation of the atmosphere through a reduction of 60 to 70 per cent (on 1990 levels) in greenhouse emissions by about the middle of this century. A further requirement, which has arisen as a result of what is now unavoidable climate change – it will take place because of past events – is a reduction in the use of drinking water for purposes that do not need pure water. Another requirement appears to be habitat protection, so that the rate of extinction of species is greatly reduced. A series of other requirements can be inferred from what has been said in earlier chapters.

GOALS, TARGETS, INDICATORS

Once the requirements for ecological sustainability are clearly identified, it becomes easier to specify the goals and targets of action and the means of monitoring their achievement.

POLITICAL CONDITIONS

Finally we can think about the political conditions that are necessary if we are to move towards sustainability – because sustainability actually means the transformation of the economy. These political conditions would seem to be something like an enhanced democracy, in which pressure from the broad base of society can reach the powerful summit. In this book we have mostly discussed the urban material requirements for ecological sustainability – the green city; the political conditions for ecological sustainability really requires another book.[11]

DESCRIPTION IS ONLY THE FIRST STEP
TOWARDS PLANNING

Norway, France, The Netherlands, Canada and the World Bank have all developed national state of the environment accounting systems. Australia has tried to follow these examples: there has been 'state of the environment' reporting at a national level here since 1996. State of the environment reporting, or accounting, is supposed to tell us in precise and measurable terms how much and how fast particular sectors of the economy, in particular geographical areas, are depleting the environment. State of the environment reporting should be linked to a *plan* first to reduce the depletion of the environment and eventually to make economic development sustainable: that is, to reduce the depletion to zero. What is lacking in Australia is a national environmental plan. The Australian state of the environment reports merely *describe* pressures on the environment, the state of the environment and government responses.

The Netherlands' environmental reporting system, in contrast, is designed to feed into a policy plan and is shaped to solve defined environmental problems. The Netherlands Environmental Policy Plan (NEPP) is a single, comprehensive, ecosystem-based policy that integrates all areas of environmental concern. The plan's aim is to 'uncouple' economic growth from environmental depletion (economic growth continues while depletion recedes to zero). This is not 'sustainability' until the uncoupling is complete, but it is a wide-ranging operational goal that everyone can understand.

In the NEPP, the planning task is divided up into categories: problem theme, spatial scale, and human activity (or target group). Problem themes are:

- climate change (the greenhouse effect, damage to the ozone layer);
- acidification (acid deposition on soil, surface water and buildings);
- eutrophication (excessive nutrient build-up in surface water);
- dispersion (uncontrolled spread of hazardous substances);
- waste disposal (waste processing, waste prevention, reuse and recycling);
- local nuisance (disturbance caused by noise, odour and local air pollution);
- dehydration (habitat change and insecurity of water supply caused by lowered water tables); and
- squandering, or inadequate resource management (sustainable use of renewable and non-renewable resources and energy).

A similar list could be compiled for Australia. Climate change would still head the list, but insecurity of water supply might well come second, followed perhaps by coastal eutrophication (excessive nutrients from agricultural run-off that disturb marine ecology) and pollution. Soil salinity (increasing salt in the soil), and the deterioration of soils generally through unsustainable agricultural practices, would also have to be high on the list.

The NEPP then identifies five geographic levels on which environmental problems (and their solutions) occur:

- local, the built environment (toxic interior environments, noise pollution, soil contamination);
- regional, the landscape (overuse of fertilisers and inappropriate waste disposal);
- fluvial, river basins and coastal areas (misapplication or overuse of fertilisers and deforestation);
- continental, air and ocean currents (acidification and smog); and global, the higher atmosphere (depletion of the ozone layer and climate change)
- Because global problems are beyond the scope of the Dutch government to solve, the NEPP promotes active environmental diplomacy.

Finally, the NEPP identifies specific 'target groups' – the economic sectors that contribute most to environmental problems and/or their solutions. The key target groups in the NEPP are:

- agriculture;
- traffic and transportation;
- industry and refineries;
- the energy sector;
- the building trade; and
- consumers and the retail trade.

For the purposes of implementation, some of the target groups are broken down even further; for example, subcategories of the industry target group include the base metals industry, the chemical industry and the printing industry.

The NEPP is fundamentally problem, plan and action based. It is described as 'implementation-oriented' policy. The state of the environment reporting is integrated with the intention to act effectively to change the way Dutch people interact with the environment, and that equals changing the economy.

Australia needs not just description of the state of the environment but a National Environment Plan to prevent its further destruction. That plan should focus equally on the use of the environment in production, and the consumption of the environment in cities; on wilderness, agriculture and *urban* nature. The green city, the green town and the green region will not be realised in Australia until there is a national will to do so. It's a question of leadership – which, at the time of writing (April 2004), we do not have.

FINAL WORDS

Andrew Marvell's poem indirectly evokes that most influential book by Ebenezer Howard, which led to the 'garden city' movement: *Tomorrow: A Peaceful Path to Real Reform* (1898). In city planning today we still need real reform, but the world has advanced by more than a century since Howard's book, and the real reform we have outlined in this book is very different from that proposed by Howard.

The sustainable city of the future is not a utopia. It will not depend on a visionary architect or a 'green' prophet. It is not 'the compact city' or the 'permaculture commune' – valuable though these important ideas are. It will not be built anew in a 'green field'. The green city will not in the first instance be a blueprint (or a 'greenprint') plan or design; it will simply be a new attitude towards the fundamentals of urban life – work, play, movement, consumption and governance. A new *out*look is needed, not an inward-looking marvellous design that promises to bring everything back into balance within a perfectly planned patch. Sustainability will be found in this new critical self-regard and the will to act among the urban citizenry and its collectives, especially power-brokers such as organisations and professions. In short, the green city will be a product of our newly sensitised and critical outlooks, not the result of technocratic problem solving. This critical or 'reflexive' mind-set must shake the foundations of the institutions and structures that shape the course of urban life.

We take a positive view of human nature – not the gloomy view assumed by market economists, who portray people as 'rational self-interest maximisers'; emotionless and free of moral or spiritual values. This view – that only material values matter – is refuted in everyday life, in the very constitution of cities as moral orders by inhabitants who constantly display concern and affection for one another and their natural setting. The innate capacity for moral good needs to be nurtured in urban policy, not assumed away or left to languish in a museum of 'primitive culture'! Citizens by and large do not want to damage the environment, and if they know what does and does not do that they will act accordingly. The green city is founded on the assumption that humans desire a place in a flourishing natural order. This moral foundation underlies a sense of common good that is the well-spring of law and institutions. What is good needs to be signalled clearly in legislation and institutional practice, not left to the murky waters of voluntary compliance. Good governance, after all, is the means by which individuals act together on common problems for the common good.

Today we have everywhere an unsustainable economy, one that seizes any and every opportunity for industrial growth, and to hell with the consequences; an economy so raddled by greed and lies that even the best of its own high priests, the economists, have lost faith in it. We have, in short, an unsustainable society, a society in which more of nature is consumed than can be reproduced. The 'growth fetish' and mindless accumulation need to be thrown out as a new enlightenment of critical self-regard dawns among the green city public.[12]

However, the sustainable city is already beginning to emerge today within the unsustainable city of the past. The public is already beginning to create it, from the bottom up. What will it be like? It is a city where there is no waste, and where the natural environment is prized as the true support of the citizens' lifestyles. It is a city where space is made for the lives and ecologies of the more than human world, and where their natural rights are recognised. Public open spaces and facilities will be plentiful, linked up and shared by humans and others. Only *public* space – not the private communal space of gated suburbs – guarantees the possibilities for real social encounter and expression that contribute to a flourishing, self-aware urban society. As we observed earlier, self-awareness is a critical prerequisite for a city if it is really to comprehend its natural foundations and its possibilities.

The green city is a place whose local economy is limited by the global ecology, and where the benefits of the environment will be fairly distributed. The sustainable city will be a city of equal human rights and equal opportunities: it will be socially as well as ecologically sustainable. The environment will continue to be consumed to provide a high standard of living for all, but consumption of the environment will not outrun its regeneration, so citizens can enjoy their lifestyles indefinitely into the future.

Starting now, the sustainable city will be made by a thousand and one small changes: in homes, in suburbs, in means of transport and communication, in offices and workshops and shopping centres. The city will be built through these small changes in how we live and work. People will reduce unnecessary travel because a journey saved is time saved. People will drive smaller and more fuel-efficient vehicles and use well-funded and highly integrated public transport systems. Walking and cycling will be given priority over powered transport. Homes will be nearly self-sufficient in power and water. The national grid will still be used for both supply and storage of power, and it will be run by organisations (public, communal or private) that invest in energy saving as much as in energy production.

The necessary changes will be implemented, supported and encouraged by governments. Consumers' lifestyles will be made possible within these environmental constraints by the lively response of many businesses. This city of the future will be accomplished by a revalued sphere of government (public sector) capable of innovative and intelligent planning, and by citizen and consumer action. There will be many shades of green in the sustainable city, but no grey. It will be a wonderful place to live.

NOTES AND REFERENCES

Chapter 1 WHAT DOES 'SUSTAINABILITY' MEAN FOR CITIES?

1   The variety of adjectives signals the importance of the concept. In a world dedicated to making more and more new things, where in art and science originality is the highest goal, 'sustainability' in general announces that some human-made ideas and objects are worth keeping and may be difficult to keep. But what is most vulnerable and most precious is not what humans have made over a few thousand years, but what has evolved on Earth over 4 billion years.

2   D. McLaren, S. Bullock & N. Yousuf, 'Friends of the Earth', *Tomorrow's World: Britain's Share in a Sustainable Future*, Earthscan Publications, London, 1998.

3   V. Plumwood, *Environmental Culture, The Ecological Crisis of Reason*, Routledge, London & New York, 2002.

4   Science has delivered wonderful things for us, but it has also produced horrors that have led to serious and episodic reversals in human health and welfare. The distinctions between the wonderful and the destructive offerings of science are only revealed over time. With genetic technology, we are still in the 'risk' period and it is right – indeed, humane – to regard this new technology with caution. We can waste a lot of time, resources and, sadly, lives by not exercising care and caution when considering the introduction of technologies that propose whole new forms of relationship between humanity and nature.

5   An example of what can happen when caution is abandoned is the crossing of a monkey virus to the human species. This occurred, and is documented, as a result of mass immunisation against polio. The vaccine culture was based on a matrix of minced monkey organs, some of which was unavoidably injected into humans along with the vaccine. The monkey virus turned out to be harmless, but there is also strong circumstantial evidence that HIV was transferred from monkeys to humans in a similar way when chimpanzees were used to culture the polio virus in the Belgian Congo in the 1950s. A trial of the oral vaccine on a million Africans was carried out at that time, and the first cases of AIDS appeared in the same locations as the trial population. Despite claims to the contrary, this charge has never been conclusively disproved. If the claim is true, the greatest plague humans have ever experienced was caused by a well-intentioned but hasty experiment. See E. Hooper, *The River: A Journey Back to the Source of AIDS and HIV*, Allen Lane, London, 1999.

6   M. Jacobs, *The Green Economy*, Pluto Press, London, 1991, p. 27.

7   'Raw' is a misleading term because much 'production' has been accomplished by nature itself prior to human processing – providing refined materials like food, timber, rocks and chemicals and digesting the waste.

8   C. Hamilton, *Running From the Storm: The Development of Climate Change Policy in Australia*, UNSW Press, Sydney, 2001, p. 18.

9   See C. Campbell, 'The peak of oil: An economic turning point for the world', in N. Low & B. Gleeson (eds), *Making Urban Transport Sustainable*, Palgrave Macmillan, Basingstoke, 2003, p. 43.

10   In an earlier work we tried to shift the vision of this crucial relationship away from that of a mutually supporting triangle (economic, social and environmental sustainability) to one of nested boxes: the environment enclosing society, which in turn encloses the economy. See Low & Gleeson, *Making Urban Transport Sustainable*, p. 17.

11   Unfortunately, too often 'the economy' or 'the market' is made into a fetish: an object of worship on account of its supposed magical powers, a principle irrationally revered. The economy, instead of being recognised for what it is – namely human beings interacting with one another and exploiting the natural world for commercial purposes, with both uses and limitations – becomes irrationally revered and mediated by a priest-hood (economists, in this case) who pretend to know what is best for the rest of us.

12   Some geologists claim to have discovered evidence in rock samples of very rapid episodes of global warming in the distant past, even over periods as short as 100 years. They do not, however, tell us what effect these episodes had on life. And of course these episodes of climate change all took place before the evolution of the human species. We must presume that such an episode would today cause the loss of at least billions of human lives as well as the rapid extinction of countless species, perhaps even the human species.

13   A recent re-examination of the satellite data suggests that the way the earlier studies adjusted the data between satellites concealed the warming trend. A more accurate adjustment has the readings in greater agreement with the climate change models (report in *The Age*, 19 November 2003, p. 14, from *The Journal of Climate Change*).

14   S. Weart, *The Discovery of Global Warming*, Harvard University Press, Cambridge MA, 2003, p. 129.

15   Weart, *The Discovery of Global Warming*, p. 186.

16   More can be found out about the carbon cycle on the Hadley Centre (UK Meteorological Office) website: http://www.met-office.gov.uk/research /hadleycentre/models/carbon_cycle/index.html.

17   These figures are taken from the official publications of the IPCC, particularly J.T. Houghton, L.G.M. Filho, B.A. Callander, N. Harris, A. Kettenberg & K. Maskell (eds), *Climate Change, 1995, The Science of Climate Change*, Cambridge University Press, Cambridge, 1996.

18   The United States ratified the Convention on 15 October 1992 and it came into force on 21 March 1994. Australia ratified it on 30 December 1992 and it entered into force on 21 March 1994.

19   N. Paton Walsh, 'It's Europe's lungs and home to many rare species. But to Russia it's £100 billion of wood', *The Guardian*, 19 September 2003, p. 3.

20   G.I. Pearman, 'Climate change', *In Search of Sustainability* (online conference): www.isosconference.org.au.

21   The major extinction events are the end of the Ordovician period (440 million years ago), the late Devonian (365 million years ago), the end of the Permian (225 million years ago), the end of the Triassic (210 million years ago), and the end of the Cretaceous (65 million years ago). See R. Leakey & R. Lewin, *The Sixth Extinction: Biodiversity and Its Survival*, Weidenfeld & Nicholson, London, 1996, p. 45.

22   B. Lomborg, *The Skeptical Environmentalist: Measuring the Real State of the World*, Cambridge University Press, Cambridge, 2001, p. 255, citing N. Stork, 'Measuring global biodiversity and its decline', pp. 41–68 in Wilson et al., 1997, uncited.

23   Leakey & Lewin, *The Sixth Extinction*, p. 244.

24 J.A. Pounds & R. Puschendorf, 'Ecology: clouded futures', *Nature*, vol. 427, no. 6970, 2004, p. 107.

25 Reported on the United Nations Environment Program website, 17 January 2004: http://www.un.org/apps/news/story.asp?NewsID=9393 &Cr=kyoto&Cr1.

26 Australian Bureau of Statistics (ABS), *Australians and the Environment*, ABS, Canberra, 1996.

27 See L. Brown, 'Feeding nine billion', in *State of the World 1999*, Earthscan Publications, London, 1999, pp. 115–32, and 'Eradicating hunger, a growing challenge', in *State of the World 2001*, Earthscan Publications, London, 2001, pp. 43–62.

28 Brown, 'Eradicating hunger'.

29 The 'more than human' world is a term Val Plumwood uses in preference to 'the non-human world'. The former is inclusive, whereas the latter is exclusive. We agree. 'More than human' is also more accurate: more species than human, more creatures than human, more of almost everything than human.

30 The very word 'nature' in one word refers to all the rest of life, in contrast to just one single species, 'human'. It contains a bias, but it is simply too convenient not to use and we will continue to do so.

Chapter 2 SUSTAINABLE HOMES AND SUBURBS

1 What follows is based on M. Mobbs, *Sustainable House*, Choice Books, Sydney, 1998.

2 Information about a range of composting toilets can be found on the internet at http://www.compostingtoilet.org/systems.cfm.

3 Mobbs, *Sustainable House,* p. 113.

4 Mobbs, *Sustainable House,* p. 111.

5 Mobbs, *Sustainable House,* p. 73.

6 Report by B. Lane, 'Home, green home', *The Weekend Australian*, 24–25 January 2003, p. 26.

7 S. Roaf, M. Fuentes & S. Thomas, *Ecohouse 2: A Design Guide*, Architectural Press, London, 2003.

8 E. von Weizsäcker, A. Lovins & H. Lovins, *Factor 4: Doubling Wealth, Halving Resource Use*, Allen & Unwin, Sydney, 1997, p. 13.

9 Australian Greenhouse Office (AGO), *Australian Residential Building Sector Greenhouse Gas Emissions 1990–2010*, AGO, Canberra, 1999, p. 4 (Fig. 3).

10 Much of the following six paragraphs is paraphrased from *Beddington Zero Energy Development*, Bioregional Development Group, 24 Helios Road, Wallington, Surrey SM6 7BZ England, 2003 (email: info@bioregional.com).

11 *Hannover Kronsberg: Model for a Sustainable Urban Community,* City of Hannover, Germany, 2002.

12 *Hannover Kronsberg,* section 3.3.

13 See *Västra Hamnen, The Bo 01 Area, A City for People and the Environment*, City of Malmö, 2003 (available in English from the City of Malmö Urban Planning and Architecture Office, 205 80 Malmö, Sweden, email: ekostaden@malmo.se).

14 *Västra Hamnen.*

15 A housing association is a form of co-operatively owned and managed housing. Housing associations take different forms: some in Sweden are provided

by local government, some are provided by non-profit private organisations.

16 http://www.urbanecology.org.au/christiewalk/factsheet.

17 Download the PDF file: www.melbournewater.com.au/content/library/ wsud/case_studies/inkerman_oasis.pdf.

18 The energy used in the daily running of the home is called 'operational energy'. The Australian Greenhouse Office estimates that the emissions generated from different operational activities are as follows: 12 per cent from space heating, 2 per cent from space cooling, 28 per cent from water heating, 5 per cent from cooking and a massive 53 per cent from running all the electrical appliances in the home. Getting that electricity from a non-greenhouse source is essential for the green city, whether from a battery of photovoltaic cells on the roof or from a remote wind turbine or biomass power station. The energy used in constructing or renovating a house is called 'embodied energy'. That is simply the total energy necessary to manufacture all the construction materials from the raw materials provided by the environment, and assemble them to build a dwelling. Bricks, for example, have first to be made from clay. Energy is used in mining, shaping and firing the clay. Going back a stage, energy is used in making the brick factory and the kiln. Energy is used in transporting the bricks to the site, and, going back a stage again, energy is used in manufacturing the truck to transport the bricks. Energy is used in laying the bricks on the building site. So there is a series of long chains of activity, all using energy, that culminate in the building in place on the site. Human energy does not directly use fossil fuel – but fossil fuels are used in feeding and maintaining the people whose labour goes into the house. The embodied energy in constructing a house can equal 20 years of operational energy in running it. Over the life of a house, renovations can account for another 20 years of operational energy. So if a house has a 100-year lifespan, embodied energy can account for up to 40 per cent of the amount of energy spent in running the house over its lifespan. Australian Greenhouse Office, *Australian Residential Building Sector Greenhouse Gas Emissions 1990–2010*, AGO, Canberra, 1999.

19 These calculations were made on the basis of figures contained in *Australian Residential Building Sector Greenhouse Gas Emissions 1990– 2010* (p. 10) and *National Greenhouse Gas Inventory 1988–1994, Summary and Analysis of Trends*, National Greenhouse Gas Inventory, Department of Environment, Sport and Territories Australia, Canberra, 1996, p. iii.

Chapter 3   NATURE IN THE CITY

1 G.C. Bolton, *Spoils and Spoilers: Australians Make Their Environment 1788–1980*, Allen & Unwin, Sydney & Boston, 1981.

2 E.O. Wilson, 'Biophilia and the conservation ethic', in S.R. Kellert & E.O. Wilson (eds), *The Biophilia Hypothesis*, Island Press, Washington DC, 1993, p. 31.

3 J.F. Wohlwill, 'The concept of nature: a psychologist's view', in I. Altman & J.F. Wohlwill (eds), *Behavior and the Natural Environment*, Plenum Press, New York, 1983, pp. 5–37 (quotation from p. 7).

4 S.R. Kellert, 'The biological basis for human values of nature', in Kellert & Wilson (eds), *The Biophilia Hypothesis*, pp. 42–72.

5 Designed by Fredrick Law Olmsted, who coined the term 'landscape architecture'.

6   R. Kaplan, 'The role of nature in the urban context', in Altman & Wohlwill (eds), *Behavior and the Natural Environment*.

7   Howard Bridgeman, Robin Warner & John Dodson, *Urban Biophysical Environments*, Oxford University Press, Melbourne, 1995, p. 16, Table 2.1.

8   *The Sunday Age*, 'From source to city, Yarra cleans up its tract', 21 December 2003.

9   E.H. Zube, 'Perception of landscape and land use', in Altman & Wohlwill (eds), *Human Behavior and Environment*, pp. 87–121.

10   H. Frumkin, 'Beyond toxicity: human health and the natural environment', *American Journal of Preventative Medicine*, 20 (3), 2001, pp. 234–40 (quotation from p. 238).

11   R.S. Ulrich, 'Natural versus urban scenes: some psychophysiological effects', *Environment and Behavior*, 13, 1981, pp. 523–56.

12   R.S. Ulrich, 'Views through a window may influence recovery from surgery', *Science*, 224, 1984, pp. 420–21.

13   E. Moore, 'A prison environment's demands on health care service demands', *Journal of Environmental Systems*, 2 (11), 1981, pp. 17–34.

14   L.M. Fredrickson & D.H. Anderson, 'A qualitative exploration of the wilderness experience as a source of spiritual inspiration', *Journal of Environmental Psychology*, 19, 1999, pp. 21–39.

15   R. Kaplan & S. Kaplan, *The Experience of Nature*, Cambridge University Press, Cambridge, 1989.

16   M. McDonnell, N.S.G. Williams & A.K. Hahs, *A Reference Guide to the Ecology and Natural Resources of the Melbourne Region*, Australian Research Centre for Urban Ecology, Royal Botanic Gardens, Melbourne, 1999.

17   R.T.T. Forman, *Land Mosaics*, Cambridge University Press, Cambridge, 1995.

18   W.E. Dramstad, J.D. Olson & R.T.T. Forman, *Landscape Ecology Principles in Landscape Architecture and Land-Use Planning*, Island Press, Washington DC, 1996.

19   D. Mugavin, 'Adelaide's greenway: River Torrens Linear Park', *Landscape and Urban Planning*, 68 (2–3), 2004, pp. 223–40.

20   R. Kaplan & E.J. Herbert, 'Cultural and sub-cultural comparisons in preferences for natural settings', *Landscapes and Urban Planning*, 14, 1987, pp.281–93.

21   E.H. Zube & C.V. Mills, 'Cross-cultural explorations in landscape perception', in E.H. Zube (ed.), *Studies in Landscape Perception*, University of Massachusetts, Institute for Man and Environment, Amherst, 1976, pp. 162–69.

22   The Kaplans have found that the most highly preferred landscape scenes of all tend to convey a definite sense of mystery; that is, they are landscapes that encourage exploration and curiosity and make one imagine what it might be like if one were to explore the landscape further. Classic examples of mystery in the landscape are to be found in those landscapes where there is a visible bend in a path or where a distant view is obscured by vegetation or landform. From an evolutionary perspective, such settings would have suggested to early hunters opportunities for finding game if only one were to explore further.

23   Kaplan & Kaplan, *The Experience of Nature*.

24   Y.F. Tuan, *Landscapes of Fear*, Basil Blackwell, Oxford, 1979.

25   G.H. Orians, 'An ecological and evolutionary approach to landscape aesthetics', in E.C. Penning-Rowsell & D. Lowenthal (eds), *Landscape Meanings and Values*, Allen & Unwin, London, 1986, pp. 1–22.

26 J.D. Balling & J.H. Falk, 'Development of visual preference for natural environments', *Environment and Behavior*, 14, 1982, pp. 5–28.
27 Wilson, 'Biophilia and the conservation ethic', p. 33.
28 A. Leopold (S.L. Flader & J.B. Callicott [eds]), *The River of the Mother of God and Other Essays by Aldo Leopold*, University of Wisconsin Press, Madison, 1991; and A. Leopold, *A Sand County Almanac and Sketches Here and There*, Oxford University Press, New York, 1949.
29 P.H. Gobster, 'An ecological aesthetic for forest management', *Landscape Journal*, 18 (1), 1999, pp. 54–64.
30 D. Cosgrove & S. Daniels, *The Iconography of Landscape*, Cambridge University Press, Cambridge, 1988.
31 S.K. Robinson, *Inquiry into the Picturesque*, University of Chicago Press, Chicago, 1991.
32 J.I. Nassauer, 'Messy ecosystems, orderly frames', *Landscape Journal*, 14 (2), 1995, pp. 161–69.

Chapter 4 SUSTAINABLE WORKPLACES

1   This paragraph and the next are paraphrased from the Sharp website: http://sharp-world.com/corporate/eco/e_activities/industry/industry_01.html.
2   D. Winter, 'Automakers deserve credit for green factories', Management Briefing Seminar, 2001: http://golfevents.meetingsnet.com/ar/auto_automakers_deserve_credit/. What follows in this paragraph contains information from this source.
3   International Energy Agency, 18 April 2001: http://www.ela.doe.gov/emeu/iea/table1.html.
4   *The Guardian*, 10 May 2003, p. 18.
5   Friends of the Earth, *Towards a Community Supported Agriculture*, Friends of the Earth, Brisbane, 2001, p. 16.
6   P. Krugman, *The Accidental Theorist*, Penguin Books, London, 1999, pp. 85, 86.
7   Colin Hines, *Localization: A Global Manifesto*, Earthscan, London, 2000.
8   http:///www.earthscan.co.uk/asp/authordetails.asp.
9   D. Burch, K. Lyons & G. Lawrence, 'What do we mean by "green"? Consumers, agriculture and the food industry', in S. Lockie & B. Pritchard (eds), *Consuming Foods, Sustaining Environments*, Australian Academic Press, Bowen Hills, 2001, p. 40.
10 From unpublished work by D. Radović, Faculty of Architecture, Building and Planning, University of Melbourne, Melbourne, Australia.
11 For example: 'Buildings and the built environment play a major role in the human impact on the natural environment and the quality of life; sustainable design integrates consideration of resource and energy efficiency, healthy buildings and materials, ecologically and socially sensitive land use, and an aesthetic sensitivity that aspires, affirms and ennobles; sustainable design can significantly reduce adverse human impacts on the natural environment while simultaneously improving the quality of life and economic wellbeing', from the UIA/AIA (Union Internationale d'Architecture/American Institute of Architects) *Declaration of Interdependence for Sustainable Development*, 1993.
12 Data in this overview is based on documentation generously provided by the City of Melbourne.

Chapter 5 SUSTAINABLE TRANSPORT

1   The term 'road safety' is a rather deceptive euphemism for road danger. There is no comparable euphemism for travel on public transport, because despite fears to the contrary, there is very little danger. Transport danger comes from individually controlled vehicles on roads. The threat of terrorism on public transport is evident since the Madrid bombing of the railways, but deaths from that cause are small in number compared with deaths from road accidents.

2   O. Ullrich, 'The pedestrian town as an alternative to motorised travel', in R. Tolley (ed.), *The Greening of Urban Transport*, John Wiley & Sons, Chichester, 1997, pp. 29–35. The World Health Organization (WHO) estimates that 1.183 million people died from vehicle crashes in 2002 (Statistical Annex to the WHO report on deaths and injuries from various causes worldwide, Table A2, p. 172).

3   R. Ewing, T. Schmid, R. Killingsworth, A. Zlot & S. Raudenbush, 'Relationship between urban sprawl and physical activity, obesity and morbidity', *American Journal of Health Promotion*, September 2003.

4   P. Mees, *A Very Public Solution: Transport in the Dispersed City*, Melbourne University Press, Melbourne, 2000.

5   There is no persuasive technical reason why wheelchair access should not be provided through rail stations, onto platforms and right into the train.

6   Zürich's public transport system is described by D. Apel & T. Pharoah in *Transport Concepts in European Cities*, Avebury Ashgate, Aldershot, 1995, pp. 127–54. The following paragraphs paraphrase their work.

7   Mees, *A Very Public Solution*, p. 123.

8   Apel & Pharoah, *Transport Concepts in European Cities*, p. 143. This passage is quoted by P. Mees (*A Very Public Solution*, p. 124), but it deserves being repeated here.

9   Melbourne Transportation Committee (MTC), *Melbourne Transportation Study, Volume 3: The Transportation Plan*, MTC, Melbourne, 1969, p. 44. In line with what was regarded as progress 35 years ago, the *Melbourne Transportation Study* also recommended 500 kilometres of new freeways!

10   *Verkehr* means 'traffic'; *Verbund* has the connotation of 'alliance' or 'coalition'.

11   A logical tangle, since Britain and Spain, which are as 'old' as they come, were excised in the presidential mind! After 14 March 2004 (the election following the Madrid atrocity), Spain presumably reverted to being 'old' Europe.

12   That governments should steer the public boat, while the private sector 'rowed' was the dictum of D. Osborne & T. Gaebler in *Reinventing Government: How the Entrepreneurial Spirit Is Transforming the Public Sector*, Addison-Wesley, Reading MA, 1992.

13   The following description is based on the publication *The Portland Region: How Are We Doing?*, published in 2003 by the Portland Metro Council, and also on a Powerpoint presentation by A.C. Cotugno (Planning Director of Metro Portland) & E. Seltzer (Director of the School of Urban Studies and Planning, Portland State University) at the *Future Urban Transport* conference in Gothenberg, Sweden, in September 2003 (organised and sponsored by the Volvo Research and Educational Foundation, Sweden).

14   There is probably not a single reader of this book who has not been affected in some way by a serious car crash. How many, though, have been similarly affected by a public transport accident?

15 N. Fairbrother, *New Lives, New Landscapes*, The Architectural Press, London, 1970.

16 This theory started with the work of engineer and economist Brian Arthur, whose example was the QWERTY keyboard. The QWERTY layout was the solution to typists hitting the keys too rapidly and jamming the mechanical arms of typewriters. A random arrangement of letters was designed to create a small pause between key hits; in effect, to slow typing down. Users learned to expect QWERTY as their keyboard and QWERTY soon became embedded in the whole vast system of production and marketing of type-writers – and word processors, which don't have mechanical arms. The theory was applied to the behaviour of political institutions by Nobel Laureate (economics, 1993) Douglass North.

17 It may well be that congestion increases to fill the road space available, but that is a separate matter, to be dealt with by the pricing of road space. The point is that improving public transport is *more* likely to reduce congestion than building roads is.

18 See E. von Weizsäcker, A. Lovins & H. Lovins, *Factor 4: Doubling Wealth, Halving Resource Use*, Allen & Unwin, Sydney, 1997, p.4.

19 C. Destefani & E. Siores, 'Automotive pollution and control technologies', in N. Low & B. Gleeson (eds), *Making Urban Transport Sustainable*, Palgrave Macmillan, Basingstoke, 2003, p. 90.

20 These points are discussed by Patrick Moriarty and Damon Honnery in 'Evaluation of greenhouse gas reduction strategies for urban passenger transport', paper for the 25th *Australasian Transport Research Forum*, Canberra, 2–4 October 2002. Methanol is 'a simple molecule containing a single carbon atom linked to three hydrogen atoms and one oxygen–hydrogen bond CH_2OH' (Destefani & Siores, 'Automotive pollution control technologies', p. 91).

21 The cost could be recovered by a few cents per litre increase in fuel tax.

22 William Black reports this research in his 'An unpopular essay on transportation', *Journal of Transport Geography*, vol. 9, 2001, pp. 1–11. The research he cites is that in B. Pearson's PhD Dissertation at the Department of Geography, Indiana University, titled 'An estimation of the potential production of agri-based ethanol and its contribution to transportation emissions'.

23 Allen Consulting Group (ACG), *Greenhouse Emissions Trading*, vol. 1, ACG, Melbourne, 2000, p. 62.

24 Car dependence may also be caused by a low fuel price or an impoverished public transport system. One cannot assume that increasing density will by itself bring about a reduction in the use of fossil fuel. Newman and Kenworthy plainly understand this and advocate a range of interlocking policies, of which higher densities around transport interchanges are just one (see P. Newman & J. Kenworthy, *Cities and Automobile Dependence, A Sourcebook*, Gower Technical, Aldershot, 1989).

25 The relative contribution to greenhouse emissions by public transport and private vehicle trips can easily be quantified but it plays little part in the quantitative 'modelling' that is regularly done for environmental impact assessments of transport projects. The modelling is heavily biased towards numerical expression of money values assigned to road trips. Perversely – there is an evil logic to this calculus – an additional trip by road is given a positive money value, so the more trips a road generates, the higher the 'economic benefit' it is credited with creating. Of course it is actually not economical to travel more. The alternative, of reducing congestion and

freeing up road space by transferring road trips to public transport, is generally discounted as impossible, undesirable, or both.

26   Lomborg writes, 'it is clear that we have more and more oil left, not less and less': B. Lomborg, *The Skeptical Environmentalist. Measuring the Real State of the World*, Cambridge University Press, Cambridge, 2001.

27   C. Campbell, 'The peak of oil: An economic and political turning point for the world', in Low & Gleeson (eds), *Making Urban Transport Sustainable*, pp. 25–41. The paragraphs following are based on Campbell's text.

28   Campbell, 'The peak of oil', p. 47.

29   *The Australian*, 'Shell of a man stages slick and the dead act' (re-reported from *The Sunday Times*), 10 February 2004, p. 23.

30   Campbell, 'The peak of oil', p. 58. This account is supported by Kenneth Pollack, Director of Gulf Affairs at the US National Security Council (1995–96 and 1999–2001): K.M. Pollack, *The Threatening Storm: The Case for Invading Iraq*, Random House, New York, 2002, p. 415.

31   Apel & Pharoah, *Transport Concepts in European Cities*, p. 249.

Chapter 6   MAKING THE GREEN CITY

1   The argument for democracy in some form is developed at length in J. Dryzek, *Rational Ecology, Environment and Political Economy*, Blackwell, Oxford, 1987.

2   K. Polanyi, *The Great Transformation: The Political and Economic Origins of Our Time*, Beacon Press, Boston, 2001 (1944), p. 145.

3   P.A. Hall & R.C.R. Taylor, 'Political science and the three new institutionalisms', *Political Studies*, 44, 1996, pp. 936–57.

4   D. Yencken & D. Wilkinson, *Resetting the Compass: Australia's Journey Towards Sustainability*, CSIRO Publishing, Melbourne, 2000.

5   K-H. Robert, J. Holmberg & G. Broman, 'Simplicity without reduction: thinking upstream towards the sustainable society' (1996), republished in *Greenprint for a Sustainable City*, City of Manningham, Melbourne, 1998.

6   The figures are taken from *Melbourne Sustainable Energy and Greenhouse Strategy*, The City of Melbourne, Melbourne, 2000, attachment 2, p. 16.

7   From the Melbourne City Council website: http://www.melbourne.vic. gov.au/greenhouse/).

8   The following is contained in *The Leichhardt Town Plan*, Leichhardt Council (looseleaf format), 2000.

9   *The Leichhardt Town Plan*, p. 7.

10   *The Leichhardt Town Plan*, p. 7.

11   Business Leaders Initiative on Climate Change (BLICC), *BLICC 2 Establishing Priorities*, BLICC, London & Amsterdam, 2003.

12   See, for example, H. Possingham, *The Business of Biodiversity: Applying Decision Theory Principles to Nature Conservation*, Tela Paper No. 9, Australian Conservation Foundation, Melbourne, and Earthwatch Institute, London, 2001, p. 16.

13   Melbourne planning scholar Paul Mees has often made this point, but the officials in the Department of Sustainability and Environment do not seem particularly interested in listening to him.

14   Landcom, *The Measures We Take*, Landcom, Sydney, 2003, pp. 26, 28.

15   Australian Institute of Urban Studies (AIUS), *Environmental Indicators for Metropolitan Melbourne, Bulletin 6*, AIUS, Melbourne, 2003. The bulletin

was written by Vera Wong in collaboration with members of the steering committee.

16   An excellent series of articles by Melissa Fife – 'The story of a tree' – tracked the death of a 40-metre high shining gum from the Errinundra forest through its felling, then as just 10 metres of it were cut for floorboards, and the rest was woodchipped and burned: *The Age*, 9–14 April 2004.

17   M. Fyfe & A. Darby, 'Tasmania: seeing the wood but not the trees', *The Age*, 13 March 2004, p. 6, and B. Ellis, 'Slaying the giants', *The Age*, Good Weekend, 27 January 2001, pp. 16–19.

18   See *Greenhouse Challenge*, Hazelwood Power Agreement, 1997.

19   See *Greenhouse Challenge*.

20   State Electricity Commission of Victoria (SECV), *The SEC and the Greenhouse Effect, A Discussion Paper*, SECV, Melbourne, 1989, p. 1.

21   SECV, *The SEC and the Greenhouse Effect*, pp. 10–14.

22   State Electricity Commission of Victoria, *Annual Report 1990/91*, SECV, Melbourne, 1991, p. 69.

23   S. Dovers, *Institutions for Sustainability*, Tela Paper No. 7, Australian Conservation Foundation, Melbourne, 2001.

24   Landcom NSW: http://www.landcom.nsw.gov.au.

25   Much of this section has been gathered and paraphrased from the work of Terry Burke and David Hayward (including unpublished course notes) at the Institute for Social Research, Swinburne University of Technology, Melbourne.

26   K. Davidson, 'Transport spending is badly off track', *The Age*, 15 May 2000, p. 15.

27   Mees notes, 'it was not until 1983 that a single authority was established to run public transport, and that body never even attempted to integrate the different modes of transport': Mees, *A Very Public Solution: Transport in the Dispersed City*, Melbourne University Press, Melbourne, 2000, p. 151.

28   See P. Mees, 'Public transport privatisation in Melbourne: what went wrong?', paper for the *National Conference on the State of Australian Cities*, Parramatta, 3–5 December 2003.

29   Absurd situations occurred with private operators competing against one another. Mees reports that 'Each operator redesigned vehicles, timetables and stops in its own livery, and began to treat other operators as rivals – a pattern that would be familiar to observers of the post-privatisation scene in the UK. For example, for many months timetables for train services operated by Hillside Trains could not be obtained from Flagstaff, Melbourne Central or Parliament stations (in the CBD) which are operated by Bayside Trains – even though the Hillside services called at those stations': Mees, 'Public transport privatisation in Melbourne: what went wrong?'.

30   Mees notes that the State's 2003–04 Budget Statement provides an allowance of around $1 billion over five years in anticipation of higher public transport costs. He writes: 'The cost blowout appears to be a direct result of "rent-seeking" by the private operators. For example, the electrification in 1995 of the 13 kilometre line from Dandenong to Pakenham, with two new stations, cost $27 million under the PTC (*Auditor-General's Report*, 1998, p. 99). But the electrification for the 9 kilometres from Broadmeadows to Craigieburn, also with two stations, is projected to cost $98 million (from 2002 State Budget Papers), plus an annual operating subsidy of $7 million': Mees, 'Public transport privatisation in Melbourne: what went wrong?'.

31   The Disinfopedia notes that 'doublespeak', a term that Orwell did not actu-
      ally use in the book, crept into use in the 1950s, meaning 'language delib-
      erately constructed to disguise its actual meaning' (such as 'collateral
      damage' meaning damage to civilians in a war): http://www.disinfopedia.
      org/.
32   See B. Gleeson, C. Curtis & N. Low, 'Barriers to sustainable transport in
      Australia', in N. Low & B. Gleeson (eds), *Making Urban Transport
      Sustainable: Transport in the Dispersed City*, Melbourne University Press,
      Melbourne, 2000, p. 214.
33   S. Weart, *The Discovery of Global Warming*, Harvard University Press,
      Cambridge MA, 2003, p. 95.
34   Royal Commission on Environment and Pollution, *Transport and the
      Environment 18th Report*, HMSO, London, 1994.
35   The following paragraphs on Curitiba are paraphrased from the
      International Council for Local Environmental Initiatives (ICLEI) website
      – http://www3.iclei.org/localstrategies/summary/curitiba2.html – and
      http://sol.crest.org/sustainable/curitiba/.
36   From the website of the International Council for Local Environmental
      Initiatives (ICLEI): http://www3.iclei.org/localstrategies/summary
      /curitiba2.html.

Chapter 7   GREEN-SHADED CITIES

1   http://www.iclei.org/europe/ECHARTER.HTM.
2   http://www.europa.eu.int/comm./environment/aarhus/.
3   http://www.context.org/ICLIB/DEFS/UIAAIA.htm.
4   http://www.context.org/ICLIB/DEFS/UIAAIA.htm.
5   http://www.context.org/ICLIB/DEFS/UIAAIA.htm.
6   http://www.context.org/ICLIB/DEFS/UIAAIA.htm.
7   *Jane's Urban Transport Systems*: http://juts.janes.com/public/juts/
      index.shtml.
8   K. van der Pijl, *Transnational Classes and International Relations*, Routledge,
      London, 1998, p. 78.
9   D. Yencken, J. Fien & H. Sykes (eds), *Environment, Education and Society in
      the Asia-Pacific: Local Traditions and Global Discourses*, Routledge, London
      & New York, 2000.
10   See N. Low, B. Gleeson, I. Elander & R. Lidskog (eds), *Consuming Cities:
      The Urban Environment in the Global Economy After the Rio Declaration*,
      Routledge, London & New York, 2000.
11   John Dryzek, Robin Eckersley and Peter Christoff are three Australians
      grappling with this problem. See, for example, J. Dryzek, *Rational Ecology,
      Environment and Political Economy*, Blackwell, Oxford, 1987; R. Eckersley,
      The Green State: Rethinking Democracy and Sovereignty, MIT Press,
      Cambridge MA, 2004; and P. Christoff, 'Ecological modernisation, ecolog-
      ically sustainable development and Australia's national ESD strategy',
      unpublished PhD thesis, Baillieu Library, University of Melbourne.
12   C. Hamilton, *Growth Fetish*, Allen & Unwin, Sydney, 2003.

INDEX